STORNOWAY
AND THE LEWS

By the Same Author

SURPRISE ISLAND
"Rich colourful reminiscences . . . funny tales, strange episodes, tragedies and adventures . . . A delightful book" Gerry Davis in the TV programme *Cover to Cover*.

THE HUB OF MY UNIVERSE
". . . emotions and real-life conflicts a-plenty . . . I for one hope he will write more." Trevor Royle in the *Glasgow Herald*.

"But most memorable of all are the intense, unforgettable impressions of a Stornoway boy — in his infancy, at school, as a journalistic apprentice and as the official scribe of some fascinating court cases." Cuthbert Graham in the *Press & Journal*.

"Altogether a wise and unpretentious book . . . We can all learn from it." Iain Crichton Smith in the *Scotsman*.

THE GAELIC VIKINGS
"From the Mutiny of the Bounty in 1789 to the Tolsta Chaolais poltergeist in Lewis via a 1930s religious revival . . .. James Shaw Grant has filled one more book with fascinating memories of his life as an editor." Cuthbert Graham in the *Press & Journal*.

". . . rich and highly enjoyable . . ." R.M. in the *Stornoway Gazette*.

HIGHLAND VILLAGES
". . . a village is not a fossilized group of buildings . . . but a living community with problems, aspirations and prejudices, arising from the past and influencing the future."

THEIR CHILDREN WILL SEE
and other stories
"They have a unique tone of voice . . . what comes over is controlled and elegiac passion." Douglas Gifford in *Books in Scotland*.

". . . there is a feeling of truth . . . an uneasy feeling because it is not the kind of truth we are used to." Naomi Mitchison in *Books and Bookmen*.

STORNOWAY
AND THE LEWS

James Shaw Grant

Humour Mystery Tragedy and Adventure
Unusual stories from the Western Isles

Published by James Thin Ltd, 53–59 South Bridge, Edinburgh, in collaboration with the author, James Shaw Grant, Ardgrianach, Inshes, Inverness IV1 2BQ

ISBN 0 9508371 3 X

Printed in the Scottish Highlands by Nevisprint Ltd., Fort William.

Contents

	page
University Blues and Pitcairn Island	1
Briogais Corduroy at the Court of King Arthur	5
His Dungarees were Illiterate!	10
The Free Dutch Soil of Lemreway	14
They Spoke in the Gaelic of Warsaw	18
A World First for Lewis	21
A Prophecy Fulfilled	24
The Spring Stampede	27
A Swedish Macleod from Skye	30
Caught in the Act	33
Thus Stornoway Flourished	36
Revolution in the Atlantic	40
A House Called Stornoway	44
A Ship Called Stornoway, too	48
The Mark of the Pirate's Knife	52
Aliens in their Native Isle	56
Two City of Glasgow Disasters	60
My Granny Made a Rug of It	64
Downing Street of the Isles	68
They Paid to Kick up Hell	71
A Bus Called Wedding Bells!	75
Mystery of a Dead Man's Dog	80
He Left His Cap on the Water	84
Kate Crola and the Lord Chief Justice	87
Espionage at Eishken	91
When the Germans Invaded Point	94
The Witch Raised an Action for Slander	97

Is the Devil a Crow or a Cat? 100

Why the "Polis" Went to Church 103

Archangels Keep Out! 106

He Might Have Been Soberer, Drunk 110

All Aboard for Gomorrah 113

The House that was Lit by a Teapot 117

Ernie Bevin Lost His Cool 120

Harshly and Aggressively Treated 123

Aztecs in Todday 127

Do It Last Year! At Once! 131

Gratuitous Amputation 135

They Crossed the Minch 139

The Milk was Black and White 142

Is It 'Awker? 145

Astrid at the Lazy Corner 150

The Story of Isidor Bass 153

How Much Panic Do You Need? 156

Scalpay Herring in Red Square 159

Twins from Different Counties 163

Boots for a Chinese Murderer 166

The Bang That Shook Up Kyle 169

Chinese Lady in the Snow 172

My Head with Oil 175

Light from a Norwegian's Torso 178

Poser for the Preacher 182

Haile Selassie in Lewis 185

Divine Retribution on a Very Modest Scale 188

The Island's Mayfly Dance 191

A Lorry Load of Social History 194

"Many a man is deeply interested in national politics who cares nothing for the affairs of his city . . . It is only a true recognition of the relation of the narrower to the wider circle which can save us from the perverted service of either . . . in the world of community it is the near relation which includes the wider."

Community by R. M. MacIver

Acknowledgements

Many people have contributed to this book in many ways. I have tried to acknowledge borrowings where they occur but the source of much of my material is long forgotten. I hope any whose names are omitted will accept this general "thank you".

In particular I wish to thank Jonathan Cape Ltd for permission to quote from Hugh Brogan's *The Life of Arthur Ransome* and *The Autobiography of Arthur Ransome* edited by Rupert Hart-Davis; Faber and Faber Ltd for permission to quote from *Memoirs of a Modern Scotland* by Karl Miller; Brown Son & Ferguson Ltd for permission to quote from Basil Lubbock's *The Opium Clippers*; John Farquharson Ltd and William Heinemann Ltd for permission to quote from Morris West's *Summer of the Red Wolf*; the Mitchell Library, Glasgow for material drawn from the files of the *Glasgow Herald*; and The Scottish Arts Council for a grant towards the cost of research.

Any profit arising from the series of which this is one will be devoted to education and/or historical research in the Western Isles.

1
University Blues and Pitcairn Island

Donald Macdonald told me once that his mother used to go to church in North Tolsta wearing his University Blue's scarf and carrying a walking stick brought home by his brother from Pitcairn Island. This epitomises the Lewis I knew in my youth. Casual links with the remotest corners of the earth: an instinct to put everything to use, acquired from a Spartan upbringing; and a generation of sons and daughters moving from the croft to academic careers as if it was the most natural progression in the world.

Donald's path began to converge with mine when he moved on from the elementary school in Tolsta to the Nicolson in Stornoway, and I moved up within the Nicolson from what we called Pryde's School — of which nothing now remains but the clock tower incongruously attached to a swimming pool — a few years later.

At that time we came under the instruction of a group of teachers who have a special place in my recollection, because of my age at the time, and the circumstances in which I got to know them. They were larger than life but not quite real. My classmates I see as normal human beings. I met them on the level and we grew old together but my teachers were birds of passage who came to Lewis for a few years and then moved on. While they were with us I was still young enough to see them as belonging to a different species from myself: entitled to respect even when I was mocking them behind their backs, or stubbornly defying them, or playing pranks in class, like popping carbide in the inkwells. Age has not wearied them, nor the years condemned, so far as I am concerned. They all moved off before they had time to change, or I was old enough to see them with adult eyes.

I have no idea what became of most of them. Dorothy Hutchings I do know about, but only because she was drowned dramatically a few hours after war was declared when the *Athenia* was torpedoed. She is embalmed in my memory. I have difficulty in convincing myself it is more than forty years since she died. She left the Nicolson a good fifteen years before that, and her sojourn among us could not have been more than three or four years in all, but I still regard her as part of Lewis, and I am sure that, until the day she died, Lewis was part of her. The intense, and in some ways claustrophobic, life of the island within an island — the English-speaking enclave in the Gaelic community — leaves its mark on all who live and work in Stornoway, for however short a period, unless they are so insensitive that they take no colour at all from their surroundings.

1

The point was well made for me in a letter I received from Stockport as I was writing this. Asking for a copy of *The Hub of my Universe* to be sent to her friend, Jean Rome, in Australia, Linda Fraser wrote: "Jean and I grew up in Lewis. She was over here at Christmas and spent most of her visit to me with her nose buried in my copy of your book so I feel she deserves one for her birthday. We, of course, were both 'incomers' — my father being Lewis Marvin, hers James Rome of the SCWS — and I for one still feel the pull of the place."

I am sure they all felt the pull of the place after they left, the teachers I am writing of — Margaret Love, Ethel Bassin, William Macneil and Alfred Barron. Even the Galloping Major. They were all deeply involved in the social life of the town.

The Galloping Major, of whom I have written elsewhere, was legendary. He could not really have existed, although in truth he did. Ethel Bassin has something of the same unreal quality. She was a Russian Jewess, or so I always believed. It was said that her real name was Bassinski, but that might have been Stornoway improving on the truth.

She was short and vivacious, with goitre-ish eyes and three feet. One leg was withered and she had an artificial limb attached to it. When she sat at the teacher's high desk in front of the class, the third foot could be seen, peeping out from below her skirt, to the eternal fascination of the pupils. She was a complete extrovert who rather terrified some of the staider Stornoway hostesses, like my mother, by her directness, and she was in no way inhibited by her physical disability. When we had a visit from a flotilla of submarines and the Nicolson staff were invited on board, Ethel Bassin was the only woman in the company prepared to venture down the iron ladder into the bowels of the ship.

While she was in the Nicolson she taught us, in accordance with the syllabus, songs that were completely alien, without the merit of being classics, like *The Lass of Richmond Hill*. But, when she emigrated to Canada, she joined the Lewis Society in Vancouver and took a leading part in the production of Gaelic ceilidhs and musical playlets based on island life. Her three or four years in Lewis had given her an identity she would not otherwise have had. Eventually she returned to Scotland and taught in various schools. She wrote a book about the work of Frances Tolmie one of the pioneer collectors of Gaelic folksongs. I bumped into her twice by chance not long before she died: first on an Edinburgh bus and then in the Over-seas Club. Our talk was all of Stornoway — the Stornoway of the twenties.

Dorothy Hutchings did not have the eccentricity of the Galloping Major, or the personality of Ethel Bassin. She was a sort of universal sweetheart for the boys. The girls may have viewed her somewhat differently, but I think she was also popular with them. The embryonic banker who put his arm round her in class may have been moved by more than mere bravado, although we did not think so at the time. *Young Woodley* had not been written then.

2

The two who left the clearest mark on the school, of that little group, were Margaret Love and William Macneil. Margaret Love was a burly, lumbering woman, with a face the colour of putty, and almost as featureless, but she could galvanise a class. She was the first to awaken my interest in the theatre although I did not realise it until now. She was associated with the first, short-lived, effort to establish a community drama movement in Lewis, and produced the first scenes from Shakespeare I ever saw on the stage. I still remember the school concert at which Falstaff came alive for me. In the dreary old picture house on Keith Street beside the Seminary. A great barn with steeply raked floor, and hard armless narrow tip-up benches covered in green American cloth. I used to sit there on Saturdays, enthralled by the exploits of Eddie Polo, or the antics of Harold Lloyd. Yelling my head off when help arrived at the critical moment, or the hero triumphed in a more than usually violent bout of fisticuffs. Ringing across the years I can still hear — although it came to me through the eyes as a cold caption in a silent film — the scorn in Eddie Polo's voice (supplied by my own imagination) as he sneered, "You coffee-coloured greaser from Mexico", and reached for his gun.

When I was in the middle of typing the previous paragraph I had to break off and hurry to Inverness Airport to see a friend. There I got into conversation with an old Nicolsonian a little younger than myself. Without knowing what I had been working on, he told me of the arrangement the country boys of his generation had with an accommodating butcher to advance them the price of a ticket for the Picture House. They lived in digs in Stornoway and when they bought the weekend meat for the landlady to cook they asked for "a piece of flank and sixpence for the P's". The butcher — who, incidentally, had spent many years ranching in South America — would add sixpence to the price when he entered the transaction in the book. He then handed the meat and a magic little coin to the expectant schoolboy. In this way stern Calvanistic fathers were induced to finance their sons' illicit pleasures without knowing that they did it. Painless extraction without anaesthetics!

For us the manager of the Picture House was more important than the banker or the minister. He was scarcely flesh and blood. A dweller on some Olympian height with the key to a magical kingdom in his keeping. I can remember the names of managers like Freer and Halley although their features have long faded from my recollection, but Will Mack was different. He still lives, and will continue to do so as long as there is anyone alive who knew him in his heyday.

He was the last owner of the Keith Street Picture House but he came straight from the music hall or circus. A brisk little man with a staccato way of talking, who always looked as if he were a Jack-in-the-box, still quivering because the catch was newly sprung and he had just shot out with a suprised look on his face.

He was old when he came to Stornoway, but he was not a day older when he left, as far as anyone could see. Associated with him were two ladies of uncertain age but youthful appearance, also clearly refugees from the cheaper music halls the cinema was killing. They called themselves the Macgregor Sisters, and sisters they may have been, but they were as unlike in height, build, colouring and temperament as two human beings could be. One was tall, well built, with long auburn ringlets. The other was short, slim, sleek, and black as a raven. Occasionally they gave a variety show, sometimes with the aid of a visiting star of very indifferent candle-power — in spite of the superlatives in the billing. The Macgregor Sisters, on these occasions, would render quite sweetly a few insipid songs while Will Mack would do his dame dance, sing in a hoarse croaking voice, and thank the audience in a speech which was rattled off like a machine gun, and invariably ended with the words, "I always do my best, and the best can do no more!"

Like Will Mack himself, but possibly with greater aid from cosmetics, the ages of the Macgregor Sisters also seemed to remain stationary while they lived in Stornoway. Many years after they closed the Picture House and left there was an article in the *Spectator* about a group of strolling players the writer had come across in Orkney. They could only have been Will Mack and the Macgregor Sisters still clearly doing their best.

Like my teachers, Will Mack and the Macgregor Sisters were very much part of Stornoway while they were there but with a subtle difference. In a strictly Presbyterian town they were looked at rather askance even by those who frequented their shows.

A friend, not long ago, reminded me of an incident he was involved in — or rather not involved in — with the younger sister. The story surfaced in conversation because an old neighbour had written me a letter in which she recalled having asked him, when she was a schoolgirl, for a "hurl" in his sidecar. He took her gladly. He had just reached the age at which it was legal to drive and he was flattered by the chance of showing off, even to a schoolgirl.

When I showed him the letter he could not remember the incident, but said he remembered clearly an occasion, around the same time, when one of the Macgregor Sisters had tried to cadge a lift in the same way. She wanted to get urgently to the laundry at the other end of the town to collect Will Mack's boiled shirt which was needed for the evening show.

"She worked very hard on it but her face was clarted inches thick in make-up. Wild horses would not persuade me to have that face in my side car."

Sixty years after the incident he was still annoyed with himself for being disobliging, which was quite out of character, and for the pettiness of his reason for being so. But was there also a note of regret in his voice for an opportunity missed, all these years ago?

The fact that he still remembers the incident may tell us more about the effect of a too strait-laced town on a growing lad than the fact that the incident happened in the first place.

2
Briogais Corduroy at the Court of King Arthur

I never really enjoyed Will Mack's concerts although I can still recall some of the songs.

"Is she short? Is she tall?
Does she cling like the ivy to the wall?
Who's the girl that's getting all the kisses
That used to belong to me?"

Why should that fragment of a sickly sentimental song be almost the only scrap that survives from a period before I was old enough to be concerned about kisses — except when I was fleeing from the too public attentions of an over-affectionate aunt?

Even now when I am enjoying a variety programme on television I have an uneasy feeling that it is a gross waste of time. I have a sense of physical and spiritual discomfort which is, in part, a reflection of the rather puritanical atmosphere which pervaded Stornoway when I was a child, but which is also a hangover from dreary nights in the old Picture House which I went to only because there was nowhere else to go.

Margaret Love's presentation of the tavern scene from *Henry IV* was a very different experience. I was so ill-prepared for seeing Shakespeare on the stage I took a copy of the play with me so that I could follow it on the printed page. I had an idea that the text, which we analysed dissected and parsed, was the real Shakespeare without which the antics on the stage could not be understood.

The rombustious performance of Fad — Billy Forsyth's uncle — as Falstaff, and the singing of Ian Smith off-stage, to create the rollicking atmosphere, soon made me forget the book in my hand. For the first time in my life Shakespeare came alive for me.

A few years later, when they were students at Aberdeen, Fad and his friend Murdigan, gave Stornoway a music hall of its own. Sui generis. Not an import. Something that could not have existed in any other town on earth. A distillation from the local cultural mix which was quintessential Stornoway. Their popular number *The Beautiful Scenes Around Stornoway Bay* sent up everything from the Gut House to the Town Council, while their lively Gaelic version of *King Arthur Ruled the Land* was enjoyed even by those who could not speak the language.

King Arthur was one of the more palatable of the English songs we sang for Miss Bassin and her successors, but I can only remember snatches of it. I recall that

> "He had three sons of yore
> And he kicked them through the door
> Because they would not sing"

It went on to describe what happened to the three. The first was a miller, and the second a weaver — naturally a breabadair in the Fad and Murdigan version. The third became

> "A little tailor boy
> Who stole corduroy
> To keep the other fellows warm."

I can still recall the gust of laughter that swept through the hall when a Stornoway audience first made the acquaintance of "balach beag an tailleir" with "briogais corduroy fo ghairdean."

Sometimes Alastair Macleod, who as Town Clerk was one of my closest friends, used to sing a parody of *When Ye Gang Awa Jeannie* as a duet with Fad. Alastair, singing falsetto, took the part of Jeannie. The song embodied a precious little bit of old Stornoway history. One verse, I was recently reminded by Alastair's brother, Willie, a well-known member of the medical profession in Edinburgh, went as follows:

> "Though you had Clabhs nan Ceidean, laddie
> With all its lights and shades laddie,
> The Castle, Clink, and Creag a' Bhodaich
> For that I would not to thee, laddie"

The riches dangled before the reluctant damsel were ill-assorted. The Clink, of course, was the gaol. Creag a' Bhodaich is a rock on the Lochs road supposed to be haunted. Innumerable murders seem to have been committed there if one aggregates the various versions of the tales that surround it. Maciver's Close on Keith Street, quite near the homes of both Alastair and Fad, was known locally as Clabhs nan Ceidean — the alley of the hundreds — because of the myriad human beings crammed into its tiny rooms and low ceilinged attics. Stornoway owes a great debt to Alastair Macleod for the way he led the Council, during his years as town clerk, in eliminating Clabhs nan Ceidean, and the other warrens, which disfigured the town in our youth. But they were part of Stornoway. My Stornoway.

On the opposite side of the road from Maciver's was another close known as the Hog (so we pronounced it). I don't know what the name signified but I have heard it suggested by W. J. Gibson, the Rector of the Nicolson, that it was a corruption of La Hogue deriving from the fact that foreign sailors had once lived there.

Of all the closes, the one I knew best was Havelock Lane, which clearly dated from the Indian Mutiny. It was a very respectable quarter when I frequented it, given over to industry and commerce. William John Tolmie, one of the bailies of the burgh, had his chemist's shop at the entrance. His brother David had a tweed business with an elegant office in what had once been a warren of little houses. David had trained as a banker in Parr's Bank in London, and had been for many years an attorney on an extensive banana plantation in Jamaica. He had travelled widely in USA, Central America and Cuba. I spent many a happy hour yarning with one or other of the brothers.

Willie John told me once that, when the close had been inhabited by hundreds of fisher girls who were joined at Communion seasons by scores of relatives sleeping on the floor, he had been faced with a public health problem. The close was too convenient a sanctuary for people hurrying from over long sermons to little houses with limited sanitary facilities — or none. He mentioned the problem to another brother, Jack, who was in practice as a doctor in town. "Leave it to me," said Jack, who was a great practical joker.

He borrowed the key of the shop, rigged up a speaking tube with two of the chemist's glass filter funnels, and some rubber tubing, and hid inside, in the darkness. The earpiece of the speaking tube was concealed in the close at a strategic point. Whenever the doctor heard someone pause outside, he began muttering maledictions in Gaelic, pretending to be the devil. Pandemonium ensued as elderly women caught short, fled through the night. But whither?

The last of the closes to disappear was at the foot of Stag Road. It was celebrated in verse by the Breve, of whom I will have more to say later, in a poem which began with an aptly borrowed line:

"The Stag at eve had drunk his fill."

It remains to add that many good men and women, and some distinguished scholars, came out of the closes of Stornoway as well as a procession of "characters" who would not have been out of place in a novel by Dickens — or Dostoevsky: their eccentricity enhanced by the ambivalent relationship in which they stood to two competing cultures. Perhaps three, because some of them were incomers carrying with them the accents of places far removed from the Hebrides.

The best loved of all the songs popularised by Fad and Murdigan was a parody of *Billy Boy* in which a succession of very localised in-jokes led to a climax in the line:

"Can she navigate a 'doosh' my Billy Boy?"

The old Picture House erupted. Dorothy Hutchings, who was sitting in front of my father with her younger sister on a visit to the island, turned and demanded an explanation. But how, in the midst of a storm of laughter, when the tears are streaming down your face, can you possibly begin to explain to an incomer a joke which depends on the juxtaposition of the English word "navigate", which conjures up a vision of exploration in distant seas, and the Gaelic word "duis" which refers to the more recondite parts of the entrails of a sheep used in the preparation of a delicacy, related to the haggis, which the elite of Stornoway regarded as rather vulgar, but still enjoyed surreptitiously, when they got the chance.

These concerts were a far cry from Shakespeare, although I don't think he would have disowned them, and belong to a period after Margaret Love had left the island — and left her mark upon it. I have a vague feeling that I saw an earlier extract from Shakespeare — the trial scene from *The Merchant of Venice* — some years before I saw Falstaff in action, but, if so, I was too young, and it all went over my head. Not so *Henry IV*. That was like opening a window on a sunny day.

Around the same time I remember going through a snowstorm to the Drill Hall to see a production of *Campbell of Kilmhor*. I don't think it would be possible for a modern audience to be moved by any play as Stornoway was by that almost mawkish highland story. The audience was completely unsophisticated: unused to theatre or television. The production was simple, almost crude. Stornoway had no electricity then. The stage was lit by real lamps with burning wicks, just as a house would be. There was no light and shade on the stage arranged by a skilful producer to simulate reality. It was reality.

When the hero — Sweedie, the local scoutmaster — was led out to die, and a shot was heard, Hughie Matheson began to sing off stage, in the distance, softly, like an echo in the mind,

"No more we'll see such deeds again
Deserted is each Highland glen . . ."

The girl lying prostrate on the stage — one of the Graham sisters, but I cannot remember which — was not simulating grief. She was crying her heart out. She was scarcely able to assume a semblance of composure for the final curtain, and many in the audience were weeping openly.

I learned that drama is not something remote and lifeless, that smells of the classroom, but directly relevant to our own lives and history.

It was then I must have discovered, although I was too young to know it at the time, that the theatre was an essential tool in the rehabilitation of the neglected, and very often despised, periphery of a nation the eyes of whose rulers, like the eyes of the fool in Scripture, were still in the ends of the earth: neglecting its own indigenous and undeveloped resources. A process of rehabilitation which had to begin with ourselves, restoring self-respect, before we could establish ourselves in the eyes of other people as an element which contributed to the richness of national life: not a parasite living off wealthier areas, as we were, and still to some extent are, so frequently portrayed.

It was later I discovered that drama can illuminate the mind of the dramatist himself. If he is writing anything of value, he is reaching out to ideas which he has not fully grasped. Perhaps does not know exist. He is exploring new and virgin territory, even although it lies wholly within his own mind and imagination.

The same is more intensely true of the poet. He is led across stepping stones of imagery until he finds himself on the far side of a river he could neither ford nor swim, in a country which he did not know existed, and which he cannot map with any precision, because it is new to him as it is to his readers, but which future generations will know intimately, and order their lives as if it had always existed.

3
His Dungarees were Illiterate!

I was not the only person whose life was altered by the small group of teachers who sojourned briefly in Lewis in my early teens. Margaret Love was the first to notice the literary potential of one of my classmates, Hector MacIver from Shawbost, a cousin of Robert MacIver, the first dux and most distinguished product of the Nicolson.

The country lads had a club in the school where they met on occasional evenings to escape from the drab surroundings in which many of them lived. Little over-crowded bed-sitters in the closes I have been writing of. The only school hostel then was the old Imperial Hotel, which was confined to girls and quite inadequate even for them.

We town boys were not permitted to use the club because we had homes to go to, and so it happened that Hector was plied with the writings of Bernard Shaw, and other moderns, as recreational reading, while those of us who were dependent on the rigid school curriculum, geared to the "Highers", were unaware that any literature existed later than Tennyson.

Hector became head of the English Department in the Royal High School in Edinburgh, and established a reputation for producing writers, although he did not do much creative writing himself, apart from a number of radio programmes.

One of his first programmes was a sound portrait of Lewis. It was brilliant and innovative technically, for its time, but it created great resentment in Lewis for the manner in which it juxtaposed the church and the pub. Some people thought it almost blasphemous to mention the two in the same programme, let alone in the same breath. We are adepts at keeping our categories apart. Not letting our right hand know what our left hand does — in a very different sense from that recommended by the Bible.

When Hector died in 1966, still a comparatively young man, Karl Miller, one of the leading literary critics of the day, who was an old pupil and owed much to him, edited a memorial volume entitled *Memoirs of a Modern Scotland.* Writers from both sides of the Atlantic of the calibre of Hugh MacDiarmid, Sorley Maclean, George Mackay Brown, Muriel Spark, Louis Simpson, George Scott-Moncrieff and William McIlvanney contributed to it.

According to Miller, Hector was not famous in the usual sense, but he did "have a kind of fame". "It went by word of mouth and seldom reached the newspapers; it was as oral as the world of his origins."

In a sense Hector was the quintessential Lewisman, embodying all the contradictions, all the paradoxes, all the conflicts of the island from which he was sprung.

So perfervid an islander that he is said to have sent back his lobster in the Cafe Royal in Edinburgh because it did not come from Lewis. So deeply at variance with the island's prevailing Presbyterianism that he boasted of having smuggled across the Minch a copy of Joyce's *Ulysses* while it was still banned throughout Britain.

According to Miller, Hector taught "as his ancestors fought — with a whole heart." To Lowland schoolchildren "he came as a revelation". "He had qualities of dignity, elegance, eloquence and fantasy that seemed not only exotic but literally portentous." "He was a stranger, a man of different temper and breeding, born to a different language, learned in a literature and song that were a closed book to Lowlanders."

Most significantly of all Miller writes, "Hector was neither right nor left, and indeed the politics of industrial societies never really claimed his sympathy. More than anyone I have known, he was unaffected by class feeling."

It is difficult for an islander to understand why Hector MacIver's lack of class-consciousness should have struck Karl Miller so forcibly. For us, Hector's stance was the norm. Karl Miller's the deviation.

I met Murdo Macfarlane, the Melbost bard, in the queue in Roddie Smith's paper shop not long before he died. I was on a visit to Lewis and had not seen him for some time. In the course of conversation he asked, "Did I ever tell you that as a lad I used to caddy for your father?" He went on to speak about the old days when Stornoway Golf Course was on the Melbost and Stenish machair, where the airport is now, and which the golfers shared with the crofters' innumerable cows. There was a bitter feud for many years between the crofters and the encroaching golfers, mainly professional and businessmen from Stornoway. On one occasion, at least, it led to violence, of a very minor kind, and some of the crofters were gaoled. On another the crofters loosed a bad tempered ram on the course and the greenkeeper was beseiged for some hours in a deep bunker, fending off the ram with a plank.

In a class-conscious community — even without the feud we had in Lewis over possession of the ground — the relationship of golfer and caddy implies a separation, a gulf, perhaps even an antagonism. In Murdo Macfarlane's world, on the periphery of which I was lucky enough to have been born, the fact that he had been my father's caddy was a bond, a link out of the past which enriched our friendship.

Of course there were traces of snobbery in Stornoway when I was a child. But they were based on town versus country, or English versus Gaelic, rather than on class, as normally defined, and did not go much deeper than the sense of superiority with which Tong looked down on Tolsta. Perhaps still does!

Once, in the thirties a group of Stornoway socialites, mainly incomers, decided to hold a very select dance in the Town Hall, by invitation only. A

11

posh do, from which the "gràisg" would be excluded. The idea was ridiculed into the ground. For weeks the popular greeting in the town was, "Have you passed the blood test?"

A correspondent, whom I do not know personally, recalled recently, in a very interesting letter, a rather similar story about her uncle, who was training to be a marine engineer. For a time he worked in Lewis, on the Leverhulme schemes. One day, while still in his dungarees, he went into a newsagent's in Stornoway and asked, "Do you sell the Literary Digest?" "Yes, but only to literary people!" was the reply. Literature and dungarees apparently were incompatible. He was so taken aback, he left the shop without his magazine.

I have to scrape around for these examples of what was, in Lewis, an aberration. Something to be laughed at for its pretentious absurdity. Perhaps the most significant fact is that, even the few who might have spoken like the lady in the newsagent's, in a similar situation, would have laughed at her for doing so. There might be personal aspirations to superiority (no doubt I had them myself) but there was nothing resembling a cohesive, exclusive, hieratic class structure, distancing itself from the rest of the community, as if everyone else had the plague.

The last word on the subject of town versus country, which was the only identifiable line of demarcation, was said many years ago, by the old bodach from the West Side, who was asked by a friend, "Do you think the poor people of Shawbost will go to the same heaven as the grand folk in Stornoway?" "No!" was the reply. "But they may go to the same hell!" And that put Stornoway pretty firmly in its place.

It was shortly after Prof Rex Knight took up an appointment in Aberdeen that I first became really aware of the gulf between the egalitarianism of the Highlands — indeed of Scotland generally — and the class-consciousness of England, and the little pockets in Scotland which ape the south. The illumination was provided by Mrs Knight. She wrote an article to the *Spectator* to say what a delightful surprise it had been to discover that her charwoman, in a rural village in Aberdeenshire, had a son who was a doctor, "and she was not spoiled by it." Mrs Knight was also pleasantly surprised because the village postman would dismount from his bicycle, and walk along the street with her, as an equal, discussing the affairs of the day. I was astonished that she was astonished, by anything so natural.

But then, I have known a crofter whose staple diet was Gibbon's *Decline and Fall* — unabridged!

I have known two "toughs", from one of the closes in Point Street, fight in the Town Hall cloakroom at a dance because of a disagreement about a quotation from Shakespeare.

And I cherish the story told me by Malcolm Smith (Safety) of the day he was battling along the sea front at Newton in a south westerly gale with huge waves breaking over the parapet, and the rain driving at him horizontally across the street. He was a bailie at the time — a very good

12

bailie, too! — and when he saw one of the burgh plumbers, perched at the top of a ladder, swaying dangerously in the wind, as he tried to repair a gas lamp, he thought he should commend his devotion to duty.

The reply from the oilskin at the top of the ladder was unexpected:

"What's the soft South-wester?
'Tis the ladies' breeeze,
Bringing home their true loves
Out of all the seas:"

Not every town breeds plumbers who quote Kingsley with such aptness and aplomb!

4
The Free Dutch Soil of Lemreway

When Hector MacIver was in Class III in the Nicolson he started a class magazine. Pupils, in those days, had no access to typewriters, let alone printing machines and photo-copiers. The magazine was written out laboriously, as the monks did in the Middle Ages, although not quite so elegantly, and the one precious copy was passed from hand to hand.

I didn't know of the existence of the magazine at the time. Hector and I went to different sections of Class III and, out of school hours, most of my time was spent with the town boys in my own neighbourhood. In fact I first heard of Hector's magazine some years after his death. More than half a century after he had written it.

The magazine, still intact after all those years, was sent to me by an actuary in Washington, who had it from one of the leading medical men in the States, who had it from a member of his family in South Africa, who found it while rummaging in the attic of a farm-house, in the veldt.

As soon as I received it, I passed the news on to the person I thought would be most interested — the British Council's representative in Buenos Aires.

It is almost needless to add that the link between us is the Nicolson Institute. The Class IV of 1924 to be precise. The year in which W. J. Gibson left, John Macrae became rector, and Alex Urquhart came to Stornoway and became our class teacher.

In that year, when the survivors from the three sections of Class III came together in one class of about 45 pupils, I was in much closer contact with Hector. We kept in touch while we were at University, although he was in Edinburgh and I in Glasgow. After that our contacts were rather intermittent.

It was during a short stay at his home in Shawbost that Hector introduced me to *A Portrait of the Artist as a Young Man*. On that occasion I took a photograph of him in a hen shed, of all places. He had rescued from oblivion an old hand-operated quern, and reassembled it in working order, in the only place available. It was really the quern I was photographing.

Another photograph of fishing boats on the beach below the village was rather sad, so many of them were then derelict. But they made a good composition, and, when I sent it to Hector, he commented that it reminded him of a painting by Van Gogh. I was flattered by the comparison, but I didn't know why.

It is almost incredible, but it is true, that I had gone through the Nicolson from the Infants to Class VI, and had spent three years at Glasgow University, taking a reasonably good degree, without ever hearing the name of one of the great artists of all time. Scottish education was good but blinkered.

The other links in the story of the Class III magazine were two Roderick Murrays. One, from the Post Office in Shawbost, became an actuary in Washington. The other, from Back and South Africa, was a doctor in the States.

The second of the Rodericks spent only a year or two in the Nicolson when his mother was home on holiday from South Africa. So far as I recall he had no nickname, which is unusual, but his younger brother was known, affectionately, as Kenny Kaffir, an appellation he owed to alliteration as much as anything else.

The British Council representative in Buenos Aires was Neil Mackay, whom I have already mentioned in connection with the Folklore Conference he organised in Stornoway when he did a tour of duty for the Council in Scotland.

Apart from his services for the British Council at home and abroad, Neil spent some years as a teacher in the Free Church Missionary College in Peru, and he has rendered further valuable service to the Free Church since retiring to Edinburgh.

At university Neil had been under pressure from the head of the Celtic Department to specialise in Gaelic and Old Norse. Instead he concentrated on Commerce and Economics. When he left university, in the middle of the great depression, the only post he could find was as a teacher of Latin in a small public school in the South of England. He had not been there very long before he was in charge of the science department, reorganising the school lab. When he went to Lima he took a PhD, writing his thesis (in Spanish!) on the philosophy of A. N. Whitehead which most people find more than incomprehensible in the original English.

Of all the boys who were with me on that Class, and who went on to university, only one — apart from myself — was able to spend his professional life in his native island. That was the late John Smith, headmaster of Sandwick School. Ian Mor, whose laugh was even bigger than his frame, was one of my most intimate friends over the years. He was a solid citizen in every sense of the term, with a tremendous appetite for fun.

I remember him telling me during the war that he grew his cabbages in the only Free Dutch soil in Europe. He was headmaster at Lemreway then, and had come on a local tradition that the soil in the schoolhouse garden was particularly good because it was the ballast from a Dutch ship. I never discovered what a Dutch ship was doing off-loading ballast in such an unlikely spot as Lemreway.

He also used to entertain me, around the same time, with hair-raising accounts of his adventures, travelling back and fore for a whole winter, on the tortuous roads of Park, in a bus with defective brakes. Fortunately the brakes went on when the driver wanted to stop. The trouble was that they would not come off. The driver kept a hammer handy under his seat. Whenever he stopped, it was handed to one of the passengers, who got out and tapped the wheels until the bus could move again.

The same driver had a weakness for his dram, although that did not deter him from negotiating the hair-pin bends on the narrow roads of Pairc in darkness, with shaded headlamps, in the war-time blackout.

One day I met Sergeant Fraser in Cromwell Steet — a stickler for duty if ever there was one. He was livid.

"I saw our friend staggering out of a pub," he told me, indicating the driver who had just passed along the street. "I warned him against driving the bus in that condition. He raised his right hand and said to me, 'My oath to God, I'll not take the bus home tonight.' Neither will he! I've just heard the bits of his bus are in a ditch near the Sanatorium. But I can't prove that he was drunk when he went off the road."

John Smith was a great admirer of Rabbie Burns, and one of the most respected figures in the Western Isles Labour Party in its heyday. The contribution he made to the life of the community is a measure of the impoverishment we suffered because so many like him had to leave.

One of the group who was lost to Lewis, although he did not go very far was Robert Mackenzie. He was headmaster in Applecross, almost within sight of his native Marvig.

At school he was regarded as an outstanding marksman. He could never resist a moving object, and went through his last year at school without knowing the time — he had thrown his watch at a mangy cat! He showed that his reputation was well founded when he went to Glasgow University and joined the OTC. When he was being told how to handle a rifle he upset the instructor by demonstrating that he was already a quicker and a better shot.

We used to have long discussions about politics. Rop's views were always highly original and pungently expressed. I remember telling him at the end of one discussion that he was the only High Tory Communist I had ever met. Which suggests that, like Hector MacIver, he did not accept the categories and frozen postures of an industrial society but made up his own mind as he went along. He was the only one of my Gaelic-speaking classmates who tried to persuade me to make good the gap in my education by learning the language, and studying its poetry.

I saw him occasionally over the years, and once spent a most enjoyable evening in his home when I visited Applecross on Crofters Commission business. His wife, a lovely woman, entertained the company well, and, in the course of the evening, I got the explanation, or part explanation, of a mystery which had lain in my mind unresolved for many years.

In the early thirties, my brother and I made a motor tour through the north of Scotland. We went into Applecross in a gale of wind and rain. At the top of the Bealach I had to open the car door for a moment. There were no passing places on the road then, and we were so close to the edge, and a drop of several hundred feet, my brother, who was driving, wanted me to

16

see what clearance we had. The wind whipped out of the car the tin basin we had for washing the dishes after our picnic meals. We found it, on the return journey, about a mile from where we lost it.

On the return journey, too, we met another car coming up the brae, laden with bolls of meal. The two cars had to inch past each other. When they were abreast the two drivers opened their windows and had a little chat.

I tried to keep out of sight but listened attentively. I had met the driver of the other car before! In Stornoway, where he was posing as a cinema tycoon, trying to raise a considerable sum of money for a film on the herring fishing industry. He claimed to have been one of the first pilots ever licensed in Britain, and produced documents which seemed to prove it.

What was he doing on the Bealach with a car load of bolls of meal?

According to himself, he was provisioning his yacht which was anchored in the bay. But we had seen no yacht!

At my Applecross ceilidh, many years later, I learned that he had been a porter in the local hotel, but disappeared abruptly when a lady arrived on the scene, claiming to be his wife.

5
They Spoke in the Gaelic of Warsaw

We also had a magazine in Class IV. This time it was typed. I had access to my father's typewriter, although hardly the skill to use it. My ingenuity was frequently exercised in trying to cover up my blunders. I was able to turn out four copies at a time of *Sparks From Class IV*. The name and the cover design were the work of Neil Mackay.

On publication day one of our precious copies was placed on the teacher's desk, just before our weekly written Latin test from "Çloggy", our absent-minded and somewhat irascible Classics teacher, who still showed the effects of shell-shock from the First World War. The magazine anaesthetised him for "a period" at least, and we quietly did our test from cribs.

One of the principal contributors to the magazine was John Macleod, from Marybank, whom we called Rover, possibly because of the almighty long walk he had to school each day. No school transport then, and no canteen. A mug of cocoa in the cookery department for those who could not go home to lunch! And even that was considered a great innovation.

John's specialty was the writing of lively parodies, sometimes multi-lingual.

> Hic jacet old Virgil
> Vir horriblisimus.
> Mortuus est Virgil,
> A year last Christmas.
> His departure from life,
> Brought relief to his wife,
> For it ended their strife,
> Which was semper saevissimus.

He took a good degree at Edinburgh, but it was difficult then, as it is now for so many graduates, to find an outlet for his talents. For a number of years he was in jobs which hardly stretched him. Just after the end of the war, I was delighted to bump into him and his very attractive young wife, on the mail steamer and learn that at last he had a teaching job that was really congenial.

Shortly before we were all due to sit our "Highers" two of the lads opted out. One morning they were missing from their place in class and we learned that they had joined the Metropolitan Police. When John Macrae, the Rector, heard about it, he commented drily, "They'll work for their breakfast now!" And work they did, to some purpose. One of them, whom we had percipiently named "Fox", became a Detective Superintendent, and hit the headlines in the national press because of his excellent work in the Jack Spot case. But who on earth was Jack Spot? His name was on everyone's lips at the time, but he has long vanished into limbo.

After the "Highers" another large group of my class-mates emigrated to Canada. They went to good jobs with the Sun Life Assurance Company which had opened up for them because of a chain of circumstances arising from the collapse of Lord Leverhulme's schemes.

The wave of emigration which followed Lord Leverhulme's abandonment of his development plans for Lewis, aroused worldwide interest. Stornoway was besieged by journalists when each of the three CPR liners sailed direct for Montreal with hundreds of young Lewismen and women. The daily press carried many photographs and human interest stories.

On the other side of the Atlantic, Canadians with Lewis blood in their veins wondered how they could help the newly arriving emigrants.

One of them, Thomas Bassett Macaulay, President of the Sun Life Assurance Company, decided to meet them as they passed through Montreal on their way to farms in the middle west. Laden with fruit and other gifts, he boarded the train, and went from coach to coach until he heard a group jabbering away in a language he did not understand. Thrilled by his first encounter, as he thought, with the language of his ancestors, he showered his bounty on a group of grateful but bewildered Poles.

No one laughed more heartily over his mistake than he did, but he took the precaution of communicating with the emigration agent in Stornoway, Stephen MacLean's father, to make sure he was better informed the next time.

Murdo MacLean was a shrewd little man, although his cockiness sometimes got him into trouble with his fellow councillors. He sent Macaulay a great deal of information about the emigrants, and the island, including a family tree, showing Macaulay's descent from Domhnull Cam, and his collateral relationship with the more presentable members of the clan who are buried in Westminster Abbey.

I don't know whether Macaulay was attracted by the blackguards, or by the "saints" in the family tree. Perhaps by the bitter-sweet mixture of the two. He was certainly attracted by the clan motto — "Dulce periculum". "Risk is sweet." No insurance man could resist that.

T. B. Macaulay was a man with a social conscience. A do-gooder, in the pejorative and offensive phrase which is so commonly used today, and which reveals the scepticism and mindless vandalism of the age. He would have responded warmly to the work of Zachary Macaulay and "the Clapham Sect" on behalf of the slaves. He would also have responded to the confident, progressive Whiggery of Lord Macaulay.

At the same time he was sufficient of a romantic to delight in the fact that

19

a remote ancestor — the "remote" is important — had scrambled up the wall of the Doune at Carloway with the aid of a couple of dirks, and cooked his enemies gently to death by throwing in bundles of burning heather as they slept below.

He would have delighted even more in the manner in which his ancestor escaped from the trap set for him by the Breve, when he lured him aboard a Dutch ship he had seized with a cargo of wine, and hi-jacked him when he was pleasantly drunk. Domhnull Cam sobered up abruptly when the ship began to roll, and he realised that they had put to sea. By then it was too late. The Morison warriors secreted on board came out of their hiding place, and, before he knew what had struck him, Domhnull Cam was tied to the mast with a sword at his breast.

The Dutchman's wine, however, continued to do its work, affecting the captors as well as the captured. At least that is a fair assumption. Domhnull Cam was landed at Ullapool and held in captivity, fettered to his son-in-law by a heavy chain attached to a block of iron like an anvil. But the guard was so lax they were able to escape and make their way to Applecross and thence to Dunvegan.

In some versions of the tale, Domhnull Cam is said to have carried the heavy chain, and the weight attached to it, as he ran. The weight was on show for many years in Dunvegan Castle. I am rather dubious about that. Dubious about the whole story, in fact. But it was just the thing to catch the fancy of a prosperous Canadian anxious to re-establish his ties with his ancestral home.

More important, perhaps, than the family tree was the book which Murdo MacLean enclosed with the package. *Glimpses of Portrona*, written by Roderick Stephen, an uncle of Murdo's wife, and a son of George Stephen, who was mate on the *Freeland* when she had a brush with pirates in "the throat of Tunis", and who afterwards married my grand-aunt, his captain's niece.

Although he was a Boddam man, George Stephen played quite a part in the history of Lewis in the middle years of last century. I have told the story of the *Freeland* in *The Gaelic Vikings*, and I will have occasion to come back to George Stephen in a later book when I pick up the story of Donald Munro, the factor who tyrannised over Lewis for a quarter of a century or more. George Stephen, so far as I know, was the first to stand up to him. He successfully resisted Munro's roguery, but it was a costly victory.

If George Stephen made Lewis history, his son recorded some. Portrona is Stornoway under a light disguise. The book told Macaulay a good deal about the town in which his father had worked as a young man. It also pointed the direction in which the main flow of Macaulay's generosity should run.

6
A World First for Lewis

Roddie Stephen, whose book so engaged the attention of T. B. Macaulay, had a brilliant career at Aberdeen University, but he had no set goal before him, and drifted into teaching, for which his sensitive, unassertive nature was completely unsuited.

He was more or less badgered into taking over the Free Church School in Stornoway, where he had received his own early education, but the discipline had become lax, and he could not cope. One of his contemporaries commented that "a hooligan situation" existed in the school. It is surprising that conditions, not unlike those we deplore in the city schools today, existed in a school in Stornoway a century ago. A Free Church School at that. It would be interesting to know the causes, but I doubt if they could be established now.

However, when the Inspector of Schools paid his first visit after Roddie Stephen's appointment, he did not comment on the lack of discipline. He commented on the wasted talents of the teacher. "What on earth brought you here with qualifications like these?" he asked.

Roddie Stephen gave up teaching, and, after a period of reflection, decided to enter the church. He was influenced, in part at least, by the revivalist preaching of Donald John Martin, the Skyeman after whom Martin's Memorial is named.

Roddie Stephen was just as unfitted for the church as he was for teaching. At least for the church of his own day. His preaching was profound, cultured, tolerant. Too Christian in its simplicity and charity to be readily accepted by congregations brought up on a diet of hell-fire certainty.

"It is better to be credulous than to be hard," he wrote once. "To credit a man with struggles he may not have made, and a confusion and perplexity he may not have experienced, than to strip him ruthlessly of every rag that keeps him warm or shields him from shame."

He never got a settled charge. The whole of his ministry was spent as a locum, here and there in Scotland, and once as far afield as Malta. Always he made friends. Always he made a deep impression on the discerning few. But he never gained the attention, or the election, of the majority.

He wrote a series of essays about Edinburgh over the nom de plume "Belinda's Husband", which, in a way, is a revelation of the unassertive nature of the man. Even as a writer he preferred to stand, as it were, in somebody's shadow.

When I was a student at Glasgow, Malcolm Macleod, in whose home I spent my Sunday evenings, read a paper to the Thirteen Club based on Roddie Stephen's long forgotten *A Plainman's Papers*. A well known literary critic who was present said it was a sad reflection on the culture of Scotland that a writer of such elegance could have lived and died almost unnoticed.

At his death Roddie Stephen left behind him, in manuscript, a series of sketches of the Stornoway he knew in his youth: *Glimpses of Portrona*. The black bound volume in a neat, spidery hand fell into the keeping of my uncle Roddie, who was co-ages with him, and one of his closest friends.

"Others have birthplaces enshrined in history, whose memories of kings, heroes, poets, splendid pageants, great events, the whole world knows," wrote Stephen. "Yet the clamour and glory of history strike lightly enough on the common heart. . . . Even in a great town the citizen has his own history, trivial and unimpressive for others, great and poignant for himself. That is the only history he has read at the sources: the rest, resounding and fateful as it may have been, is but a secondary study, a pale reflection in comparison.

"Portrona has its interest and sacredness for the children it cradled. It can stir thoughts that range far and dive deep, though for most they come back with few words or none. Sombre, bare, much forgotten by the sun as it may be, it is to us what no other place can be."

Portrona was published as a series of articles in the *Stornoway Gazette*. Later, to fulfil Roddie Stephen's dying wish, it was published in book form. The profits were to go to the Endowment Fund of Lews Hospital. Whether there were any profits I do not know, and very much doubt, but the book proved to be something of a goldmine for Lewis.

The reference to the Lews Hospital Endowment Fund in the preface fired T. B. Macaulay with a desire to do something really big for the island from which his father had set out as a young man to found the family fortune in Montreal.

Gift after gift flowed into Lewis. The Hospital. The Library. The burnt-out Town Hall. Bursaries for students. And then, most ambitious of all, a project to reclaim the Lewis moors, as he had reclaimed the wastelands of Quebec at his farm outside Montreal.

One of the worst bogs in Lewis was chosen for the experiment, on Arnish moor, just above the river Creed. Experts were gathered from all over Britain. Machinery was imported from Germany. Monsters, such as Lewis had never seen before, crawled across the moor, digging drains, churning up the land.

I remember one day going out to see an experiment with a new technique for cutting drains with high explosive. The fibrous top layer of the Lewis peat proved too tough for the dynamite and the experiment failed. When they found they could not cut a clean edge, as they did in other soils, the engineers, in disgust, thrust their remaining sticks of dynamite as far down in the peat as they could put them, a dozen or so together, one on top of the other.

We all retired to a safe distance while they prepared to fire the lot, in one almighty explosion. But the explosion never came. There was a dull, muffled rumble. A small piece of turf, about a foot square, was turned back slightly, like a dog-ear on a book, and that was all. The explosion spent itself dispersing the buttery peat below. When we ventured back near the site, we could hear, like a cataract underground, water pouring in to fill the unseen cavity beneath our feet.

In spite of that, and other set-backs, oats and celery and potatoes were growing on the bog within two years. The first occasion on which cereals and root crops had been grown on black peat in so short a time anywhere in the world.

Agriculturalists came from all over Europe to see the miracle. Even from Russia. On two occasions, at least, Macaulay came from Canada in a blaze of publicity.

One hot summer day the peat was so dry that a field of potatoes caught fire. Not the potatoes, or the grass, but the field itself. Whether the fire was sparked off by a cigarette butt, or whether the bottom of a broken bottle acted as a magnifying glass, I do not know, but the field smouldered over a wide area for many hours until a downpour of rain finally dowsed it. And that was on a stretch of bogland where you could not have walked without wellingtons, and perhaps not even with them, in the height of summer, a few years before.

But the Lewis bog was not easily conquered. Unseen below the surface the wooden box drains, laid at so much expense, were warping as the peat dried out and shrunk. The whole development had been carried out too quickly, in an attempt to produce results for Macaulay's first visit.

When the drainage system broke down the bog returned, but, instead of heather, there was now a wilderness of rushes. Instead of the natural moorland there were the ugly fingermarks of man, the botcher.

I am quite sure Macaulay would have seen the mistake, and made a fresh start, if there had been time. But the American Depression cast its blight over the Western World. Macaulay's benefactions came to an end. Even the income from the shares with which he had endowed the Library, and other institutions, dried up.

Quite apart from that, the advisers who crowded round him, attracted by the Lewis experiment, pressed him to put his money into projects of their own. And so the Macaulay Institute of Soil Research at Aberdeen and the Institute for Animal Genetics at Edinburgh, came into being.

No doubt these achieved more for Scottish agriculture than the reclamation of the Lewis moor would have done, even if it had been successful, but these benefactions would probably never have come the way of Edinburgh or Aberdeen if Macaulay's interest in Scotland had not been fired by the love of a Lewis minister, whom the world regarded as a failure, for the Stornoway of his boyhood.

7
A Prophecy Fulfilled

Even after the experiments had ceased, the Macaulay Farm remained in use for quite a number of years, producing a fair proportion of the local milk supply. But the deterioration continued, and eventually it was abandoned as an agricultural subject.

At that point the wiseacres who had decried the experiment from the start were able to preen themselves on their prescience. They forgot their Bibles: "Except a corn of wheat fall into the ground and die . . ."

Although the grandiose Macaulay experiment had failed, the North of Scotland College of Agriculture, which had managed the farm, continued the work on a modest scale, financed in part by funds which Macaulay had provided.

The crofters had never been really interested in the farm. With complete realism they saw that reclamation which required the use of massive machines and vast amounts of capital, was not for them. In the lean years after the collapse, the College looked for cheaper ways of improving the moorland herbage, which might be within the crofters' reach.

While Macaulay had tackled the worst bit of moorland in Lewis, the College tackled the best. They looked mainly for skinned land from which the peat had already been cut to feed the fires of countless generations. Although good by Lewis standards, it was still miserable and unproductive land. Some areas, where the sods had not been replaced when peats were being cut, as by township regulations they should have been, carried no herbage at all. It was a black wilderness.

Even on the choicer bits, which had a carpet of heather and moss, the College was trying to reclaim the most acid land in Britain, in one of the windiest zones in the world, with nearly two hundred and fifty rainy days in the year, and, just to complicate things completely, a high risk of drought in early summer when moisture was needed most.

Eventually the College satisfied themselves that good grass pasture could be established on skinned land in Lewis, if shell sand was applied to kill the acidity, and grass seeds and fertilisers were spread across the surface — without drainage and without tilling. At first the grass grew strongly in the shelter of the heather, but gradually the shell sand killed the heather off, and what had been moorland became a good green sward.

The College adviser under whom this experimental work was carried out was Angus Macleod, an unassuming but remarkable man. He was a typical easy-going Highlander, never showing signs of haste or urgency, never showing emotion, except perhaps when singing a Gaelic song, and scarcely even then.

I have been told that, shortly after he came to Stornoway, he had arranged for some reason to call on Kenny Maciver, one of the leading figures in the fish trade. When he knocked at the door in Francis Street it was answered by Kenny's mother, rather a grand lady in the manner of the wealthier Stornoway families of the time. She assumed the stranger must be the cook's boy friend who was also expected to call, and showed him into the kitchen. Angus sat patiently by the kitchen fire, waiting for something to happen, while Kenny fretted and fumed upstairs and wondered why he had not kept his appointment.

The same unruffled phlegm served Angus well on the golf course. For many years he was one of the most consistent trophy winners in the Stornoway club.

In spite of his easy-going ways — perhaps because of them — he got the confidence of the crofters, and persuaded them to try his method of improving the peat bogs by surface treatment. The first major experiment was carried out in the village of Barvas, where grass seed cleanings were used to cut down cost. Even with this third rate seed, the experiment succeeded, and the field was still providing good secondary pasture more than twenty years later.

A more ambitious experiment was carried out on a hillside at Bragar. On that occasion I went over with my camera to photograph the crofters at work, spreading shell sand, fertilisers and grass seed over some twenty acres of broken ground with no mechanical aid more sophisticated than a bucket.

When Angus was due to retire that was about all that had been done in the way of surface seeding, but, when he spoke at his retirement presentation in the Masonic Hall, he painted a poetic picture of Lewis, the heather isle, transformed into a green isle of rich pasture.

It was not an occasion for pouring cold water on idle dreams, and we let it pass, although, in our superior wisdom, we were a little cynical both as to the achievement and the prospects. But, within a very few years, Angus was proved right. In an incredibly short space of time more than ten thousand acres of new pasture was created in Lewis, and even townsfolk who hadn't as much as a garden to give them an interest in agriculture, pointed out to visitors the green fingers reaching into the moorland as one of the most interesting features of the landscape.

This revolution in Lewis agriculture, which changed the attitude of the people almost as markedly as it changed the landscape, was brought about by the conjunction of three circumstances.

Angus Macleod was succeeded by a young Islayman, Archie Gillespie, with fire in his belly and a flair for leadership. The Crofters Commission, which had just been set up, offered grants for land improvement, and, in the background, providing continuity between Angus Macleod's work and Archie Gillespie's, there was John Grant, the Regional Director of the College, never obtrusive but always there.

Most of the work of land improvement in the early stages was carried out communally, and some astonishing things happened during the boom. Men, and often women, worked like coolies, carrying hundreds of tons of shell sand and fertiliser up precipitous hillsides. They even built rafts to ferry sand and other equipment across lochs and arms of the sea.

Squatters, who had no legal right in the land, were permitted to share in the new pasture, provided they paid their share and gave a hand with the work. People who were too old to be interested themselves voluntarily signed documents to show that they were consenting parties to the development, because it could not go forward without the approval of a majority of the crofters in a township.

If Archie Gillespie found a township unresponsive to his suggestion that they should carry out an improvement scheme, he never argued with them. But, in a short time, he had the township ringed with schemes carried out by more forward-looking neighbours, and he had little to do but wait for the laggards to come seeking his help.

In a short time some of the lorry drivers began to buy tractors and spreaders to mechanise the work. The pace of reclamation increased. One small firm had no less than five crawler tractors and spreaders at work at the height of the boom.

Then, just when things were going well, the government changed the rules of the Lime Subsidy Scheme, because of large scale frauds by big operators in the south, who were claiming payments for non-existent lime, spread on imaginary fields.

The new regulations imposed so much paper work and caused such long delays in the payment of subsidy, the small firms could not cope and the movement lost its impetus. Eventually the lime subsidy was withdrawn altogether.

Having destroyed the land improvement movement in the Hebrides when it was going well, the government had to start again from scratch, twenty years later, under the so-called Integrated Development Programme.

8
The Spring Stampede

There was a surge of land improvement in Shetland at the same time as in Lewis but it followed a very different pattern. Instead of communal schemes, the work was carried out by individuals, on areas of common grazing land apportioned to them by the Crofters Commission.

This may indicate a difference in attitudes to co-operation. It certainly reflects a difference in the lay-out of the townships. In Shetland many of the crofts stand apart like separate farmsteads, while in Lewis the crofting village generally consists of a straggling line of houses, quite close together, on tiny crofts.

The three mile stretch of villages in Ness, which shade into one another with no distinction visible to the stranger, apart from the road signs, is almost an urban sprawl. In Lewis, and the rest of the Hebrides for that matter the croft is designated by a number in a township, but in Shetland a great many of the crofts have individual names, often with a Viking flavour.

The Noop of Norby sounds as if it had come straight out of the sagas, or the novels of Selma Lagerlof, whose *Story of Gosta Berling* has resonances from our own Viking past which we can still discern behind the Celtic mist.

The Noop of Norby remains in my memory because, when we carried out an apportionment, so that the land could be reclaimed, one old crofter told us it would be the first time a plough had gone into the soil there since the day in the sixteenth century when they were ploughing with oxen and there was an eclipse of the sun. The crofters, so he assured us, took to the hill, thinking it was the end of the world, and abandoned cultivation of the area for good.

I have no idea whether the story is true, but I like to think that the Crofters Commission were able to make progress by turning the clock back three hundred years.

The sub-division of crofts, especially in Skye and Barra, makes a township list look like an exercise in mathematics. In the Crofters Commission I often found myself faced with the question whether a croft designated as, say, $\frac{1}{2}8$, in a particular township, should be amalgamated with its neighbour, which might be $\frac{1}{2}9$ or $\frac{1}{3}9$ or the other half of 8.

Lewis, by and large, avoided this absurdity, possibly because of the prevalence of squatting. The crofts remained intact, nominally at least, but the young folk built houses on their parents' land or on the common grazings, without the consent of the estate, and sometimes in defiance of the estate's specific prohibition, although latterly the estate gave up the struggle and connived at what was happening.

Although the crofter generally tolerated the existence of the squatter, he was fiercely opposed to any organised attempt to give squatters a legal title. One of the angriest scenes in Lewis since the Crofters War occurred in the 1930s when the Factor to the Stornoway Trust Estate, Edwin Aldred, who had come to Lewis with Leverhulme and settled permanently, went to Tolsta to mark off the land held by squatters so that he could regularise their position.

The Trustees had to drop that idea quickly, but there was seldom any opposition from the crofters to individual squatters getting a title from the estate to a small piece of garden ground, when they required it, so that they could get grant aid from the County Council for house improvements.

When I was a youngster there were about two thousand squatters in Lewis. Two thousand families with as little legal right to the land they lived on as gypsies, but forming a settled population, and an integral part of the villages in which they lived!

The squatters were very much at the mercy of the Grazings Committee elected by the crofters. Generally they paid the township a levy for the privilege of grazing stock. This levy was quite illegal. The crofters had no authority to sublet the landlord's land. It made complete good sense, however. The crofters were paying rent for all the land in the township, including the land the squatters were occupying. The squatters were also generally given a right to cut peats, by the crofters, again illegally, but sensibly.

The Crofters Acts have always proceeded on the basis that there is a landlord-tenant relationship, and that the crofter's rights are strictly limited, while the crofters, in Lewis at any rate, have acted in the belief that they own their crofts, subject to the payment of rent to the landlord, and conformity with the customs of the township administered by the Grazings Committee or the township in general session.

The attitude was neatly encapsulated once at a Land Court case I reported where the Member of Court, who was taking the hearing, explained to a crofter from Tong what the Crofting Acts had to say on the point at issue. The crofter listened respectfully and then replied, "That may be the law, my lord, but it's not the law in Tong!"

The principal duty of the Grazings Committees, in the days before the crofts were all fenced off from each other, was to fix the date on which all the township stock must be removed to the sheiling, to protect the growing crops, rest the inbye pasture, and make use of the grazings on the higher ground which had little value except at the height of summer.

When we lived on Lewis Street, I was scarcely aware of the existence of the crofters and the significance of their seasonal arrangements, but, as soon as we moved to Matheson Road, there was a change.

Early in May I would be awakened, morning after morning, at first light, by the lowing of cattle, the hysterical baaing chorus of driven sheep, the barking of innumerable dogs, the shouting of human voices, directed at the dogs, in command, or at errant stirks or ewes, in sheer exasperation. Behind the vocal sounds was the steady patter of hooves and the tramp of many feet. I can hear it as I write, the memory is so vivid.

Sometimes I would look from the bedroom window to see the crofters of Point, village after village, each on the day appointed by the Grazings Committee, going out en masse to the summer sheilings round Beinn a' Bhuinne.

Most of the Lewis villages have direct access to their hill ground, but the townships of Point — Knock, Aignish, Swordale, Bayble, Garrabost, Flesherin, Portnaguran, Portvoller, Broker, Eagletown Melbost and Branahuie — had to drive their stock through Stornoway to get to the 19,000 acres of their General Common Pasture on the far side of the town.

The animals moved forward in a loosely regulated stampede. They had the scent of spring in their nostrils, and perhaps a recollection of tasty moorland pasture from previous years. But they were bewildered by the maze of streets into which they were driven, and tempted by the gardens — the only greenery in sight. They were also excited, rather than restrained, by the innumerable drovers who waved sticks and shouted as they dashed hither and thither, to block a street, a gate, or even an open house door.

Generally a group of women followed, barefooted, knitting as they went, and carrying on their backs in creels such household goods as had not been already transported to the sheiling by cart or gig.

Going to the sheiling or airigh was a migration of the whole village, or at any rate of the younger folk. The airigh itself was a drystone hut roofed with turf or heather, with recesses where bracken or heather could be spread for bedding, and little apertures in the inner wall for storing the milk and crowdie and butter.

Some airighs were primitive indeed, but others were fairly elaborate and provided most of the simple comforts of a crofter's house of the period, including tables and chairs brought out from home for summer use.

9
A Swedish Macleod from Skye

There is — or at least there was — one airigh on the Uig road, just south of Garynahine, which was of considerable historical or archaeological interest.

No one in Lewis paid any particular attention to it, but, shortly after I became editor of the *Gazette*, I met a Swedish professor who had come to the island specially to see it. He maintained that it was the only building in Europe erected within living memory on Bronze Age principles.

The building of the airigh had been recorded, he said, by Capt Thomas of the Ordnance Survey, who took a great interest in the traditions of Lewis when he worked here last century, and whose wife was one of the ladies who helped to build up the Harris Tweed industry in the early years. The distinguishing feature of the airigh was that it had been built with a corbelled roof. An arch without a keystone, so to speak.

I went to see the airigh some time after that, and took some photographs of it. It was no longer in use, but was still intact. The last time I passed along the Uig road, however, I did not see it. I didn't leave the car to have a thorough search, but I have an uneasy feeling that we have obliterated a little bit of Lewis, perhaps of European history, to make space for a fank.

Many years after I met the Swedish professor in Lewis, I called on him at Uppsala University. On the way north from Stockholm, the car broke down. We were standing disconsolately by the roadside, Cathie and I and some friends, when a smart little two seater, driven by an army officer, pulled over and offered assistance. The officer did, that is. In the course of conversation we mentioned that we came from Lewis. The Swedish officer stood to attention, and said smartly, "My name is Macleod and I come from the island of Skye!"

Further questions established that his people had gone to Sweden in the wars of Gustavus Adolphus around 1610. Swedish-Hebrideans have even longer memories than Hebridean-Swedes. Our Scandinavian names are confined to the map. Their Scottish names are still often on the front door. The professor we were going to see was a Campbell! He will appear again in the story in a context far removed from archaeology.

My own first visit to an airigh as a child was to Anna Pope's (Mrs Macdonald's) summer home just above Loch Bhat an Dip. I went in the sidecar of my father's motor cycle: one of the very few motor vehicles of any sort in Lewis then.

Anna was one of the kindest women I ever knew, and everyone in the family loved her, but I think some of the would-be aristocrats of the town looked at her a little askance because she had, in their phrase, "gone native". She had married a draper's assistant, (a close friend of my father) and they lived on the family croft in Point. They must have been pretty tight for money throughout their married life, but Anna kept open house for all who called, and, when her husband set up a drapery business of his own, he bankrupted himself in a very few years by his easy-going generosity. And was no doubt despised for it by some of those who had taken advantage of him.

I was not aware of any of these things when I went to the airigh as a child. It was sheer adventure to eat oatcakes and bannocks, heaped high with strongly flavoured moorland butter, and crowdie, in a rough stone hut such as I had never seen before, miles away from town, in an open landscape of heather and little blue lochans, stretching away to the Harris hills. A day of undiluted pleasure like that can enrich a whole life.

My contemporaries in the Nicolson who lived in crofting villages were, of course, much more familiar than I with sheiling life. Neil Mackay has told me of visits he paid to the sheiling with his granny when he was a lad in Breasclete. He did not romanticise the sheiling as it is romanticised in Gaelic song, and in the recollection of many an emigrant. Indeed as it is romanticised in my own memory of that day at Bhat an Dip.

Neil was well aware of the labour, the inconvenience, and the constant struggle with inclement weather in a hut which was proof against neither wind nor rain, and which generally had two doorways but no doors — the leeward doorway always stood open while the windward was laboriously blocked with turf. Until the wind changed!

Apart from having to take all the furniture and utensils from home, Neil told me that some Breasclete families had to take a considerable quantity of grass to humour cows which were temperamental at milking time, although in earlier days the popular cow's "comforter" had been the backbone of a large fish.

The sheiling, of course, had its attractions. The change of scene was as welcome for the humans as the change of pasture for the cows. It was a favourite time for courting. There were fishing expeditions to the nearby lochs. Informal ceilidhs in the gloaming. And occasional nights of special revelry.

On the last night at the sheiling, Neil told me, the night of the flitting, "oidhche na h-iomraich", all the young folk gathered at one of the airighs for a meal and a dance to the music of the melodeon and the pipes.

Next morning, on the day appointed by the Grazings Committee for the return to the village, the thatch would be stripped from the airigh, leaving the building open to the elements for the winter. The bedding and all other disposable rubbish would be burnt in a sort of ritual bonfire which they referred to as the "teine-leadhainn". The cattle, who, according to Neil, knew the signal as well as watchmen on the Borders knew the beacon fires, would set off, of their own accord, for the green pastures of the village from which they had been separated so long.

With all its grinding poverty, the life of the old crofting township had a rhythm which was civilised and humane, but the sheiling system began to break down even before the First World War when the girls, feeling the pressures of a money economy, elected to go instead to the East Coast fishing ports to gut herring — a cold, dirty, disagreeable repetitive job, if ever there was one, although it never broke their spirits or repressed their gaiety.

One can still identify the sites of the old airighs on the hillsides by the green patches where they were situated, and where the soil was enriched by the droppings of cattle over many years. But not many people could point out the knolls as Neil's granny did, recalling the vanished families whose ancient airighs the greensward marked.

The habit of going to the sheiling lingered on among the older folk long after it had ceased to be an essential feature of village life. Well into the fifties I visited a sheiling in Skigersta where an old lady, then over eighty, was busy cutting peats so that the fuel would be ready when she came back the following year.

On a hillock nearby a young lassie from Australia was playing the bagpipes — a sight which would have been considered incongruous, if not indecent, in the heyday of the sheiling, when piping was exclusively a male occupation.

Along the road from Stornoway to Garynahine, after the Second World War, there sprung up a colony of more than a hundred corrugated iron or wooden shacks, where families from Point and Stornoway took up residence in the summer. Seeking out by some atavistic instinct the old sheiling ground in the heart of the moor, rather than the beaches which might seem, if one did not know the social history of the island, a much more attractive setting for a holiday home.

10
Caught in the Act

On T. B. Macaulay's first visit to Lewis he sailed direct from Montreal to Stornoway on the CPR Liner *Minnedosa*. On board with him were more than a hundred Lewis men and women coming home from Canada and USA to see their families, and a fair sprinkling of others coming, like Macaulay himself, to see for the first time, the island from which they were sprung.

It was almost the *Metagama* emigration in reverse. I doubt whether any port in the Kingdom, the size of Stornoway, has thus been used as a terminus by trans-Atlantic liners, in both directions, carrying locally generated traffic. So far as I know it was the first organised visit home by Lewisfolk who had settled in America and made good.

Long before the *Minnedosa*, of course, there had been a two-way traffic between Lewis and America. Many of those who went as trappers to Hudson Bay eventually returned to Lewis, some of them bringing their Indian wives with them, and there were seasonal visitors, like the Quebecers who went out in summer to work on the Great Lakes but came home in winter when the Lakes were frozen, although they lie far to the south of the Hebrides, where the Gulf Stream permits us to grow semi-tropical plants in sheltered places, out of doors, in the latitude of Labrador.

In more recent years there has been a steady stream of visitors back and fore across the Atlantic by air, but there has been nothing quite like the *Minnedosa* before or since.

The trip was organised by Murdo MacLean, who seldom missed a trick in his business as shipping agent, and very often did some good for the island in the by-going, although he did not always get credit for it. He needed all his shrewdness. In a place with Stornoway's capacity for fun his business was subject to hazards which would have been unthinkable elsewhere.

Many years before the *Minnedosa*, when he was organising the emigration of domestic servants to some of the top families in the States, he caught Aeneas Mackenzie, the shipbuilder, and a leading figure in the community, trying to steal from his office some sheets of CPR notepaper. When challenged, Aeneas gaily admitted that he had intended to forge a letter from Murdo to another leading citizen, asking him, in suitable terms, to travel to America with a party of girls, as guardian of their welfare and their morals, while another letter would inform the press that the invitation had been sent.

The point of the exercise was that the intended recipient of the invitation maintained a facade of Victorian respectability, but it was well known locally that there were brats about the place who bore his likeness, although they didn't bear his name.

There was an air of carnival gaiety about the *Minnedosa* trip, a lightheartedness which I don't think Lewis has ever quite caught again. On board ship the visitors were riding high. The collapse of the American stockmarket was just a few months ahead, but they hadn't the slightest premonition as they rollicked along.

They improvised their own song, and sung it on every excuse:

Stornoway! Stornoway!
That's where we long to be.
We've been happy here and there,
We've been happy everywhere,
But in Stornoway we long to be.

In Lewis it was the first break in the clouds after the war, the *Iolaire*, the collapse of the Leverhulme schemes, and the mass emigration which followed. It was the first indication that the island was not down and out. That it was making a comeback, even if it was only as the sentimental capital of a far scattered race. A secular Jerusalem. A place of pilgrimage.

Macaulay, who was accompanied by his daughter and her family, gathered his grandchildren about him on the deck when the hills of Uig began to show blue above the horizon. The homeland he had not yet seen himself, where the villages of Brenish and Valtos and Mangursta lie between the Atlantic and the hills, round some of the loveliest beaches in Europe.

"There", he said, "is where your ancestors were born!"

The solemnity of the moment was shattered by a matter-of-fact Canadian voice: "Grandad, what are ancestors?"

Later, when a reporter asked him how he felt on first seeing the hills of home, Macaulay replied, "Are you a Scot?"

"Yes", said the reporter.

"Then you know how I felt!"

It is very easy for islanders to slip into a sickly sentimentality on occasions like that — especially for island journalists! There is, however, a happy mean between the ancestor worship of the Chinese and the modern detachment, not only from ancestors, but even from parents, and sometimes from children, which gives each individual the completely selfish idea that the human race begins and ends with him.

The instinct in man is not only natural but healthy that he should wish to know who he is, whence he came, and whither he is going, but, if present trends continue, man will soon be like the mule, without pride of ancestry or hope of posterity. A lonely nomad pursuing personal success from place to place like an outcast with neither home nor tribe.

The week or fortnight after the *Minnedosa* dropped anchor outside Arnish Light was a busy one for my father. There was a succession of events. The unveiling of a plaque marking the birthplace of Sir Alexander Mackenzie the great Canadian explorer. The presentation of an illuminated address to Macaulay on a hilltop in Uig overlooking the home of his ancestors. And, of course, the opening of the new Town Hall.

During the opening ceremony, Provost Bain apologised to Macaulay because the Council could not offer him the Freedom of the Burgh, as they had not the legal power.

Macaulay had done his homework. He knew the circumstances in which Stornoway had been granted a charter only to have it withdrawn. "My own ancestors were among those responsible for that," he said.

Next day the *Daily Express* reported him as having said "My own ancestors were the mongrels responsible for that."

The error was not due to an attempt to embellish the news. Anyone familiar with Pitman's shorthand can guess that it arose from a badly written outline. Anyway it amused Macaulay.

A few years later it came to light that, although Stornoway's charter as a Royal Burgh had been withdrawn before it had come into effect, there was another valid charter establishing the town as a Burgh of Barony under which it had the right to elect free burgesses.

On a subsequent visit, when Macaulay was in Scotland to receive an honorary degree from Edinburgh University, he got the Freedom of Stornoway as well.

11
Thus Stornoway Flourished

T. B. Macaulay was telling no more than the truth when he admitted that his Lewis ancestors had been a little bit unruly in their day — as were my own ancestors, their great rivals, the Morisons of Ness. But he was wrong in blaming the unruly conduct of the natives for Stornoway's loss of its Royal Charter.

The real reason was the fear felt by the douce burgesses of Inverness, Dingwall, Cromarty, and the other Royal Burghs along the Moray Firth and further south, that their pockets would suffer, if Stornoway was given the privilege of foreign trade, especially in fish.

As the records of the Convention of Royal Burghs show, they thought the people of Stornoway would "debar the inhabitants of the rest of the frie borrowis and the whole natives of this Kingdome frome the benefeit of that fisching, to the vtter vndoeing of the whole cuntrey and destroyeing of all trade both outvard and invard." The typical cry of the monopolist throughout the ages!

The mainland burghs were also afraid that the Earl of Seaforth, who had obtained the Charter for Stornoway, would bring in "straingers' and plant them "thair, with power to theme to trade and trafficque."

The Commissioners to the Convention of Royal Burghs in 1628 grossly exaggerated the risk to their own trade of giving Stornoway access to the export market, but they were right in assuming that, if the disability under which Stornoway laboured was removed, the inhabitants would be enterprising enough to take full advantage.

When White, of the General Excise Office in Edinburgh, gave a paper to the Highland Society of Scotland in 1790, he singled out the inhabitants of Stornoway for their initiative and perseverance in the fishing industry.

"It was after the Union," he wrote, "that the merchants in Stornoway had full scope for their laudable pursuits; then it was that the herrings which they caught might lawfully be sent to the British West Indies, and be exported thither, and to all other lawful places, attended with the encouragement of a bounty; and from that time the people of Stornoway have been gradually advancing.

"Some twenty-five or thirty years ago all the fish they caught were carried for them to their port of destination by hired vessels. Now they can show in their harbour, in the fishing time, upward of thirty sail of stout handsome vessels, from twenty to seventy tons burden, all their own property.

"Their town is a pattern of neatness and cleanliness; and when a stranger enters their convenient mansions, he will have set before him a piece of well-dressed Highland mutton, some choice fish, and a bottle of port, the produce of the hospitable landlord's industry. To the everlasting credit of these industrious fishers and merchants, it falls to be recorded, that they have made their pleasant hamlet rise into view, and display upwards of a hundred slated houses, besides inferior ones, from their gain from the sea. Thus Stornoway flourished . . ."

Eighteen years before White's visit, the Incorporated Trades of Stornoway — smiths, tailors, weavers, carpenters, wrights, coopers, shoemakers, masons, dyers and hecklers — registered their armorial ensigns with the Lord Lyon. Stornoway was the only burgh in Scotland, apart from Aberdeen, to do so, which one would think is a fair indication that Stornoway, at that time, was a prosperous community — and a proud one.

Fortunately for Edinburgh, Glasgow, Dundee, Perth and Inverness, whose trades used arms which had not been registered, the Lord Lyon did not enforce the Act of 1672, under which he could "escheat to His Majestie" all the moveable goods and gear on which such fabricated bearings were represented, and have the users "incarceret in the narrest prisone."

Although the Incorporated Trades had their arms registered in 1772, the Burgh Commissioners were not so careful when Stornoway became a Police Burgh in 1863, and began to use the Coat of Arms which was popular in my own day on tourist souvenirs from the town. It was not only unregistered, it seems to have offended all the rules of heraldry, to judge by the acid tones in which the Marquis of Bute criticised it, in a book he wrote in 1903 on the Arms of the Baronial and Police Burghs of Scotland.

Stornoway came in for further criticism when Innes of Learney began to tighten up on the use of arms and took legal action against Aberdeen for having an unauthorised armorial seal on the Provost's chain. Stornoway, at that time, was listed among the 78 delinquent burghs using unregistered coats of arms. Ten years later Stornoway was listed among the 16 Police Burghs still refusing to conform to the law as interpreted by the Lord Lyon.

Finally, in 1958, the Town Councillors caught up with the Incorporated Trades of 1772, and had the Burgh Coat of Arms properly registered, to mark the 350th anniversary of the granting of a Charter to the town as a Burgh of Barony. Stornoway, in fact, became the first burgh in Scotland to use the distinctive coronet for Burghs of Barony designed by the Lord Lyon. But we didn't enjoy the use of it for long. Twenty years after it was granted, the burgh was swallowed up in the new local authority area of the Western Isles, and lost its separate identity.

It was just about the time my father came to Stornoway, in the eighteen nineties, that J. L. Robertson "discovered" the long forgotten arms of the Incorporated Trades. He gifted a set of reproductions to the Town Hall, together with the arms of the United Corporations — "gules, two dexter hands in fess, couped above the wrist grasping each other, proper, with the

37

mottoes, 'Grace, Peace and Unity' above and 'God's Providence is our Inheritance' below."

They perished in the Town Hall fire with the rest of the building, but were replaced in the new Town Hall, and I often thought there was a certain irony in those clasped hands above the platform, when the hall was used for ratepayers' meetings, and grace, peace and unity were patently absent from the proceedings. But "God's Providence is Our Inheritance" always seemed to me an ideal motto for a seaport town dependent on the vagaries of herring fishing.

Stornoway's seaborne trade was not always innocent, however. In 1954 I had a call from Dr Hellerstrom, a Swedish historian. He was trying to unravel the history of an organisation of carpenters, founded in London in the reign of Queen Elizabeth, rather on the lines of the Freemasons, but with a political background.

The organisation flourished in Sweden, where the carpenters became "timmermen", and still exists, or did in 1954, although it has lost its political motivation. In Elizabethan days, however, the English court used the organisation to stir up trouble for the Scottish Crown, and Stornoway was a focal point in the conspiracy.

The purpose of Dr Hellerstrom's visit was to trace a hill called "Nuan" near Stornoway, as the Society's records show that a number of Swedish carpenters were engaged in shipbuilding there. I cannot understand why anyone would want to build ships on a hill, but there is an island called Eilean nan Uan, near Holm, which used to be a busy herring fishing port, and on the Bleu map, it is described as "Ylen na Nuan".

The tradition of fishing in other peoples' troubled waters lingered on in Lewis. When the Home Guard was formed in 1940, all the rifles at Lews Castle and the various shooting lodges round the island were commandeered for use. There was little else available! In fact, in some parts of Britain, at that time, the Home Guard were armed with pikes!

The Stornoway police made a surprising contribution to the pool of arms. They produced fifteen short cavalry rifles which were quite serviceable although a little rusty. They were part of a consignment smuggled into Lewis in 1908 when the Ulstermen were arming to resist incorporation in a United Ireland.

Peter Liddle, the farmer at Gress, had formed a band of volunteers to assist the Ulstermen. They were supplied with arms and ammunition, and used to meet secretly in one of the local hotels to drill. When the police got wind of their activities the cases of rifles were opened and the arms dispersed for hiding. Some years later, when there was an amnesty for holders of unlicensed firearms, Peter Liddle handed his share of the cache over to the police — the fifteen cavalry rifles used to arm the Home Guard thirty years later.

I don't know how the arms were smuggled into Lewis in the first place, but I do know that the Captain of the Antrim Iron Ore Company's boat, the *Glentaise*, which visited Stornoway weekly in my childhood, was

38

regarded as a hero in Ulster because of his activities as a gun-runner in the troubles of that time.

If he had not been so successful Ireland's troubles might have been sorted out by now. Or, at least, they would be the troubles of Eire not of the UK!

12
Revolution in the Atlantic

It would be about the time of White's report on Stornoway that the first generation of seafaring men of whom there is record in my mother's family were voyaging to Archangel, Riga and Lubeck, to the British West Indies, and the coast of Africa — to say nothing of Tahiti — not only with salt herring but with dried cod and ling of which there was then, and later, a considerable export.

I remember as a youngster seeing thousands of ling spread out on Sandwick beach to dry until the flesh became as hard as a board. When steeped in water, and boiled, it regained its original texture. Eaten with mealy potatoes, mashed up with butter, it made as satisfying a dish as I have ever tasted.

Ling could also be seen drying on the wall along South Beach, although Sandwick was preferred because, while the fish lay on the big round pebbles, the air could circulate freely below, speeding up the drying process.

Could you leave hundreds of pounds worth of fish today to dry in the sun on a beach or wall, unattended by day or night? There was a lot more real poverty, even actual hunger, around when that could be done without fear of theft than there is today. Crime is not a function of poverty. It has other and deeper springs.

It must also have been around the time White wrote that the children of Lewis first began to hear the sound of the ocean in huge, brightly coloured tropical shells, as I did when I was a child, or wonder at trinket boxes made of porcupine quills, or inlaid eastern work, or red painted Riga bowls, which seamen brought home to wives and sweethearts in long, narrow, bleached white canvas kit bags, like the one my brother fell heir to eventually, and took with him to a Scout camp at Evanton, no doubt with a greater sense of adventure than my grandfather experienced when he carried the self-same bag to the Indies or the Coromandel coast.

Although Stornoway has been the principal port and gateway of Lewis from Viking times or even earlier, it did not have a monopoly of the island's trade. The villages round Loch Roag, especially Carloway and Valtos, from which Macaulay's ancestors had come, were prosperous fishing and trading ports up to the First World War.

Even in my own day they were still visited regularly by cargo vessels and puffers. I remember, from holidays in Uig, the bustle which prevailed when a cargo vessel came into Loch Roag. I also remember the temporary shortages in the shops which could precede its arrival. Stornoway was a long day's journey away, and the villages were much more self-sufficient.

One of the principal seafaring and trading families of Uig were the Nicolsons who founded the school. They moved across the island from Uig to Stornoway — an indication of the change taking place in the pattern of trade — before spreading their tentacles to the woollen mills of Yorkshire, the cotton fields of America, to Australia and Shanghai.

There is a story that, when the family was established in Stornoway, they presented a bell to the church at Balnakil. A very special bell! It came from a pirate ship! I have never been able to verify the story, nor can I even recall clearly where I first heard it, but I have often wondered whether, by any chance, the bell at Balnakil came from the *Jane* of which I have written in an earlier book.

The story of another Uig family was brought forcibly to my notice one day early in the war by Murdo MacLean, the shipping agent, who asked me to go with him to the pictures. He wanted company. I don't think he had ever been in the pictures before. He had no time for that sort of thing. He regarded the cinema as frivolous, not in the sense a member of the Free Church might, but because it distracted his attention from business.

The film he wanted to see was *Atlantic Ferry*, based on the story of the Cunard Line, with, so he assured me, Michael Redgrave playing the part of a "Lewisman" and Valerie Hobson the part of a "Lewiswoman".

The Lewis link with the Cunard Line is through the Macivers of Liverpool whom Murdo, an ardent Uigeach, claimed were an Uig family. William Matheson, whose say-so I would take on any matter of Lewis genealogy, describes the Macivers as an off-shot of the Macivers of Gress. Actually both are right!

The truth of the matter would appear to be that there were two families of Macivers from Uig, closely related, and with their roots in Gress, who were prominent in the maritime life of Liverpool. They got to Liverpool by a natural progression, trading first between Uig and the Clyde, then between the Clyde and the Mersey.

The first family moved from Uig to Dunoon early in the 18th century, then moved to Greenock, and finally to Liverpool. They were said at one time to have had a virtual monopoly of the trade between Glasgow and Liverpool. David Maciver, the father of the second family, according to an account of Clan Iver, published anonymously in 1873, was lost at sea when the ship he commanded sank in the Bay of Biscay in 1812. Two brothers were in the navy. One commanded HMS *Swallow*, a vessel of 14 guns.

David's three sons, for some reason which I cannot explain, were brought up in the American Consulate in Greenock. One of them went to America and died there at the age of 33, a comparatively wealthy man. The other two brothers, David and Charles, went to Liverpool, and became the partners of Samuel Cunard in establishing what must rank as the world's most famous shipping line.

This association gave rise to the belief in some quarters in Lewis, where the clan Maciver is known but the clan Cunard is not, that the name of the line is really a corruption of the Gaelic words "cuan ard", the high ocean, which would be both poetic and apt, but which has no foundation in fact.

Lewis, in fact, has a double link with the Cunard Line in that Charles Maciver, the younger of the founding brothers, married Mary Ann Morison, daughter of Daniel Morison, Comptroller of Customs in Glasgow, who was descended from Rev Kenneth Morison, minister in Stornoway in the early years of the 18th century, and, through him, from the Breves, giving Ness a share in the story.

According to the film the two Maciver brothers were rivals for Mary Ann Morison's affection. She was first engaged to David, the elder, but at a great ball in Boston, celebrating the inauguration of the line, Charles supplanted his brother. Whether the rivalry of the brothers is fact or fiction I do not know. It may owe more to the imperative of the box-office than to the facts of history. So with some other exciting incidents in the film, like the great storm in which the "coffin ship" *Anne of Liverpool* was lost with Charles Maciver on board. For a time he was given up as lost. Or the tense scene in which Charles risked his life to free a jammed paddle wheel. Or David's dash through a fog to avert a collision between the *Britannia* and a drifting light buoy.

Even when one makes allowance for anything Hollywood may have added to the story, the inauguration of the first regular service across the Atlantic was both dramatic and significant to a degree it is hard for us to realise in the age of *Concorde*.

In the early years of last century mails were carried across the Atlantic by government brigs which took six or seven weeks on the voyage. Samuel Cunard, an American business man, conceived the idea of replacing the brigs by steamships which could maintain a regular and much speedier service. Not steamships as we know them today. Wooden hulled paddle steamers. Squat and unmanageable. Cockleshells in an Atlantic gale.

The idea grew too big for Cunard to finance. Napier, the famous Clyde engineer, told him to consult George Burns, the Glasgow shipowner. Burns called in the Macivers of Liverpool. Between them they cobbled together the package which became the Cunard Line.

When David Maciver died, a comparatively young man, his place was taken by his brother Charles. Clement Jones in his book, *Pioneer Shipowners*, makes the significant comment that it still remains an open question whether it was Samuel Cunard or Charles Maciver who was the real builder of the line.

Charles Maciver certainly was a masterful man. One of his biographers says he had the look of a man born to command. During the reign of Napoleon III in France there was a scare that Britain was going to be invaded. Charles Maciver recruited a company of volunteers in Liverpool, and paraded through the streets of the city at the head of a thousand men.

When one of his captains asked leave to take his wife on a voyage with him, Maciver said "Do as you please! You know the rules!" When the captain and his wife arrived on board they were handed complimentary tickets for a first class state-room. Somebody else was on the bridge!

In 1839 the partners got a government contract for the carriage of mails, on condition that their vessels were available as troopships in time of war — a tradition which has lasted down to our own day.

In 1840 the first Cunarder, the *Britannia*, made the crossing from Liverpool to Boston in 14 days and 8 hours. There was great jubilation at the end of the voyage. A new era had dawned on the Atlantic. In the winter, when Boston harbour froze, the local inhabitants, at their own expense, had a channel cut through seven miles of ice so that the mail would not be delayed.

The Lewis connection with Cunard was reinforced more than a century after the *Britannia* made her maiden voyage when a Stornoway man, Donald Maclean, became Commodore Captain of the line. The original Lewis link, attenuated by time, could also still be traced — the Chairman of the line, Sir Percy Bates, was married to a grand-daughter of Charles Maciver.

I may be dreaming, but I have a feeling that the celebrated Mrs Perrins, who struck Lewis like a whirlwind in the fifties and sixties, was a close connection of Sir Percy Bates. She certainly had connections with Liverpool and the Cunard Line.

13
A House Called Stornoway

Donald Maclean was not the first Lewisman to command the "flagship" of the Cunard Line. Alick Ryrie, a member of a well known Stornoway seafaring family, was captain of the *Hibernia*, the first Cunarder that ever entered New York Harbour.

Originally the Cunard run was from Liverpool to Boston, but, in December 1847, it was decided to extend the service to New York. The Lewis Captain was the guest at a great commemorative reception, given by the leading merchants and businessmen of New York. The New York *Herald Tribune* described his pioneer voyage as "one of the most important events of the year", because of its effect in promoting commerce between the two countries.

Although Alick Ryrie made maritime history on that voyage, his career began, a little inauspiciously, as an apprentice on the London convict ship *Surrey*.

It is interesting to speculate how the Ryries came to be in Stornoway, but I am afraid I have more questions than answers. When I think of the matter, I am reminded of a crofter I knew, whose broad Aberdeenshire accent struck me like a blow in the face, at a meeting of soft-spoken Hebrideans, but who was clearly a settled, and respected, member of the community. "How did you come to land up here?" I asked him, afterwards. "I came ahint a woman!" he said succinctly.

The first of the Ryries may also have come to Lewis "ahint a woman". He certainly married a Stornoway wife, but there was a prior link in the chain which was probably more significant. He may have come "ahint a regiment".

Alick Ryrie was a son of Capt Phineas Ryrie, who served in Egypt with the Old Soldiers of Uig, in what became known in the Uig tradition as "Cogadh nan Turc".* Phineas, then a lieut, was one of the unfortunates taken prisoner at the battle of El Hammed. Whether the officers were sold into slavery with the men, I do not know, but all of them were released sometime later, when a truce was signed. By that time those who had not been involved in the Battle of El Hammed were stationed in Sicily, and, presumably, Phineas Ryrie rejoined them there.

The old soldiers were back in Britain, briefly, in 1808, before going to the Low Countries, where they remained until 1816. The Uigeachs were not

*For the history of the Old Soldiers of Uig see *Surprise Island*.

44

involved in the Battle of Waterloo but they were, for a spell, on garrison duty in Brussels. They, and the other Highlanders in the regiment, were so popular with the Belgians for "the mildness and suavity of their manners, and their excellent conduct", that the Mayor presented a formal petition to the army, asking that they should not be replaced by other troops.

Whether Phineas Ryrie was with the Uigeachs at Brussels, as he had been at El Hammed, I cannot be sure. According to William Matheson's genealogies, in *The Blind Harper*, he married in December 1809, which might suggest that he was invalided out of the regiment after the battle of El Hammed. On the other hand, he may have got married during a period of leave, or his bride may even have joined him in Brussels.

In any event, she was a Lewiswoman, Catherine Morison, daughter of Roderick Morison, a merchant in Stornoway. According to Matheson, he was also tacksman at Mellon Udrigle, and was drowned in the Minch while travelling between his two properties. He is buried at Ui.

The really significant point in the story, however, is not that he married a Stornoway wife, but that he was so well-known in the Uig tradition that there was a little rhyme, a rabhd, about him in circulation, half a century after his death, when the youngsters who chanted it would have had no recollection of the man it referred to. Murdo MacLean once recited it for me. He translated it as, "Capt Ryrie was a wealthy man and a gentleman, and he walked very carefully."

Once settled in Stornoway, the Ryries quickly became part of the local community. Capt Phineas was one of the subscribers to the Stornoway Academy, established in 1817, a fact of which I was reminded a number of years ago by an ex-moderator of the Free Church, Rev Angus Finlayson, whose great-grandfather, Norman Macfarlane, of Marvig, married one of Phineas Ryrie's daughters.

There is a tombstone in Sandwick Cemetery which shows the strength of the link which bound the Ryries to Lewis. One panel of the elaborate monument records that "here lie interred the bodies of Phineas Ryrie, Late Capt of the 78th Regiment, aged 51 years; William Ryrie, late Lieut of the Royal Marines, aged 45 years; and Robert Ryrie, aged 36 years, all of whom expired at Stornoway".

I have always assumed that Phineas, William and Robert were brothers, but Basil Lubbock, who wrote *The Opium Clippers*, and other well-known nautical books, once told me that they were cousins. I think he was mistaken, but either way, they must have been a close knit family, and much attached to the little seaport, where the tide had cast them ashore.

The same stone records, on other panels, that Capt Phineas's widow, Catherine, died in Liverpool in 1861, and was taken to Stornoway for burial. Presumably she had gone to live with her son, Alick, who captained the *Hibernia*.

Another son, Robert, who died in London, was also taken to Stornoway for burial. In fact the only member of the family named on the tombstone who was not buried in Stornoway was William Donald Ryrie, who died at

Heloun in Egypt in 1900, and was buried in Cairo. He was aged 77, and presumably retired. Whether he died while on holiday in Egypt, or whether he lived there permanently, I do not know, but he certainly did not lose contact with Lewis.

It was he who, on a visit to Stornoway, in December 1874, got wind of the misuse the notorious factor, Donald Munro, was making of the Ness Disaster Fund, at the expense of the scores of widows and children dependent on it. He exposed Munro, in a pamphlet written from the Colonial Club in London, setting off a chain of events with many ramifications, which I have tried to unravel in *The Hub of My Universe*. I will come back to it when the time comes to explore the manner in which Donald Munro was given a sort of ossified immortality, in an obscure three-decker Victorian romance, which would have been completely forgotten, if I had not stumbled on an old newspaper cutting, in my father's album, with a cryptic annotation in shorthand, which set me rummaging in obscure corners of the National Library, with the invaluable help of one of the librarians, Iain Maciver, whose parents were school and university friends of mine.

Apart altogether from the names on the Ryrie tomb, the fact that someone was sufficiently interested in the Lewis connection to erect it, sometime after 1900, is illuminating. The Ryries were both incomers, and birds of passage. None of the three who first settled in Stornoway could have lived there for more than thirty years, probably a good deal less. And yet, nearly three quarters of a century after the family had scattered, the second or third generation were treating Lewis as their ancestral home.

I have mentioned elsewhere more recent instances of this disproportionate attachment to Lewis, as compared with other resting places, in the history of families on the move. Linda Fraser (or Marvin), whose letter I quoted from earlier, says it is 'an emotion which sounds romantic and impossibly 'Scotch-mistish' but is nevertheless quite real".

The outstanding example of it is the manner in which the official residence of the Leader of the Opposition, in the Canadian Parliament, has come to be called *Stornoway House*.

Victoria Stewart, of the Lake St Louis Historical Society, in Quebec, for whom I inadvertently solved part of the mystery, told me she was very angry when she began to make enquiries, a few years ago, and found that "no one in the nation's Capitol knew the origin of the name". That did not surprise me. The official guide to Ottawa didn't even know what the name was, when he pointed the house out on a coach tour of the city. I had to tell him!

"After much digging", Victoria Stewart writes, "I came up with the name Perly-Robertson, and started to chase along this family's path. Finally I made contact with not one but two Perly-Robertsons — twins! The difficulty with these two gentlemen, who grew up in the house in question, is that they couldn't agree as to what side of their family came from Lewis!"

In short, their father called his house "Stornoway", because his grandmother was a daughter of Hector Sinclair, who was tenant of Goathill Farm — at the end of the 18th century!

The interesting point for me is that Hector Sinclair was not a Lewisman. As the name suggests he belonged to Caithness. Nor was his wife a Lewiswoman. She belonged to Petty, near Inverness. They stayed in Lewis for only 25 years. They gave up the farm, around 1822, following a lawsuit with the Earl of Seaforth, in which they were represented by the great Lord Cockburn, whose *Circuit Journeys* still makes pleasant reading.

When they returned to the mainland, they took two farms near Inverness — Stratton from which we get our milk, and Balnafettack from which we get our vegetables.

Why did a family, whose contact with Lewis was so tenuous, and ended rather unpleasantly in a legal wrangle, decide to call their house "Stornoway", a generation later, when they were prosperous businessmen on the other side of the Atlantic, and half a continent away, forby?

Obviously there was a deep attachment to the island which was passed on from parent to child. A brother of the man who built the house and called it "Stornoway", visited Lewis on at least one occasion, and wrote *The Annals of Lodge Fortrose*, a mine of information about the history of the town. He was John Ross Robertson, and, according to Victoria Stewart, was "one of the finest writers we have had" in Canada.

In the introduction to the *Annals* he gives a very emotional account of the family's departure from Lewis, on a day of drizzling rain. An event which happened many years before he was born!

He showed the strength of the tie which bound him to the island in a more practical way when he furnished two wards in Lews Hospital, stipulating that the children of local Freemasons should be treated free. That gesture had repercussions — Lodge Fortrose decided to make an annual contribution to hospital funds, which they had not previously done.

14
A Ship Called Stornoway, too

William Ryrie, the Lieut of Marines who was a veteran of the Peninsular War, also married a Lewis woman, a Mackenzie. When she was widowed, she too moved to Liverpool, with her family of three boys and three girls, to set them up in life.

The journey from Stornoway to Liverpool, around 1835, in a coasting schooner, took a fortnight, but for the three boys it was the start of a much longer voyage — they all went eventually to the Far East.

Liverpool was the obvious place for a Lewis family to make for, at that time, and in these circumstances. It was one of the most important seaports in the country, from which many Lewismen normally sailed — my grandfather among them — and there were two sources of influence which a Stornoway family — some Stornoway families anyway — might hope to tap.

Apart from the Macivers, of the Cunard Line, there was old John Gladstone, later Sir John, the statesman's father, who presided over a shipping empire which spanned the globe. He had sugar plantations — and slaves! — in Demerara, but his fortune was amassed in the Far East. As a young man, he was the first shipowner in Liverpool to send a vessel to Calcutta, when the monopoly of the East India Company was broken. An act of foresight that paid him handsome dividends. His wife, Anne Robertson, was a native of Stornoway.

Basil Lubbock, in his fascinating book *The Opium Clippers*, which I picked up purely by chance, in an Edinburgh bookshop, many years ago, not knowing that it was a treasure house of local information, says that the most famous vessel in the China tea trade, up until 1850, was Gladstone's *John o' Gaunt*. Wily Canton merchants, sending their wares by slower and cheaper vessels, still labelled the tea chests "per *John o' Gaunt*". They thought the magic of the name would raise the price.

For many years the captain of the *John o' Gaunt* was John Robertson who, according to the *Nautical Magazine* for 1843, was so well known for his quick and regular voyages, the Admiralty asked to see his charts of the China Seas.

John was a brother of James Robertson, the Stornoway midshipman who stood near Nelson on the *Victory*, when he was killed at the battle of Trafalgar. The news of the battle caused great anxiety in Stornoway at the time. It came first from a passing vessel which put into the harbour under stress of weather. The crew knew only that there had been a great sea battle with Napoleon's fleet and Nelson was dead. The storm which drove the stranger in delayed the very irregular packet which plied between Poolewe and Stornoway with the mails — carried thirty miles from Achnasheen on the postman's back because there was no road! It was a fortnight after they heard that Nelson was dead before the Robertsons learned that the battle had been won, and their son was safe.

These two notable seamen were sons of James Robertson, the Collector of Customs, who went to London to haggle with the lawyers over Mary Carn's fortune, when her brother, the first Surveyor General of India died, and his widow married on the voyage home.

I don't know what the relationship, if any, was between Capt John Robertson and his employer's wife, but he was certainly the centre of a Lewis colony in Liverpool shipping circles. When Evander Maciver from Gress visited Liverpool, to see his cousin Kenneth Maciver from Coll, who was in an office there, he met John Robertson "and other Stornoway friends." Evander made his first railway journey on that occasion, from Liverpool to Manchester. The first passenger-carrying railway in the world had been opened just nine years before, and from Manchester to London Evander had to travel, in the old way, by stage coach.

Among the "Stornoway friends" clustered round John Robertson, and John Gladstone, were the Ryries. Basil Lubbock quotes in his book from a large packet of letters which passed between the Ryrie brothers, their mother and their sisters, which somehow came into his possession. Robertson is mentioned in two of the six letters quoted.

In the second of them, Alick Ryrie, writing from Hong Kong, says, to his sister in Liverpool, "He (Robertson) told me that when he went to Liverpool last year he only remained there two hours, which was the reason he did not call on you, but next time he may have more time."

The other letter is even more interesting. Writing to his mother this time, Alick says, "I suppose Robertson's new ship, the *Stornoway*, is not far from Bombay by this time."

The letter is dated December 1850. It was in the previous year that Robertson, having left Gladstone's service for that of the rising star in the Eastern trade — Jardine Matheson — had gone to Hall of Aberdeen "with an order for a new clipper that was to be the fastest thing possible for her size." Lubbock says the *Stornoway* is generally regarded as the first of the genuine Aberdeen tea clippers. Other sources say she was the first British ship to wrest the blue ribband of the China trade from the famed American clippers.

There used to be a painting of the *Stornoway* in the Reading Room of Stornoway Public Library, when it was housed in the Town Hall. I presume it still survives. The frame, like the picture, enshrines a piece of Lewis history. It is made from oak from the timbers of Nelson's *Victory*, presumably provided by the captain's brother who had been with Nelson when he fell.

The *Stornoway* was named by Jardine Matheson as a compliment to Sir

James Matheson, one of the founders of the firm, who had purchased the Island of Lewis just five years before the order for the vessel was placed.

The Matheson connection opened up a new field of employment for Lewis seamen. It was a trade in which they were hard-worked and not overly well paid — some of the Ryries seem to have been quite hard up at times. But there were opportunities of making a fast buck, or even, for some, a considerable fortune.

Matheson himself had gone to China almost by accident, and somewhat in disgrace. His uncle, who employed him in Calcutta, told him he had no further use for him, because he had carelessly forgotten to forward an ·important despatch. Whether his uncle really intended to sack him or not, I cannot say, but Matheson took him seriously, and went off to arrange his passage home. Listening to words of wisdom from the captain of the first vessel he tried to get a berth on, he changed his mind and went to China.

He couldn't have had much in his pocket when he landed in China, a young man in his early twenties, but, when he left China in 1842, still in his middle forties, he was a man of immense wealth. I don't know how much he took out of the firm in hard cash when he left, but the stake he had still invested in it was worth more than a million dollars. The interest on it was paid to him, in London, in cargoes of tea, which he could sell on the open market, making a double profit.

When his ship docked at Bombay, on the way home to Britain, eighty of the leading Parsee merchants in the city gave him an illuminated address, and a gift of plate, valued at £1,500, which, in present day money, would be something like £40,000.

While amassing a personal fortune, James Matheson found time to take a very active interest in social and educational enterprises in Canton. He established the first English language newspaper in China, *The Canton Register*, and was the principal supporter of a missionary school. He was undoubtedly a philanthropist, but there was another side to his activities. One of his first associates in China was an eccentric Pomeranian missionary named Gutzlaff, who claimed to have converted more Chinese than any other man in history, and almost certainly dosed more Chinamen with pills! His missionary activities were sufficiently important to gain him an entry in the *Encyclopaedia Britannica*, but the association earned Matheson the reputation of going round China with the Bible in one hand and opium in the other.

There is more than an element of truth in the charge. Matheson himself stated in print that "the command of money which we derive from our large opium dealings, and which can hardly be derived from any other source, gives us an important advantage." And the address from the Parsee merchants, which was read aloud at a glittering function in Bombay, by Bormanjee Hormusjee, specifically thanked Matheson for the help he had given him "at his own risk and responsibility" . . . "after the affair of the opium trade in 1839".

The "affair of the opium trade" was the start of the first Opium War which lasted until 1842 — one of the most discreditable incidents in British commercial history.

Lubbock records that the supercargo on one of the first opium voyages made by a Jardine Matheson vessel, with Gutzlaff and his Bibles on board, was named Alexander Robertson. Whether he was a Lewisman, like his namesake Capt John, I have no idea, but I am sure there must be some connection, whatever it is, between Matheson's friendship with the Bombay merchants and the fact that my mother, as a child, knew two wealthy Indian boys — she called them princes — who regularly spent their summer holidays in a house on Shell Street. I cannot recall their names, although I heard them from her on many occasions, but they were undoubtedly Parsees.

15
The Mark of the Pirate's Knife

The attitude of the commercial nations of Western Europe to opium was best defined by Warren Hastings. "A pernicious article of luxury which ought not to be permitted — but for the purpose of foreign commerce only!" Succinct and cynical!

The question, of course, is not how we look at the opium trade today, preening ourselves self-righteously, but how we would have acted, if we had been standing on the waterfront in Hong Kong, 150 years ago, like young James Matheson from Lairg, without a penny in our pockets, and a Chinese gold mine before us.

The glamour of the era, when China was being opened up to the West for the first time, can still arouse us. It is well caught in *The Thistle and the Jade*, a lavishly illustrated book, published by Jardine Matheson & Co, to celebrate a century and a half of trading. I had the book on loan recently, from one of the most successful Lewis businessmen of the present day — Murdo Macleod, whose group of companies are accredited agents for major transportation firms throughout the world, and have close business ties with Jardine Matheson.

The Matheson family's involvement in the direct management of the firm was relatively short lived, although the name is still retained. Not long after James Matheson had returned to Britain, to start a new career as MP and Highland laird, his nephew, Donald, who had succeeded him, began to agonise over his part in the opium trade, and left the firm for good in 1848. He was a strong supporter of the English Presbyterian Church, but not without his own share of commercial acumen: he was one of the founders of the Rio Tinto mining company.

It is interesting, and perhaps significant, that, while the personal conscience of Donald Matheson persuaded him to leave Jardine Matheson, very shortly after Lord Ashley declared in Parliament that the opium trade "was utterly inconsistent with the honour and duty of a Christian Kingdom", and the firm withdrew from the trade completely in 1870, it was not until 1917 that the British Government, which had not only condoned the opium trade but encouraged it, finally entered into an agreement with China for its gradual — and conditional! — suppression.

Of the three Ryrie brothers, Alick seems to have been the only one involved in the opium carrying trade, and he was the unlucky one!

He began his career in Gladstone's ships, making use, no doubt, of the Lewis "mafia" to gain a foothold. Later he switched to Jardine Matheson & Co, whose "employ", he wrote in a letter home, "is far before any other in China." According to Basil Lubbock, whose books are a mine of information, he was employed by them as an officer on the opium schooner *Sidney*. Later he was an officer, and finally captain, on the firm's American-built schooner *Mazeppa*, which was regarded in the forties as one of the smartest on the China coast.

Alick was highly regarded by the firm. His brother Phineas, in a letter home in 1854, to tell the family that Alick had been given a new command — the *Audax* — writes, "He is a great favourite with Mr Jardine, indeed, so much so that he speaks publicly of the high esteem in which he holds Alick — this from a man who is proverbially reserved in his communications is something to be proud of. I hope Alick won't hear of it, though — it may make him vain."

A few years earlier, Alick himself, in a letter home, had complained, for reasons which do not emerge, "I have been misfortune's child ever since I have been afloat, and wonder if my luck will change." It didn't. Within a year of his promotion to the *Audax*, the vessel was lost with all hands.

Phineas, the youngest of the Ryrie brothers, was employed by a firm of merchants in Hong Kong, who had at least one tea clipper, but he does not seem to have been a seafaring man. Both he and Alick regarded the oldest brother, John Mackenzie Ryrie, as something of a stick-in-the-mud, but, in the end of the day, he proved to be the most successful of the three.

Basil Lubbock told me, many years ago, that John Mackenzie Ryrie was born in Stornoway in 1820. He was apprenticed to W & F Shand of Liverpool, shipowners and West India sugar merchants. He served a five year apprenticeship in the *Grace*, a full-rigged 300 ton vessel, then served successively as 2nd mate, mate and captain, before taking command of the *Marian*, an Eastern trader belonging to the same firm.

While he was on the *Marian* we find him writing home from Whampoa, "I don't know what I am going to do as yet. There is nothing here but California business" — connected no doubt with the gold rush! Around the same time Phineas was writing home about the "absurdity" of John remaining on the *Marian*. "He is so wedded to old world notions that there is no driving them out of his head."

At last they persuaded him to make a move, and enter the service of Jardine Matheson. He does not seem to have been involved in the opium trade, but he did command two famous tea clippers, the *Cairngorm* and the *Flying Spur*.

In the autumn of 1858, there was a fleet of fast vessels lying at Hong Kong, awaiting the signing of a peace treaty, which would release a large quantity of tea, lying in the hongs, or warehouses, on the Canton River, at Whampoa. These were exciting and dangerous times. Although peace was in the offing, the local Chinese ruler tried to wipe out the British community in Hong Kong, by sending in a cargo of poisoned flour. When that failed, he tried to inconvenience them by ordering all the Chinese cooks to leave. The grand ladies of Hong Kong were left to the tender mercies of the ships' cooks in the harbour to cater for their parties.

53

Ratification of the peace was like the starter's pistol at the Olympics. There was a mad rush to Whampoa to load and sail. According to Lubbock, it was the first occasion on which there was an agreed bonus of £200 for the first ship to dock. Jardine Matheson's representative was the *Cairngorm*, captained by John Mackenzie Ryrie. Douce and careful though he was, he carried away two stunsail booms, in strong winds, on the China coast, then felt his way through the mudflats in the Banka Straits, inch by inch, in the darkness, taking soundings all the way. Another captain, who was becalmed in the same place, said afterwards it was almost as bad as the legendary voyage of the clipper which couldn't swing the yards because the trees were so close the monkeys' tails were fouling the brace blocks.

When it came to the pay-off, the *Lammermuir*, the largest vessel in the race, was first to reach the Downs — six hours ahead of the *Cairngorm* at the end of a 92-day voyage. But, by the time the vessels had docked, the *Cairngorm* was 40 hours ahead of the *Lammermuir*, and the first fixed bonus in the history of the tea trade, went to the Lewisman.

From the *Cairngorm*, Ryrie went to the *Flying Spur*. "A beautiful little vessel", according to Lubbock. He commanded the *Flying Spur* until he retired, by which time, he "owned a good many sixty-fourths in her, and made money."

Despite the excitement, and the glamour, of their lives, their letters home were concerned with family and domestic matters, as seamen's letters generally are.

"Phiney had a letter from John yesterday." "I saw a glimpse of Alick. The *Mazeppa* was going down the river as I was coming up." "I see (through the telescope) that the *Mazeppa* is in."

An appeal to their mother for a dozen pairs of "good worsted socks" for the winter, or a complaint that she had forgotten to send flannel singlets in October, or a gift of money for the girls "to buy their spring dresses, with my love".

The Ryries were in at the start of the Lewis connection with the China trade, but it continued long after they were dead. When I was still a student in Glasgow, Rev N. C. Macfarlane had an article in the *Gazette*, recalling the captains he had known in his own youth.

Men like Kenneth Macaulay, from Uig, who sailed out of Fraserburgh, and whose son founded the Sun Life Assurance Co of Canada. Or another of the same name, whose brother William "became one of the big men in Bombay."

He had quite a lot to say about Capt William Morrison, who commanded a vessel belonging to the father of the founder of the school. His son was also a captain. I knew him well as the legendary Capt Tom, who was sent to sea in his youth, because they thought he was dying of consumption, was invalided ashore because he had a bad heart, and lived to make the century, or pretty near it. He was harbour master in Stornoway and a Bailie of the Burgh. My father used to amuse us with stories of his nautical approach to legal matters, when he sat on the bench, in the burgh

54

court. When a tinker appeared before him, charged with letting his horse stray, he was not asked did he plead "guilty" or "not guilty". In a good quarter-deck voice, Capt Tom demanded, "Did you set this horse adrift?"

Macfarlane also recalled Capt John Mackenzie who "built the first slated house in Newton." His daughter, Hectorina, was a great temperance reformer, and one of the formidable ladies who dominated Newton in my childhood. Then there was Capt Murdo Morrison, who lived on Keith Street, and bore on his face the mark where a pirate, catching him asleep in his bunk, thrust a knife from cheek to cheek.

16
Aliens in their Native Isle

A footnote to the Lewis involvement in the opulent world of tea and opium is provided by a newspaper cutting I have before me, headed: "Chinese God that Vanished". "Now in Hands of Veteran From Lewis".

The veteran from Lewis was the late Willie Martin, well-known in London-Highland circles for half a century, but that is almost the only point of certainty in the tale. I don't even know the date of the cutting, or the source. Although I would guess that it came from the *People's Journal* around 1940, judging by the banal love story of which there is a snippet on the back.

The cutting relates to an exhibition in London on behalf of a Chinese charity. One of the most interesting exhibits was a Chinese Buddha, standing three feet high, loaned by Capt W. A. Martin, who had been at one time recruiting agent for the London-Scottish.

"Originally the statuette occupied a place in the home of a Scotsman who had been prominently identified with the Far Eastern trade", said Captain Martin. "How it came into his hands I do not know, but I believe the Chinese offered 15,000 dollars for its recovery when it first disappeared.

"After his death it was given to me by his widow. I was only 12 or 13 at the time. Evidently she disliked having it in her home, fearing it might bring about some misfortune. I cannot say it has ever brought me any ill luck — or good luck either."

Parts of the statuette were made of solid gold, and I would guess, and it is only a guess, that it came from the collection of Sir James Matheson. Martin's father was in the Matheson's employment, and the family home was in the Castle Grounds. Any transaction which took place when Willie Martin was 12 or 13 years old, almost certainly took place there. And he would have been just about the age he mentions when Sir James Matheson died in Mentone, leaving his Lewis estate in the hands of his widow.

I know Martin's age because he and my uncle Roddie were veterans of the Wet Review, which took place on the occasion of Queen Victoria's Golden Jubilee. I still recall my uncle's vivid description of the deluge which soaked the participants, and the burst water main, in the middle of the parade ground, which assaulted them from below. In fact I'm not sure he didn't say "a burst sewer". Anyway, as detachment after detachment approached the gusher, the line divided, until the Lewis contingent approached, and Johnnie Anderson gave the command, "Right into it boys!''. There was a great cheer as the Leodhasaich marched through the fountain, without breaking rank or losing step.

They went home by train, immediately after their sousing and, according to my uncle, they would all have died of pneumonia, if a Lewis woman, who had a pub in the city, had not supplied them liberally with whisky. It was a strange story for an ardent temperance advocate to tell, until, perhaps catching the query in my eye, he added, "We stripped naked in the carriages, and rubbed the whisky into our skin, to restore the circulation." And that must be the strangest use a Lewisman ever made of a bottle of whisky.

Whether I am right or wrong in my assumption that the golden Buddha had been brought from China by Sir James Matheson, it is certainly true that a considerable slice of the money he made in China was invested in Lewis, one way or another.

I use the word "invested", deliberately.

When he purchased Lewis, there were less than 45 miles of very rough track in the whole island, and only one gig. He built over 200 miles of road, good by the standards of the day. He also subsidised the first steamer service linking Lewis with the mainland — the *Falcon*, which plied between Stornoway and Ardrossan. He provided the town of Stornoway with both water and gas. He built 32 schools in the rural areas, and a Ladies' Industrial School in Stornoway, in the building, still known as the Seminary, where Duncan Morison has his home.

I remember my aunts telling me how lucky they were when they trudged from Newton to "Lady Matheson's School" on the corner of Keith Street and Scotland Street. Every child had to bring a peat, each day, for the school-room fire. While their friends carried their load all the way from Newton, my aunts went empty-handed. They had a relative living beside the school, and helped themselves to a peat from her stack, when they got to their destination. That's what relatives were for!

It has been estimated that Sir James Matheson spent over half a million pounds on his Lewis Estate, including the purchase price, a vast sum of money, at that time, and all the product of his Chinese trade.

But it was not a gift to the people of Lewis. Not by any means. A writer in the *Celtic Magazine* of 1882, while praising Sir James Matheson's liberality, calculated that, if one excludes the Castle and the Grounds, which were in his personal occupation, the Lewis rents gave him a return of around $3\frac{1}{4}\%$ on his capital outlay. Which, with the interest rates prevailing at the time, was a pretty good return on an investment in the peat bogs of Lewis.

About £12,000 of the total was spent on assisting 2,231 Lewismen and women to emigrate. The emigration was "voluntary" in that it was not induced by a physical clearance, but by economic pressures, which were producing the same movement of population, at the same time, all over Europe.

The Lewis communities overseas which resulted from the process of emigration, over a period of more than a century, are dotted around the map of America, like stars in the heavens, in different stages of evolution, from red hot suns, bubbling with communal activity, to black holes from which the last remnant of Gaelic has disappeared.

Even where active Lewis Societies have ceased to exist, however, individuals tend to keep their family ties. I met a man in Winnipeg once who had a list, in his notebook, of the 56 cousins he hoped to see on a visit to Scotland. The other day I had a letter from D. J. Macrae in Wisconsin, whom I have never met, in which he mentioned several of the Lewis relatives with whom he is still in touch, among them Jessie Cameron, with whom I was associated in the Gaelic Drama movement in Inverness, and Calum Macleod, with whom I sat on the Board of Grampian television.

The point that is really relevant to my present theme is that he recalled the days in his youth when Duluth, where he was born, had one of the most active Lewis Societies in the whole of North America. His father, Alex Macrae, had been the secretary for many years, and a regular correspondent of my father's. When I was a boy, Duluth seemed as much part of the Lewis scene as Miavaig, from which Alex Macrae had emigrated in 1898, and he himself was almost one of the family, his letters were so frequent and so carefully read.

Before it is too late, someone should get round to collating the history of these Lewis communities, making it easier for the scattered remnant of the second or third generation to re-establish the link with Lewis, as many of them now seem to wish to do.

Such a study would throw up one or two surprising lines of enquiry. Murdo Macleod, when he acknowledged the return of the Jardine Matheson book, *The Thistle and the Jade*, suggested that I should investigate the underground route, leading to a pub in Detroit, through which many Lewismen and women got into the USA, without the appropriate documentation, in the days when the Ford Motor Company was the mecca for jobless islanders.

I first came across this trail one evening in Stornoway, when I was on my way home from the office. The shops were closing for the night, and, as I passed J. and E. Macleod's, I saw a very old friend, standing behind the iron gate, which she had just locked.

"They've got you behind bars at last" I quipped.

"It's not the first time I've been behind bars," she replied, and I knew she meant it.

"When were you locked up?" I asked, a little incredulously.

"When I tried to get into the States without a visa!" she replied.

When Cathie, on a visit to the States, expressed surprise that a friend she met had never revisited Lewis, although she was clearly well-to-do, and very homesick, she was told, "She daren't! She came into the States without a passport. If she leaves, she'll never get back."

Just before the Second World War, when everyone was edgy about spies and saboteurs, and the authorities were tightening up, sometimes to a

58

ridiculous extent, one or two Lewismen, home for an extended visit from the States, were confronted by a policeman, and told that they had overstayed their welcome.

Having taken out American papers, they were aliens in the house where they were born.

The bureaucrats do strange things to us when they get control.

17
Two City of Glasgow Disasters

A truer picture of conditions on the Atlantic in the pioneering days of the steamship can be gained from the disasters than the successes. There too Lewis names are to be found.

The Captain of the *City of Glasgow*, which was involved in one of the great disasters and mysteries of the sea, was Kenneth Morison, a son of Lt John Morison RN of Aignish, who was one of the links in the chain of circumstances which gives credence to the tradition that one of the mutineers of the *Bounty* was a Lewisman.

The *City of Glasgow* was an experimental vessel with two engines geared to one propeller shaft. It was owned by the Inman Line and plied the Atlantic successfully for four years proving that screw-driven steamships could more than hold their own with the paddle ships with which the Cunard Line had inaugurated the Atlantic mail service.

On March 1st 1854 the *City of Glasgow* left Liverpool for Philadelphia with 480 people on board, including the crew. She was never heard of again.

As for so many other things I am indebted to William Matheson for my knowledge of the Lewis link with the vessel, but when I came across the reference in the Appendices to his book *The Blind Harper*, I had a problem on my mind. Had I ever heard of the *City of Glasgow* disaster before?

I had certainly heard of the wrong one: the collapse of the City of Glasgow bank in 1879 which precipitated the passing of the Limited Liability Act! The collapse of the bank had repercussions for Lewis. I remember hearing as a youngster that James Mackenzie's shop, the principal store in Lewis at the time, was badly hit by the crash, although it managed to survive.

Of that recollection I am sure, but whether I also heard in my boyhood of the loss of the liner I cannot say, although I would expect it to have been spoken of in the seaport town the captain came from, even half a century after the tragedy occurred.

The story emerges vividly from the files of the *Glasgow Herald* of the period. The vessel sailed and the vessel vanished. There was no trans-Atlantic communication by telephone or telegraph then. It was three years after the *City of Glasgow* was lost before the first — and unsuccessful — attempt was made to lay a submarine cable across the Atlantic. It was twenty years after the *City of Glasgow* was lost before Marconi was even born.

One only knew that a vessel had reached its destination when it got safely back to its starting point, or some other vessel reported its arrival. The Atlantic crossing, even in favourable conditions took about a fortnight. Given a speedy turn-round, the *City of Glasgow* might have been expected back a month after it sailed.

In the middle of March, even before any anxiety was felt, the *Herald* had the first ominous news. "Accounts of numerous marine disasters have been received in New York", the paper stated. Numerous disasters! In peace time! We hardly know we are living today.

The *Cornelius Grinnel*, on arrival at New York, had reported seeing two other vessels abandoned in a sinking condition. Half the crew of a third vessel were suffering from frost-bite when they landed.

These reports did not create anxiety at the time. They related to a period just before the *City of Glasgow* sailed, and she was a good and speedy ship, by the standards of the day. She could steam at 12 knots!

On April 7th came another report from New York. Four emigrant ships had been lost, and two more were missing. A fortnight later, the owners of the *City of Glasgow* thought it necessary to write a letter to the *Times* to allay the fears which were being expressed. By then it was known that she had not reached Philadelphia by the 9th of April — five weeks after she had sailed.

"We believe the vessel to be detained in the ice on the banks of Newfoundland and unable to make her way out of it," they wrote. In corroboration they stated that the steamer *Baltic* had been three days in the ice, and the screw steamer *Charity* nine days. "A sailing vessel some years ago, in the same place was 30 days in it without being able to move."

The owners assured enquirers that the vessel was mechanically sound, and the compass had been adjusted just five days before she sailed. She had food and water for 60 or 70 days, with economy, and although she had coal only for 26 days' steaming, she could sail to the westward under canvas if the need arose. Sailing vessels which had left Liverpool as much as a month before the *City of Glasgow* were only then arriving at their American destinations.

On the 12 May the *Herald* reported that "the gloom which has for several weeks prevailed by the continued absence of any tidings of the *City of Glasgow* screw steamship, Captain Morison . . . has now been painfully increased by the arrival of mail packets from the other side of the Atlantic not communicating the least intelligence of the long missing ship.

"An almost general opinion is now entertained among the members of Lloyds that the worst has befallen the noble vessel and her unfortunate passengers and crew" added the *Herald*.

All berths on the vessel had been taken. She was carrying 111 cabin and saloon passengers, and 293 steerage passengers. The crew of 76 was made up of the Captain and 4 officers, a surgeon, a purser, 4 engineers, 6 firemen, 5 coal trimmers, 10 stewards and waiters, 1 stewardess, 4 quartermasters and 30 ABs.

"It was Captain Morison's first voyage in her as commander although he had served many months in her in the position of chief officer. He bears an unexceptionable character for ability and care in his profession and had had considerable experience in navigating the Atlantic."

For days after the vessel sailed the weather had been propitious, and the expectation in Liverpool had been that she would make a speedy voyage. But then came reports from other ships that the ice had been greater than had been experienced for many years. The *City of Westmoreland*, which sailed a few days before the *City of Glasgow*, calculated that the ice extended in one direction for 347 miles in a nearly compact mass with numerous icebergs two or three hundred feet high.

Then came the unexpected twist to the story. The steamer *Baldaur* put into Queenstown, and the Captain reported that, on the voyage, he had seen a large steamer of which he gave a detailed description — hull and funnel black; inside painted drab; paddle boxes yellow; fore and foretopmast sail yards; nothing on the mainmast. The *City of Glasgow* had no paddle boxes, but there were structures on the deck which might have been mistaken for paddle boxes, and they were painted yellow. In all other particulars the description fitted.

The vessel the *Baldaur* saw had a strong list to port. The Captain saw no people or smoke. The strange vessel appeared to alter course towards the *Baldaur*, but almost immediately disappeared. The *Baldaur* sailed across to the spot where the vessel had last been seen and found nothing but a large quantity of biscuits and boxes floating in the sea.

When the Baldaur first sighted the stricken ship there was a barque alongside, but the barque steered away to the south.

Is it possible that the *City of Glasgow* was trapped so long in the ice that the crew and passengers took to the boats and perished in them, while the vessel herself eventually broke free and drifted to the point at which the *Baldaur* saw her sink?

It was probably the *Baldaur's* story which led to a report on the 19th of May that the passengers and crew of the *City of Glasgow* had been rescued and landed on the coast of Africa. The report created some excitement in Liverpool, but the *Herald* treated it with the scepticism it deserved.

A few days later it was found to be "a hearsay tale vended by an Irish newsmonger fishing for popularity as an express agent". A scoop that never was.

The mystery of the *City of Glasgow* led me on to another puzzle.

When I was visiting in Kalamazoo I picked up a book — a sort of American version of *Whitaker's Almanack*, but much more voluminous as one might expect. A compendium of useful and curious information.

As I thumbed through it, I came on a list of the world's greatest shipping disasters. I looked for the names with a Lewis connection. The *City of Glasgow* was there, and the *Norge*, of which I will have something to say later, but there was no mention of the *Iolaire*, the most poignant of them all.

I studied the list carefully. It seemed to relate only to civilian or peacetime disasters. I decided that, although the Great War was over when the *Iolaire* was lost it was treated as if it had been a wartime casualty.

But later, in the Mitchell Library in Glasgow, when I looked up Charles Hocking's standard *Dictionary of Disasters At Sea* I discovered that the *Iolaire* is also omitted there.

Hocking's is a much more exhaustive work than the American list. It claims to be authoritative. It covers war as well as peace. All the familiar names are there, the *Arlington Court*, the *Jervis Bay*, the *Rawalpindi*. But no *Iolaire*.

I wonder why?

18
My Granny Made a Rug of It

I was still a student when T. B. Macaulay came to Lewis, from Montreal, on his first and historic visit, but I was on holiday, helping my father with the *Gazette*. I was present at most of the functions of that crowded week — the welcome on board the liner *Minnedosa*; the opening of the Town Hall; and the unveiling of the plaque to Sir Alexander Mackenzie. But I missed the most significant of all — the gathering on a hilltop above Valtos at which Macaulay was given an illuminated address by the people of Uig.

Before mounting the platform Macaulay was greeted by the four oldest men in the parish, led by Hector Matheson, hale and hearty despite his 97 years.

The official address of welcome was given by a distinguished Uig preacher, Rev Dr Maclennan, Edinburgh, who repeopled the village for his hearers with the men he had known in his youth. I wonder if anyone in Uig can identify them today?

"In yonder glen there is a clachan in which lived a group of men of singular integrity and charm of character — two of them Macaulays. Over that knoll is the ruins of the home of the wise man of my boyhood, whom we all revered. Down below us there was the home of our philosopher — clear visioned, of reverent faith, intensely proud of his parish and of Lewis — so full of humour that he made us all his friends.

"Round to the left lived our tailor par excellence. He plied a pointed needle and a sharp pair of scissors, but also a sharper tongue and a more poignant wit. There were a few who feared the tailor but a great many more who loved him.

"Up the brae from the tailor was the home of our model saint — a worthy scion of the Macaulay clan. I can barely remember Angus. As I got the story — he happened to waken at an early hour of a summer morning when he noticed a number of sheep in his neighbour's growing grain. He ran out as he was and drove them into his own grain close by, and leaving them there he went in to dress himself comfortably, and then chased the sheep beyond the village bounds."

Dr Maclennan belonged to a remarkable family. One of his sisters who was born deaf and dumb, was trained in Edinburgh, and went out to America where she became a teacher of the deaf and dumb.

An older sister, also deaf and dumb, did not have the same opportunity, although she was just as well equipped intellectually. When I got to know her, many years after Macaulay's visit, she was housekeeper to Norman

Macleod, the minister at Uigen, who was a close friend of my uncle, Roddie.

On one occasion, when my uncle was visiting Norman, I took him over in the car, and stayed the night with them in the manse. In the evening the housekeeper came into the sitting room with two candles, a new one, and a tiny stump. She handed the new one to me with a sign to suggest that I was getting the big one because I was tall. She gave the other to my uncle with a deprecating gesture about his lack of inches.

My uncle, who knew her well, and her capacity for telling a story or cracking a joke without the use of speech, shook his fist at her playfully. Immediately she signalled that she was giving the big candle to me because I was young and would want to read in bed, while my uncle being old would want to sleep.

Her hand held above her forehead indicated a minister — a high hat! A characteristic gesture would then identify the particular minister she had in mind for anyone who had ever seen him in the pulpit. We had a hilarious time while she imitated various ministers and my uncle guessed whom it was she meant. The climax came when she imitated my uncle himself with a gesture he had no idea he ever used, but which Norman and I recognised immediately.

Then she gave us a graphic account of an incident in the village, some time before, when a neighbour, who was afraid of the noise made by his new Aladdin lamp, panicked and threw it out the door, whereupon it exploded, confirming, as he thought, his fears.

Next morning I met Norman coming home with a poached salmon. He had not caught it himself: one of his parishioners had given it to him. Norman had no scruple in accepting it, but as he had to pass the keeper's house on the way home, he thought it wise to hide it under his jacket, to avoid embarrassment all round. When I met him, about six inches of the tail was dangling below his jacket, so that his guilt was much more obvious than if he had carried the salmon openly in his hand.

The salmon was duly cooked for dinner and brought to table, on a large ashet, covered by a tureen lid. My uncle knew nothing about the escapade, and Norman, with a wink at me, asked him to say grace. He knew that my uncle invariably ended with the formula, "For the mercies which Thou hast provided, Lord, make us truly thankful." With an appropriate flourish Norman, on cue, unveiled the fish, and we all set to with a hearty appetite.

This was before the days when poaching had become commercialised and greedy. My uncle was no more disturbed than the rest of us that the fish had been come by illegally. Indeed he told us that on one occasion he had gone poaching venison himself. He set off from Stornoway by boat, for Parc, leaving his father in charge of the little draper's shop he had at that time — a sad come-down, surely, for a shipmaster to be standing behind the counter! They shot a fine stag and set off for home. They had eluded the keepers but they still had to get past the Stornoway police. They touched first at a quiet spot, some distance from the town centre, and put ashore a

65

scout. He ran quickly and quietly along South Beach, turning off the street lights as he went, and the carcase was brought ashore under cover of darkness.

The mission safely accomplished, my uncle set off back to his shop. At that time shops were open until nine or ten at night. Elated with his successful venture, he vaulted over the counter. A bloody palm print where his hand touched the counter brought him quickly back to earth. My grandfather was not disturbed. Indeed he might have regretted that he was too old himself to join the party. It was different with my grandmother. She was a woman of very strict principles, and gave my uncle a frightful row, but, he added philosophically when he told me the story, "That did not prevent her from curing the skin and making a rug of it."

I have a feeling that the rug was still in use when I was a child, but I cannot be sure. I am working here in the area where the line between true memory and imagination, working on what I was told, is thin and fragile.

The poaching escapade could not have been long before my uncle left home to study for the ministry. His conversion had not been easy. He told me how he sat for hours on the rocks at Battery Point agonising over it. Although he became a preacher of great sincerity and power he was completely free from complacency. He had no time for glib emotional revivalism or rigid Sabbatarianism.

His decision to enter the ministry some time afterwards was just as abrupt as his conversion had been protracted. He showed my brother the spot he had been walking on when he made up his mind, in a flash. Where Mitchell's garage is today. It was then a plantation of trees.

Standing on the same spot, many years later, I had a curious discussion with an elder about religion, and in particular about the day of judgment. As we spoke, a drunk man staggered off the pavement in front of a bus. There was a screech of brakes. The bus swerved. It missed him by inches.

"Do you not agree," said the elder, "that if that man had been killed, at that moment, and in that condition, he would have gone straight to hell?"

"No I don't!" I replied. "And what's more, if you believe that, you may be in greater danger of going to hell than he is!"

He looked at me in amazement and we parted, but we remained good friends. I think my uncle would have agreed with me if he had still been around the spot where he took the snap decision which set his course for fifty years of preaching. Certainly he never lost his sense of fun. I recall him at a Christmas party, when I was a child, demonstrating the Highland Schottische with an abandon and lightness of foot Will Mack would have envied. I wonder what the Free Kirk would have thought of it, or even some of his own elders in the Church of Scotland?

When he was in his eighties there was still nothing he enjoyed more than a game with the children at a Sunday School picnic, and I recall him in his nineties, just after his retiral, saying with a smile, "It's time I stopped chasing the girls!" as he romped round the table with the daughter of a young minister, home from Canada, who had been his assistant for a time.

66

His sense of fun was certainly aroused by Norman Macleod's salmon. We were still laughing over it when the housekeeper came in to clear the table. With an unmistakable gesture, she asked us if we had seen the big fish. We nodded. She shook her head dolefully and went back to the door. There she straightened herself, threw out her chest, and strode purposefully towards Norman. A policeman come to arrest him! She placed her hand on his shoulder. Then, just as suddenly, she became Norman himself, cowering and miserable, walking from the room in handcuffs. Not a word spoken, but the whole incident graphically portrayed.

I was not surprised when, a few years later, a pawky friend from Uig, commenting on the decline in bus traffic from the decaying villages, told me there had been nothing on the bus with him that morning, coming into town, but a hunchback, a dummy and a box of lobsters, but they represented the brains, the business ability and the wealth of the community.

The lobsters were the wealth, the hunchback was the man of business, and the brains of the parish were represented by Norman's housekeeper. If she had had the power of speech she would have given an even more eloquent and amusing welcome to T. B. Macaulay on that Valtos hilltop, than her brother, the eminent preacher who had come from Edinburgh for the occasion.

Be that as it may, it was a very happy occasion, as were all the public events during Macaulay's historic visit. But out of sight, behind the scenes, there was a different little drama going on. The sort of drama that is inevitable in municipal affairs, when councillors "dressed in a little brief authority", begin to take themselves too seriously.

My father, as a reporter, was privy to it all, and regaled us at mealtimes with a blow by blow account of the in-fighting, adding a delicious tartness to the flavour of the week.

But, to pick up the threads of that story, I must go back to Lord Leverhulme — or Lord Leverhulme's ghost!

19
Downing Street of the Isles

When Lord Leverhulme bowed himself off the stage with a princely gesture, handing the town and parish of Stornoway, the Castle and its grounds, and three salmon rivers, to the feuars and crofters as a free gift, it was his intention that the Provost of Stornoway should have an official residence in the Castle. A sort of Downing Street of the Isles.

It was also his intention that the Castle would replace the burnt-out Town Hall, and the Art Gallery which he intended to build at the head of a broad avenue sweeping up from the harbour to Goathill.

The dream was never realised. It was too grandiose for the real world. The extravagance of Lord Leverhulme's own regime, in the period between the making of the gift and the transfer of control, left the estate burdened with debt. In the early years of the Trust, the Trustees exhibited all the petty parochial stupidities of a small town at its worst, squandering the resources they did have in bickering among themselves.

But, for one short spell in 1929, the Castle was used as Lord Leverhulme intended. The Provost moved into residence, and there he entertained the town's distinguished guests, T. B. Macaulay, and the members of his party — much to the amusement of the townsfolk who found some difficulty in visualising Louis Bain in such mock baronial splendour.

Before the advent of television, national politicians could always escape the too close scrutiny of their fellow men, and become legendary figures judged on their policies and their achievements. The provost of a small town, however, never gets far enough away from the electorate for his blemishes to be obscured, or even softened by distance. He never becomes a sort of abstract public figure. Everyone knows him better than he knows himself. However much they value his services to the community, they see no reason to forgo the opportunity of extracting the maximum amount of fun from any situation in which his artificial dignity is involved. To them he is all wart and no Cromwell.

Many years later, when a small group were forming the Arts Association of Lewis, in an effort to bring good music and drama to the town, Lucienne Doig, the plump, vivacious, highly cultured, French wife of the local MOH, who always seemed to be quivering with excitement, enthusiasm and friendliness, and a general inexplicable hurry, which contrasted with our leisurely island ways, burst out, with that little tang of French in her accent which gave piquancy to the comment, "Why should zee Town Council not help? In France zee Town Council runs the theatre!" A weary Lewis voice replied, "In Stornoway, the Town Council is the theatre!"

Louis Bain was a fishcurer. A shrewd judge of boats and herring and men. He traded successfully to all the Baltic ports, and to the USA, where the large Minch herring, well cured in brine, were much in favour with European immigrants, who had carried with them a taste for Stornoway herring, acquired in more straitened circumstances in their Polish, Latvian or Lithuanian homes.

He was the German, and, I think, the Danish vice-consul in Stornoway, and discharged his duties competently when the need arose, as it inevitably did from time to time, in the nearest seaport to a wide area of the North Atlantic.

He brought the same qualities of solid, unimaginative, shrewdness to the affairs of the Town Council, the Harbour Commission, the Hospital Committee and the Lifeboat Committee, but he always spoke of the surgeon, newly appointed to Lews Hospital under the Highland and Islands Medical Service which, in so many ways anticipated the National Health Service, as the "surgent", which gave his critics something to mock.

When he had to rebuke one of his fellow councillors for making obscure but offensive allegations against another, he rapped out, "We must have no aspirations in this council," which reduced the town to ungovernable laughter. But none of those who loved to take the mickey out of our public men were prepared to take over the onerous task of running the town. If they had been, I doubt if they would have done it so well.

There was a good deal of lively politicking in the Council before the arrangements were made for entertaining Macaulay and his party. It was only possible to lodge them in the Castle because Louis Bain's brother, John, a banker in Chicago, was prepared to foot the bill. John Bain had been the largest contributor to the Town Hall building fund apart from Macaulay.

Louis Bain's term as provost was due to end before Macaulay arrived, and John Bain's largesse, it was feared — and may well have been hinted — was liable to dry up if another councillor usurped his brother's seat.

At the same time, some of the other councillors could not bear to contemplate the prospect of Louis Bain serving another three years as provost, while they stood impatiently in the wings awaiting the chance to don a bailie's ermine (donated by Lord Leverhulme) or the provost's golden chain (donated by Stornoway Gaelic Choir when Stornoway had one of the finest Gaelic Choirs in Scotland and a provost of real stature).

Eventually a compromise was arrived at. Louis Bain was re-appointed provost, but there was a gentleman's agreement that he would retire gracefully when the festivities were over, "to let the honours go round". The Council invented the principle to cope with their problem, without seeming to realise that it exposed the pettiness of their own ambition, and debased the whole idea of public service.

So, at the end of a year, having had his hour of glory, Louis Bain stepped down to make way for Alex Maclennan, a native of Marvig who had built up a very successful merchant's business in the town. He was a squat, broad shouldered man, with a head which drooped forward as if none too securely attached to his shoulders.

He was unctuous and deep, and was known as "Holy Alex" because of his rather ostentatious attachment to the Church. Once, when the candidates at a Town Council election agreed to post their election addresses all at the same time for a fair fight, Alex stole a march of them by getting his off a day before the deadline. "We'll have to call you Wily Alex now!" said one of the others, not so much in anger as amusement that a colleague had run true to form. Alex let the gibe pass. He liked to live in peace with his neighbours, even if he was outflanking them. His love of compromise, as I have already related, cost the town thousands of pounds in the "Mitchell Case", the legal tussle over Stornoway's golden acre, and his anxiety to have a flamboyant obituary in the *Stornoway Gazette* led to my own appointment as a Justice of the Peace while I was still a comparative youngster — "wet behind the ears" as the saying goes.

The principle of letting the honours go round was not pursued so consistently as to give Stornoway the distinction, which it might have had, of being the first burgh in Scotland to appoint a woman as provost.

Julia Fraser was probably the ablest member of the Council intellectually in her day. Able but unpredictable. Eloquent and polished but, at times, a little bitter. I don't know whether the bitterness came natural to her, like the grace of her carriage and features, or whether she had gone sour through being trammelled by so many people who disliked her for her sex. I rather suspect it was a bit of both.

On one occasion she lost her temper with her critics and told them to go to hell. The Council solemnly censured her for using language inappropriate to the Council Chamber. When the motion was carried she stormed out of the meeting, but paused at the double doors, before she slammed them, to tell her fellow councillors, "You're just a lot of dirty dogs!" To which Hughie Matheson the baker, replied, "And the female of the species is more deadly than the male." Fortunately the door had closed, and she did not hear him.

The whole incident was ironical and absurd when one thought of the language some of her critics used regularly themselves.

Not long afterwards one of them was called from his place of business to sit on the bench. A tinker had been arrested for being drunk and incapable. Instead of pleading guilty in the normal way, and paying his 5/- fine, the tinker protested his innocence. The Bailie was aghast. He would have to fix a date for trial, the Fiscal told him, and come back to hear the evidence. The Bailie did as he was bid. Then, as the tinker walked from the Court, he glowered after him, and said in a voice which rang through the building, "I'll make the bugger sweat for it, bringing me back here a second time!"

A later generation of Stornoway councillors were more gracious and less sexist. They not only made Nan Urquhart Provost, they made her a Freeman of the town.

70

20
They Paid to Kick Up Hell

Not long after the opening of the Town Hall, my father began to receive disturbing anonymous letters from Chicago, sometimes enclosing newspaper cuttings.

John Bain had been a plumber to trade, but in Chicago he had built up a very prosperous business, and finally went into banking. He never forgot Stornoway. He was very generous to his sister and her family who lived on Matheson Road, in a house called Englewood after the district in Chicago where he had his home.

He was also generous to local causes. In those hard days Lewis was very dependent on the generosity of expatriates of the first and second generation, like John Bain, and T. B. Macaulay, and William Macaskill, a brother of Ivor Macaskill the butcher, who had also prospered in Chicago. Lewis Societies in various cities in the States and Canada contributed regularly to island charities like Lewis Hospital.

John Bain was outstanding among the givers, but, like many another American banker, he got into difficulties in the great Depression. Lewismen who had banked with him for sentimental reasons, suffered serious losses. There were suggestions of irregularities in his banking operations. I never knew the full facts, but I always had the feeling that John Bain had been manipulated by younger and slicker operators. His easy-going generous bonhomie, and his inexperience of banking, made him vulnerable to exploitation.

In any event, when the Town Council discovered, largely through the efforts of Provost Smith, back in office for a second term, and W. C. Mackenzie the historian, that they could confer the freedom although Stornoway was not a Royal Burgh, John Bain was omitted from the initial list, although, in happier times, he would certainly have been on it.

The freedom was conferred on T. B. Macaulay, W. C. Mackenzie, himself, and Malcolm Macleod, Govan, who was one of those who had built up the Lewis and Harris Association of Glasgow and An Comunn Gaidhealachd.

A few years later, when the dust had settled, and John Bain came to Lewis on a family visit, he was made a freeman of the Burgh at a discreet ceremony in the Council Chamber. I always thought it was an act of magnanimity which reflected credit on the city fathers. By that time the flow of John Bain's benefactions had ceased. The councillors had nothing to gain, and the gesture itself was controversial. They could so easily have skipped it.

The involvement of Canadian and American Lewismen in the affairs of the community, at that time, was well illustrated when there was a controversy over the affairs of Lewis Hospital.

In the days before the National Health Service, despite the assistance of the Highlands and Islands Medical Service, the Hospital lived from hand to mouth.

The generosity of the ordinary people of the island was remarkable — as it still is today for a wide variety of causes, putting much wealthier communities to shame. In addition to annual gifts of cash, every village in the island had a regular collection of eggs for the hospital. Every sample of herring presented in the Fish Mart at Stornoway was gifted to the Hospital, and sold on its behalf. But there was a limit to what a poor community could do.

At one stage, a political element crept into Hospital affairs. People who saw shortcomings — and there were shortcomings! — instead of trying to raise the funds which would have put things right, attacked the Management Committee for not doing what was beyond their power to do.

The criticism was picked up by some of the leading supporters of the Hospital on the other side of the Atlantic. I remember my father writing urgently to J. T. Mitchell in Toronto to defend the Hospital Managers from some of the mud being slung at them. There was a real danger that an essential source of funds for the Hospital might dry up because the controversy was being exaggerated by distance. At home we were closer to the facts and the personalities concerned. We could also see the political roots of much of the agitation.

In this, Mitchell was a key figure. He was an Uigeach who had become one of the leading figures in Canadian journalism but who still kept up a lively interest in affairs at home.

Nearly twenty years after the Hospital row we were still in touch. He asked me to write an article for the Magazine of the United Scottish Associations of Canada, which he was editing. I told the story of three Canadian servicemen who visited Lewis on furlough during the war. Some of his readers refused to believe me!

The first Canadian was a Cree Indian who established his title as heir-at-law to a piece of land in Ness. One of his grandfathers was a Niseach, Donald Macleod. The second was a soldier, and a boxer, named Macdougall who was identified by his relatives in Bernera, despite the fact that contact between the families had been severed for nearly a century, following the elopement of a farmer's daughter with a crofter's son.

The third was an airman named Martyn who had only three items of information about his pedigree, all doubtful, or untrue. His ancestors, he said, came to Lewis as survivors from the Spanish Armada, which is improbable. They were evicted from Lewis by the Duke of Argyll, who never had anything to do with the island. And they crossed the Atlantic in their own boat, which is unlikely. But a few hours after his arrival, his cousins — in Shader (Barvas), I think — were showing him the ruins of his grandfather's house. "This could not be done anywhere else on earth, and it's all to the credit of our people," wrote Mitchell. There is also nowhere else on earth where a minor dispute over a cottage hospital would excite the attention of busy professional men, in the heart of another continent, five thousand miles away.

The controversy came to a head at the annual general meeting of Hospital Subscribers. Everyone who contributed 10/- a year to the Hospital was entitled to attend the Subscribers' Meeting at which the accounts for the year were presented, and the Management committee appointed. In normal times few subscribers bothered to attend. It was all left to the Management Committee, and it was often difficult to drum up new members to fill vacancies as they occurred.

On this occasion it was different. Scores of subscribers who had never bothered to attend before came up to slate the management, or listen to the fun. The meeting, normally held in the Sheriff Courthouse, had to be transferred to the Town Hall. Scores of people who had never been subscribers before forked out ten shillings for the privilege of kicking up hell.

I was not able to attend the meeting myself. I was helping my father, but I was still a student. I was a charitable institution myself, dependent on my parents to pay my way through college and in no condition to be a hospital subscriber. In fact I could not even afford to be a member of the Students' Union at the University. It was different with my father. The meeting had been closed to the press, but no one could prevent him from attending as a long-standing subscriber. When he went in, his notebook and pencil went with him.

When he came home that evening, he was chuckling delightedly. The Management Committee had been subjected to a violent fusilade of criticism. Their attempts to defend themselves were treated with derision. A motion comprehensively condemning them was carried by a large majority.

Having denounced the Committee as incompetent nincompoops, or worse, the meeting then proceeded to re-elect them en bloc for another term in office!

I have always been a little chary, since then, of protest movements. It is so easy to work up a head of steam. So difficult to harness it to anything productive. When it comes to doing the world's business those who shout loudest do least. It's the dull, plodding men and women, who are not afraid of detail, hard work, and an unremitting grind who count in the end of the day. We may laugh at them, sneer at them, revile them, but we couldn't do without them.

The Hospital did gain from the controversy, of course. It was richer by all the crisp new ten shilling notes the agitators had handed over for the privilege of feeling self-righteous.

73

We got another pay-off as well. At a Hospital concert held around that time, Alasdair MacGregor, the writer of romantic travelogues about the Highlands, made an impassioned attack on the Hospital Management Committee for conditions in the nurses' quarters at Lewis Hospital. If I remember aright he said there were only two armchairs for the whole staff, and one of them had a broken leg.

What he said was of little relevance. He was immediately followed on stage by Fad and Murdigan, the local comedians, and, as they crossed to the footlights, one asked the other in a conversational voice, "I wonder what MacGregor was doing in the nurses' quarters anyway?"

The audience laughed. But they rolled in the aisles when MacGregor came storming back on the stage to explain!

By that time everyone had forgotten what he had been complaining about in the first place.

That was the great beauty of Lewis. However fierce the controversy might be, it was always seasoned with laughter. No one took anyone too seriously. However much we criticised our public men, we still adored them. They were all characters. Not good. Not bad. Each a distinctive blend of both, with a bouquet of his own, which one rolled a little lovingly around the tongue as one passed on the latest story about him that was going the rounds.

I can think of no one in Lewis I ever met who was completely colourless. A cipher of the office he held, or the job he was doing. Most of them had a history. The women perhaps mainly of the hopes and despairs of a quiet domestic life which, on the surface, seemed to be slipping placidly along. The men, however, could often talk of adventures, sometimes on an epic scale, in the far corners of the globe.

Few among them were more colourful than the bus drivers who took over from the carters when petrol ousted the horse. But they demand a chapter to themselves.

21
A Bus Called Wedding Bells!

There was a social revolution in Lewis when the rural buses first came on the road. Town and country were brought dramatically closer together. The practice of walking long distances to visit friends or transact business came to an end. Many more people travelled around the island to the half-yearly communion services, but they tended to come back the same night, or make a shorter stay than in the past. The old tracks across the island from Ness to Stornoway via Back or from Harris across the hills to Uig fell into disuse.

The long established tradition in the Nicolson that each of the senior classes would have an end of the term trip to Arnish by Coachman's boat, for a picnic, was replaced by trips by bus to Coll, Gress, Barvas or Dalmore.

Coachman's boat? It is only now, as I write the words, the incongruity strikes me. What have coachmen and boats to do with each other? Presumably, at one time, the round tubby red-faced gentleman who ferried us to Arnish had been a coachman, but when I knew him he was back to his more natural element, the sea.

It was not only at picnic time the habits of the schools were changed by the bus. It was no longer necessary for pupils — and teachers! — to walk, or cycle, at weekends between distant villages and the town. A retired headmaster said to me recently, "I used to meet your mother-in-law every Friday when I was a pupil in the Nicolson. She was cycling from Tolsta, where she taught, to her home in Tong. I was walking from Stornoway to my home in Tolsta."

A good fifteen miles on foot on Friday evening, and then again on Monday morning, before a hard day's graft in school.

Then he added with a smile, "I don't know if she ever realised that every kid in Tolsta learned to ride on her bicycle. She kept it in the barn at the end of the house she was lodging in and we borrowed it when she was asleep."

She would have enjoyed that story!

One of the first buses to go on the road in Lewis was a huge truck which had been stationed in Stornoway during the war, by the Red Cross to carry the wounded from the mailboat to their homes. Some time after the end of the war it was taken over as a bus by John Mitchell, Shawbost, who had no doubt learned a good deal about vehicles when he was a Lieutenant in the Army Service Corps.

I cannot recall the Red Cross truck myself, although I must have seen it as a child. I am reminded of it by Donald Macleod, writing from Fort

William to recall the "good laughs" he had with Johnny Mitchell over his adventures in those pioneering days.

The early buses had no windscreen wipers. No starting handle. No accumulator. The lights were pretty poor at the best, and varied with the speed of the engine. Going down a brae, when you had to close the throttle and apply the brakes, they practically went out. Driving a bus was a game of Blind Man's Buff in which everything went dark just when the vehicle was threatening to get out of control as you approached a hairpin bend, at the foot of a brae, with the river beside you.

What the buses lacked in convenience they made up in other ways. "Johnny Mitchell wouldn't pass an old man or woman on the way to Stornoway," Donald Macleod recalls. "He would stop the bus and his word was 'leum a steach!' (Jump in). And it wasn't done for money. At the end of the journey 'Moran taing!' (Many thanks) was good enough."

"John was full of wit and humour," he adds, recalling an occasion when someone ruined an engine by running it without enough oil in the sump. Instead of the expected rocket, John said to the culprit drily, "As long as you don't run it without petrol!"

Most of the buses coming on the road at that time were individually owned in the crofting villages and many of them were locally built. The practice was to buy the chassis and get a joiner, or even a boat-builder, to erect a body on it. The story that some of the buses were clinker built and caulked, is no doubt apocryphal, but each was an idiosyncratic hand-made job, completely different from every other. One was known affectionately as "Wedding Bells" for the merry din it made bouncing over water-bound roads. I remember, as a child, running from a football match at Goathill Park to see it, when I heard the sound of its approach.

The seating consisted of two plain deal planks set lengthways so that the passengers faced each other and travelled sideways, while all the paraphernalia the bus driver was taking to the village pressed down upon them. A mountain of goods disintegrating into a miniature landslide with the jolting, shaking and swerving on roads as rough as the bed of a river, and the sudden stops and starts as anarchistic sheep, unused to noisy engines, darted out of the ditches and dived between the wheels.

Bolls of meal, tins of paraffin, boots, coils of rope, yarn for tweed, sheep dip, or kegs of butter, danced around the passenger compartment, to say nothing of the smaller purchases which the driver, as general factotum for the village, had made during his stay in town, and which might range from a pitchfork or a tarasgair to a tin of Epsom salts from Roddie Smith's, Kenny Froggan's or Willie John's.

Even after the Traffic Commissioners were established to bring some order out of the national chaos in the bus industry, the Lewis drivers went their own sweet way, serving the community as best they could, and ignoring bureaucratic regulations as far as they might. On one occasion, when the police made a round up, and took all the operators in one district to court for ignoring their time-tables the proceedings quickly got into shoal water. The witnesses were too deeply indebted to the bus drivers to say anything incriminating. Besides, they knew that mainland rules made little sense in island conditions.

One bus driver pled that he could not understand English, and the court interpreter had to be sworn in. The effect was rather spoiled when one of the key witnesses, forgetting a crucial date, asked the accused, in English, in a whisper which everyone heard, "Was it a Thursday, John?" John, who had just persuaded the Sheriff that he knew no English, ignored the question and gazed stolidly in front of him, but some imperceptible signal must have passed between them for the witness recovered his memory and gave the answer expected of him. Expected by the accused, that is. Not by the Procurator Fiscal!

The easy-going ways of the Lewis bus drivers provided good material for the *Gazette* cartoonists: Iain Campbell, the effervescent art organiser, and Nick — P. C. Nicolson from Tarbert, who deprived the island of a considerable talent when he emigrated to Africa. In one cartoon the driver was depicted explaining to a prospective passenger, "Sometimes she goes at one. Sometimes she goes at two. Sometimes she goes at three. But now and then, she's late." Another depicted the confusion of the tourist who asked where the bus was going and was told, "Back!"

By that time the buses had become relatively sophisticated. They had time-tables — whether they kept to them or not. They had destination boards — whether they changed them or not. They even had conductresses.

Being conductress on a Lewis bus was something of a liberal education. The passengers were not self-contained individuals frozen into their own thoughts, as you might find in the city. Every journey was a ceilidh on wheels. And the journey home after the pubs had closed was a very animated ceilidh indeed.

In "One Man's Lewis", the Breve has a lively description of a New Year's Eve journey in the Point bus, with 'the conductress refusing sippers from forty-four bottles at once", "a Rudhach sleeping in the passage, breathing long and rum", "the well-beloved oaths flying with each back-slap, and the botul mors travelling to and fro like searchlight beams in an air raid."

In wartime there was the added interest of a possible interception by the Home Guard on exercises. The men in uniform trying as best they could to maintain their dignity as they went through the prescribed farce of examining their neighbours' credentials, while the passengers exhorted them to deal with the German spy under the back seat.

The owners of the buses were as rugged and individualistic as the buses they drove. One of the most interesting parts of my job as a reporter was meeting the fleet as they rolled into town, not too early in the morning, to chat with the drivers, who, although they were busy men, always had time to spare in the civilised island way.

There was Morrison from Borve, a dark, square-built, rather solemn looking man, but with a lively sense of humour, and his own highly original approach to politics, religion and life in general. His views were compounded from his observations as crofter, fisherman, merchant, and bus owner in Lewis, and lumberman in Canada — or was it in USA? In any event, I was fascinated by his story of the long talks he had in his lumberjack days with the man who occupied the next bunk to him in the camp, who was then a communist and a labourer, but subsequently became a lawyer and a Nazi, and ultimately was one of Hitler's closest advisers.

There was Dollag from Point, a round, jolly, good-natured man, so tickly that he was terror-struck before he was even touched. His progress from shop to shop, doing the errands for a whole village was often punctuated with screams of laughter, as the shop girls, knowing his weakness, tormented him in the friendliest possible way. No one enjoyed their attentions more than the victim! I sometimes heard the commotion as I passed Hughie Matheson's shop on Francis Street, a favourite rendezvous.

"Shoyan", or perhaps more phonetically "Shoy-yan", was another round, and comfortable-looking man, who generally wore leather leggings as if the bus were still a horse. He was quiet, leisurely, humorous and philosophic. A man who drove so sedately that on one occasion a passenger asked if he could get out and walk because he was in a hurry.

"Forty" from Tolsta was alleged to be almost blind, but, if he was, he must have had his own in-built radar. He drove his bus for more years than I can remember round some of the worst hairpin bends in Lewis, in all sorts of weather, without a serious mishap.

The Breve, if I may quote from his book again, paid a tribute to "Forty" which was really a tribute to the whole of the breed.

"A bus is, in miniature, the whole life of a community in Lewis, or it was before amalgamation brought an impersonal efficiency," wrote the Breve, " 'Forty's' bus was of such an order.

"Sometimes the sadness of death came with the bus, a coffin met with mourning and brought out with tears and the wailing of women. Sometimes there was no end to mirth for a wedding party coming from town, with the wherewithal to sustain an all-night festival — whisky and white lace, beer and conversation lozenges.

"With equal courtesy, he would welcome on the pier the wanderer returning, or see into MacBrayne's loving hands the lads and lassies going south in peace or war.

"By the laws of chance and average, any man in such a length of driving should have at least one accident; yet 'Forty' never had, unless we count the time it is alleged he fainted when some wag shouted to him that he had run over and smashed a full bottle of whisky. If someone were to come forward and maintain that, in September 1931, he broke a hen's leg at Coll, we would not even deign to reply.

"Those were the grand old days when, of a morning, with Logan's bus behind, and a pint beckoning in front, the vehicle went careering past Tinkertown in a whirl of dust, the passengers meeting the seats occasionally with a protesting of the lower spine. A fine miller's dust would come in off the roads, but what recked the rubicund Jehu in front, his moustache dreaming of froth to come?

"Varied were the cargoes, both up and down the line. Ministers travelled warily, with unsteady-legged calves disputing the available space between a bag of peats and a man from Gress. School teachers pretending they didn't know enough Gaelic to understand what some well-oiled Tolstonian was saying to the bus load in general, belligerent crofters going up to town to knock blazes out of the Manager of the Labour Exchange, old women going to the dentist or optician and not at all as sure of the bus as of the carts of former times. These and many more sat, and talked, and sang, and swore, behind the placid 'Forty', and seldom was he flurried. He was phenomenally cool. We are quite sure that, in his heydey, had a ghost come aboard, 'Forty' would have accepted the fact as everyday, collected his fare at leaving, and merely nodded his head once or twice in silent rumination.

"Somehow or other, all 'Forty's' buses had a liking for bridges. Seldom on the way home would a bridge be passed without ceremony, and, if he sometimes forgot, there were those who would remind him.

"What he was, and his history, is the transport history of any part of Lewis, during those happy-go-lucky years of go-as-you-please, do-as-you-please transport. It had its points and its advantages, especially when the bus owner was such an adaptable and human character as 'Forty'."

So wrote the Breve. And what he wrote is true. But, remember the ceremony of the bridges! I will come back to it later in an unexpected context.

22
Mystery of a Dead Man's Dog

Although they had a special place in the social life — and the humour! — of the island, the home-made buses of the twenties were not the first motor vehicles to carry passengers in Lewis and Harris. The transition from horse to "horse power" was pioneered by the Hendersons and Murrays in Lewis, and the Camerons in Harris but they were rather a different species. They were not the ancestors of the modern bus so much as of the little red vans which carry our mails, and the astonishing fleet of taxis, in line astern, in the centre of Stornoway, at the witching hour on Friday nights when spirits are abroad.

Their vehicles, too, were anything but home-made. The Camerons wagonette was an eight-seater Albion while the Hendersons at one time boasted an "Austrian Daimler". When they took it to Tarbert on a trial run, old Donald Henderson declared it came up the Clisham "galloping".

I remember old Dol Henderson a little vaguely. Perhaps more vaguely even than I think. It was said that he had a magnificent watch but could not read the time. When anyone asked him what it was, he presented the watch to the enquirer's scrutiny with the comment, "I canna see without my glasses." The story may be quite apocryphal: an example of the Lewis habit of cutting down to size anyone who got so far above his fellows as to stable twenty horses, and then acquire an "Austrian Daimler" when horses became redundant. When I picture him at Bob Scott's garage, where I most frequently saw him, the watch chain is much in evidence in my mental picture, but I think that is sheer imagination, importing the story I heard so often into my visual memory where it does not really belong.

During the First World War, Harris had only one steamer per week from the mainland and the Camerons put an eight-seater Albion on the road between Tarbert and Stornoway for the convenience of servicemen who would otherwise have lost most of their leave. Their first driver was Donald Mackinnon, Northton, who died, in his nineties, when I was working on this book. One night when Donald arrived in the office and began to empty his pockets Mr Cameron was astonished at the amount of money he produced.

"How many passengers had you?" he asked.

"About fifteen!" said Donald a little vaguely, which might have indicated that he had even more, all packed into an eight-seater wagonette.

"How did you manage down the Ardhasig brae?" asked Mr Cameron.

"Fine!" said Donald nonchalantly. "The weight was so great the back step was hard on the ground!"

There was no fear of the wagonette getting out of control — it would have grounded first!

Mr Cameron's son, Tom, now living in retirement in Tarbert, near the family hotel which he ran for so many years, reminded me, when he told me the story, that the steepest gradient between Tarbert and Stornoway at that time was one in three and a half. The Clisham was a frightful climb, nearly a mile long, tortuous, pot-holed, single-track with no passing places, snaking along the edge of a precipice for much of its length. The Ardhasig was almost as steep, and a vehicle careering down the hill had to negotiate a hairpin bend across a bridge at the foot.

"On the way to Stornoway," Tom Cameron added a little surprisingly, "a stop was made on the Harris side of Airidhbhruaich to fill a bucket of stones to scare the dogs in Balallan. We all had good shots as we had plenty of practice."

I never heard of the dogs of Balallan which so troubled Tom Cameron and his drivers. I don't suggest that they didn't exist. They assuredly did but, for a very good reason, which I will come to in a moment, they did not impinge particularly on my consciousness as a lad.

There were dogs in every Lewis village then. Dogs in every Lewis household. The strange monsters which came snorting and snarling along the roads, called cars, were an affront and a provocation to them. I wonder what the dogs called the cars? Were they aware they were something new and unprecedented? The canine equivalent of creatures from outer space?

The dogs of Balallan, which had to be kept at bay with a bucket of stones by Harris motorists when they ventured north, or, for that matter by Lewis motorists when they ventured south, are a vivid reminder of a vanished island.

An island in which every inch of arable land, or so-called arable land, was cultivated. A changing landscape of little patches, black and glistening in the spring with the new cut furrows; green in the summer with the growing crops; golden in the autumn when the barley and oats were ripening — if the weather permitted ripening — and black again in the winter when the harvest was in.

Every croft had its own cow or cows. Bottled milk was unheard of. Bread was almost unknown, outside Stornoway. And the fish travelled in creels on the backs of barefoot women towards the town, instead of in the opposite direction in hawkers' vans, or the freezer compartment of a travelling shop.

It wasn't a better island over all but it was certainly a different one. And one of the biggest differences was the vast population of dogs. Like the sands of the sea for multitude, as the Bible puts it. The only reason the dogs of Balallan have not remained in my memory is that the dogs of Tolsta eclipsed them all.

There must have been about a thousand people living in Tolsta when the first cars appeared on the Lewis roads. I am prepared to swear, although I know it is untrue, that the inhabitants were greatly outnumbered by the

81

dogs. That is what my recollection tells me. As you passed through the village they came swarming down like ravening wolves. Snapping at the wheels. Snapping at each other. Young dogs. Old dogs. Black dogs. Brown dogs. Grey dogs. White dogs. Dogs with every possible permutation of colour in the canine spectrum, in every conceivable pattern of patches and splatches. Dashing ahead to ambush the car at the next bend. Dashing back impatiently to yell defiance at the monster. Sometimes leaping high along the side as if getting at the driver's throat. But never getting under the wheels. And never relenting until utterly exhausted.

It was not only numbers that gave the dogs of Tolsta pre-eminence. The dogs of Balallan came "peching" up from the lochside to attack a monster on the skyline. Even at that, Tom Cameron needed his bucket of stones. But in Tolsta the motorist was trapped like Mackay's army at Killiecrankie when Dundee's Highlanders rose from the heather and came roaring down the hill.

The dogs of Tolsta were not notorious. They were fabulous. Even while they were still real. The Breve has celebrated them in prose and verse. In a more leisurely age a Gaelic Homer might have immortalised them as the wrath of the gods. Thunder and lightning materialised in flesh and blood.

Just as the Harris drivers stopped at Arivruaich to arm themselves for the battle of Balallan, so my old doctor Jack Tolmie stopped his car at Coll or Gress to get ammunition for the even greater battle which awaited him in Tolsta. He approached the encounter not so much with fear as with relish. I don't think the worthy doctor ever ceased to be a boy. The moving targets of Tolsta were better fun than the bottles and cans in the harbour which no doubt had filled his stone-throwing boyhood, as they later filled my own.

In the middle thirties, when the house cow was beginning to disappear at least in the villages round the town, and cars were so numerous that the dogs were becoming a real nuisance, if not a danger, the police decided to tighten up on the granting of agricultural exemption to all the dog owners in rural Lewis. Seven and a tanner (37½p) was quite a consideration to a Lewis crofter in the pre-war years and there was great resentment when the squeeze began. Many of the crofters argued the case for exemption with great eloquence, and considerable ingenuity, before a somewhat less than sympathetic sheriff. At length he was forced to concede that, according to the Act, any crofter who had a "plurality of animals" was entitled to claim exemption.

He was then forced to concede, a little reluctantly, that two was a plurality. There he drew the line.

"This lady has only one animal," said the Inspector of Police, when the next applicant came forward.

"That's not true!" said the old lady stoutly. "The cow calved since the police were at the croft."

She got her exemption, but the Sheriff refused to anticipate events when the next applicant — from Sandwick — declared, "The cow is going to calve."

82

Cows in Sandwick? Yes and in Stornoway, too, at that time, and indeed much later.

Apart from the comedy, the dog court provided a mystery. One application for exemption from dog licence carried the "signature" of a lady who was dead, the number of a croft house which was vacant, and related to a dog which did not exist.

That may have been the Lewis penchant for practical joking. The lads of the village taking a rise out of the police. But what can one make of the application in the name of a man who had been dead for nineteen years. Over that period it appeared his dog — if dog there was — had been solemnly granted exemption year after year.

But who applied for exemption?

And why?

23
He Left His Cap on the Water

Although I knew John Mitchell as a bus driver only by hearsay, I knew him well after he came into town to manage the garage owned by his cousin, Dondy Maciver, a brother of Robert Maciver who became one of America's most distinguished writers on sociology and politics.

Later John Mitchell opened his own garage and became one of the most successful business men in the island. He was one of the most enterprising men I knew, and the most phlegmatic. And, as I have said before, he was very generous. An unusual combination of qualities. When I knew him first there were no petrol pumps in the island. We got our petrol laboriously from the barrel. The colour gave us a clue to the quality. The first lead petrol was tinted blue. Another grade was red.

An important side line for the garage was the charging of batteries, or accumulators, both for cars and for radio sets. That is after the buses had evolved far enough to have batteries, and radio reached the Western Isles.

One lunch time, when John came back into the garage, he noticed that the bank of batteries was fully charged. Some of them were gassing vigorously. He hurriedly switched the engine off. But it didn't stop.

John tried everything he could think of. Ignition off! Petrol off! Disconnect the fuel pipe! Still the engine rattled on. then the head mechanic, Jimmy Munro, came in. Realising what had happened, he gave the switchboard a thump. The engine immediately stopped.

Munro knew that the switch had a habit of jamming, and, when it did, the whole apparatus ran in reverse, like an electric motor, with the batteries driving the engine, instead of the engine charging the batteries.

"And to think that I was just beginning to wonder if I had discovered the secret of perpetual motion!" said Johnny, nonchalantly.

Around the same time, one of the West Side bus drivers had trouble with his lights. He took his battery in to be charged, suspecting that that was the trouble. It wasn't. He had just got as far as Laxdale with his recharged battery, when the lights failed again. He had only one passenger, and he had a bottle of whisky. The two of them polished the bottle off, and then lay down in the back of the bus to sleep until daybreak.

In the small hours of the morning, the driver wakened. There was a full moon. He reckoned he could get home without lights. With his passenger looking on encouraging him, he began to crank the engine. No self-starters then! When at last it fired, and they were able to resume the journey, the driver looked up at the moon with a heartfelt, "Thank the Lord you weren't charged by Johnny Mitchell!"

Whether the story is true or apocryphal I have no idea. Either way, no one would have enjoyed it more than John Mitchell himself, if it ever came to his ears. For myself, I have a vivid recollection of the circumstances in which I heard the story, but I cannot date the occasion within twenty years. That's the way my memory works.

I was told the story by my cousin, Jack Ross. He was visiting us, while home on holiday. I can visualise the room, and the particular chairs we were sitting in at the time, but I cannot say whether it was in the late twenties, when he was at college and I was still at school, or in the late forties, when he was recounting his harrowing experience as a chaplain with the British forces: one of the first to come face to face with the horrors of the Nazi extermination camps.

The light-hearted story about the buses of our youth might well have been the antidote to more gruesome recent events. Be that as it may, and despite my confusion about timing, I can still hear Jack's characteristic chuckle as he came to the punch line of the story.

Jack was quite a few years older than me. I was never one of his playmates, but I used to hear from my brother and others of the daring with which he would scramble over the timbers under the wharves, even when they were greasy with clinging green seaweed, and despite the fact that he did not have the full use of one of his arms.

Peter MacLean once told me "Jack Ross was like Nelson. He knew no fear." Peter went on to say that, on one occasion, when a sailing ship came into the harbour — one of the last of the tall ships still in commercial use — the boys dared each other to scramble up the rigging. Jack, despite his disability, astonished them all by climbing the rigging up one side of the ship to the top of the mainmast, scrambling over the ball of the mast, and down the other side.

It was the physical counterpart of the moral courage he showed many years later when he persuaded his reluctant parishioners it was their Christian duty to accept an open prison in their midst.

If John Mitchell was the pioneer among the bus owners, one of the most colourful was Murdo Kennedy of Orinsay. One could write a book about him, but what stays in the memory is the tragic manner in which he lost his life. Having negotiated one of the worst roads in Britain, day and night, summer and winter, for many years, he lost his life fishing, with three neighbours, a few hundred yards from his home. They had set a net for herring, and struck a shoal too large for them to handle.

It was squally weather, and, when the wreckage was recovered, it was clear that an attempt had been made to cut the overladen nets adrift before the boat was overwhelmed.

A few weeks later, another small boat from Orinsay was sunk with the loss of three more lives, so that, from a small village of fourteen crofts, seven heads of families, all experienced seamen, were drowned within sight of home, within a single month.

The sole survivor from the second disaster was the only man on board who could not swim.

It is not often that I have seen a Lewisman show emotion of any sort, but Angus Nicolson, a weather-beaten fisherman, as hard and grey as the gneiss which has enabled Lewis to endure the fury of the Atlantic, broke down and sobbed, when he told a Fatal Accident Inquiry in Stornoway how he had been saved.

"We pulled out with four oars," he said, speaking a little stiffly in his second and secondary language. "There wasn't much wind and there was no sea at all, but we were taught by our fathers, when we were very young, to be careful in Loch Shell with the WSW wind, because it was bad with round black squalls, so, when we gave her the sail, we had a reef in.

"My brother was steering, and I was at the sheet. He asked me for a match and I said, 'Hold that until I get a match out of my pocket.' When I turned round to give my brother the match, I felt this. Well! I don't know how I felt it! It was cold and it was something unusual. It came from the other side of the sail. From the bow of the boat. And it pressed her under. She went down by the stern."

When Angus found himself in the water, he shouted, "I'm lost!". His brother Donald, a powerful swimmer, came across to him with an oar.

"I didn't keep that oar very long," Angus told the Court. "But the next thing I knew, I found myself on two oars with Carmichael. I spoke to him, but he made no reply. I saw him slipping off the two oars and going down. He left his cap on the water.

"My brother was swimming round me all the time. I said to him, 'John is lost!' He was our uncle. He said, 'Yes, Angus. Every man for himself now. You follow me. We will go to the boat.!' "

Angus clung to his two oars, kicking with one foot. The other foot was hurt. Eventually he was cast ashore.

"I could see my brother," he said. "He was still swimming. I was in a bad state. I was saying to myself I would just stay there and die — I felt like that! — when I heard my brother shouting 'Angus! A boat!' When I heard him, I tried crawling the best way I could until two women came along and found me."

At this time the fourth man, Kenneth Kennedy, was still swimming towards the shore, but when Angus shouted to him to ask was he making any headway, he said "No!"

"Do you think your brother exhausted himself swimming about trying to help others?" asked the Fiscal.

"I believe my brother was trying . . ." replied Angus, but he broke down, unable to finish the sentence.

"To help Kennedy?" suggested the Fiscal, gently.

"To help his own brother, anyway," said Angus.

24
Kate Crola and the Lord Chief Justice

Islanders are probably at their best in times of danger at sea, but they have other qualities, and here I am thinking of the women as well as the men. Perhaps the women even more than the men.

Not long after the Orinsay disasters I had to write an article for a national weekly on the village of Crola, on the boundary between Lewis and Harris, which had come into the news through the unlikely medium of the New Year Honours List. Calum Macaskill, the local postman, had been awarded the BEM to mark his retiral.

Crola, now uninhabited, is more than five miles from the nearest road, across a trackless and featureless moor, rimmed by the hills of Uig and Harris. You pass Morsgail Lodge, follow the shore of the loch to a group of ancient beehive huts and then strike into the moor, with nothing to guide you but the stones set up at intervals by successive postmen as markers in the mist. For many years Calum Macaskill had carried the mails to a still more isolated township at Ard Bheag, which has now also vanished. He had walked many thousands of miles across very rough terrain, in all sorts of weather, without, so far as I know, ever missing a trip.

The Head Postmaster from Stornoway had to go to Crola on a dark, wet January day to make the presentation. I was told afterwards that as he plodded across the moor accompanied by a friend from Stornoway, and guided by the postman who took the mails from Morsgail to Crola, they came on a little lochan in the middle of nowhere. They were wet and disconsolate. "I think you could do with a dram," said their guide. He lifted a stone by the side of the loch and produced a bottle of whisky, obviously cached down against just such an emergency.

While they were resting, and enjoying the dram, two women came in sight from the direction of Crola. They had walked across the moor from Uig some days before on a New Year visit, and were now making their way home.

"I better give them their Hogmanay," said the guide.

He lifted his magic stone again and produced a bottle of port.

I quite forgot to ask whether he also produced glasses!

On the day I went to Crola, however, the sun was shining, with a sharp bracing breeze, and Cathie came with me for the walk.

The population of Crola at that time was seven. Three bachelors. Three old maids. And a minister. Someone suggested it was time the minister did something about it! He was only a temporary resident. He had been stationed in Lewis with the RAF during the war, and got to like the island so much he came back every summer to fish and play golf on a course he improvised himself. It must have been the most exclusive golf course in the world, but I wonder what the greens were like!

Calum was working on the croft when we arrived. All his suits were hanging out on the fence to air in the sun and the breeze. I had a long chat with him about his experiences carrying the mails back and forth across the moor. Then I said I would like to take his photograph. "Wait!" he said and hurried across to the fence to put a jacket on. "I would like you to wear your medal," I said. Before getting the medal he went back to the fence again to get his very best jacket. The first was not good enough to wear with the medal he got from the Queen.

We then walked up the hill to talk to the legendary Kate Macdonald. I had always wanted to meet her. Old, gaunt and grey, living in one of the most isolated villages in Britain, in a very modest cottage, she was still one of the most remarkable women I have been privileged to meet.

With customary island hospitality she prepared tea and oat cakes for us, and as we ate, I asked her about her brother Murdo whom I had met once or twice and with whom I had corresponded for many years.

So far as I know, Kate had never been educated except in the village school in Crola. Her youngest brother Murdo was sickly as a child and could not go to school at all. Kate taught him at home. As he grew up, his health improved somewhat and he was able to work for many years as postman between Crola and Morsgail. The whole community latterly seemed to consist of postmen, retired or active, employed to carry letters to one another.

Murdo's interest was not in the postal service but in philosophy. Despite the fact that he had no formal schooling, he was widely read, and wrote in a slightly pedantic, but highly intelligent way on a variety of subjects. He corresponded with many distinguished people — including a number of professors — whom he met while they were fishing at Morsgail, and he sometimes contributed sane, perceptive letters to the *Stornoway Gazette* to lighten the turgid, pseudo-religious squabbles which sometimes monopolised the correspondence columns.

When he died, in his middle thirties, not long before my visit, he was waiting to go to Glasgow University having passed his entrance examination, with a view to entering the ministry.

Duncan Maclean, a Scarpach now living in Ardrishaig, told me once that he knew Kate Crola and Murdo well in his schooldays. He spent his holidays with relatives in Crola and Luchair, and was in and out of their home.

On one occasion Murdo came to Tarbert, and Duncan went with him to call on Angus Macdonald, caretaker at the Leverhulme Memorial Hall. Angus had a lively mind himself, but he was in a relaxed mood, leaning on a cue at the billiard table when his visitors arrived. Murdo had no time for frivolity. He went into action right away.

"Well, my friend, what do you think of the political situation in the world at the present time?"

Duncan, as a schoolboy, thought the greeting pedantic. Later he came to realise that a man of Murdo's intellectual capacity, holed up in Crola, must have been, in Duncan's own expressive phrase "like the hart in the Good Book that panteth after the waterbrooks."

When he was a little older and better able to savour Murdo's conversation they walked across the moor together from Crola to Hamnaway to see Duncan's aunt, the gamekeeper's wife. On the way they discussed Carlyle's Essay on Burns, and the writings of Emerson Fosdick, the American theologian.

I wonder whether the keeper's wealthy and aristocratic employers on their stalking or fishing expeditions maintained the same standard of conversation as the postman and the keeper's schoolboy nephew?

Duncan's attention, however, was not wholly on Carlyle and Fosdick. Their route took them past the Brenish and Mangursta shielings then still in use. "I like to think I gave at least one ear to Murdo," said Duncan "while I pictured the blue-eyed girl from Mangursta I had seen washing in the burn that tinkled past the shieling door."

"In the spring a young man's fancy . . .". Even when he is walking across the moor with a homespun philosopher.

The difficulties with which Murdo Macdonald had to contend were extreme because of his ill-health and the isolation of Crola, but many even of those who had the opportunity of going to school in rural Lewis and Harris, in the early years of the century, faced difficulties which today we find it hard even to visualise. Cathie has told me of a contemporary of her father's who used to say to his mother, at night, when she was smooring the fire, "Leave me a flame". The flickering glow from the burning peat was the only light he had to study by.

After Murdo's death, Kate lived alone in the family house, in a dying village, keeping in touch through the radio news, interested in everything at home and abroad, and as well informed as if she were living in the heart of a city. Hers was a wasted life, perhaps, in material terms, but not, I think, an unhappy one, although, at last, old age compelled her to go to live with relatives elsewhere in Harris, leaving the abandoned crofts to be obliterated by the heather, and the houses to become another memorial to a vanished race, like the mysterious beehive houses I had passed on my way to visit her.

The Post Office and the individual postmen gave a great service to these remote communities, at the time I am writing of. They had a regular service, and the loads were not light — most of their meat and groceries came by parcel post. In addition, Kate told me, the postman, presumably as an obligement, carried her accumulators back and fore across the moor so that she was never without her radio. It was quite an obligement to carry someone's accumulator — in essence a box filled with lead and sulphuric acid — a few hundred yards to a local garage or radio shop. What does one say of a neighbour prepared to carry it five miles across the Uig moor?

No one ever thinks of erecting a memorial to the Kate Macdonalds of this world, or the postmen who bring them their household necessities, but, ironically, there is a memorial not far from her home — a large stone with the inscription "Lord Kemble, Lord Chief Justice of England, sat here, 3rd September, 1853".

I've never actually seen the stone myself. The inscription was noted for me by Ian Maclean who spent a lot of his time roaming the hills of Uig. The story he was told in Uig was that there had been a dispute about the boundary between Lewis and Harris. The case reached the House of Lords, and the Lord Chief Justice came to the island to see the territory for himself. He came by sea and landed at Kinresort.

The memorial stone was erected on the instructions of Sir James Matheson. When the question arose of transporting it across the moor from Morsgail one of the worthies of the parish — Calum Mor an t-Sruth — said he would take it on his back, if he got double pay.

He carried the huge stone five miles across the moor on his back, and then walked five miles home to collect his double pay — four shillings!

In modern money — 20p.

25
Espionage at Eishken

The internal combustion engine brought about two transport revolutions in Lewis. The first when the bus displaced the horse and cart. The second when the private car displaced the bus.

In the twenties, when the home-built buses began to ply, Lewis became, for the first time, an integrated community. No longer an island with a hundred villages, and one town, but an extended city — like Los Angeles — of which Stornoway was merely the shopping centre. The social life of the island was enriched, and the basic egalitarianism was not disturbed. There was nothing more democratic than a Lewis bus.

The second transport revolution had less fortunate side effects. It increased still further the mobility of the community. The interchange between village and village, and village and town. The multiplicity of private cars was clear evidence of rising prosperity. At the same time, the coming of the private car differentiated those who had a car — perhaps two or three in the same household — from those who had none. Compared with their neighbours, carless families were relatively worse off, at the end of the second revolution, than they had been at the start of the first.

Up to the war, and for some time after it, it was most unusual for a teacher, even the headmaster of a large rural school, to have his own transport. It was almost unheard of for a teenager to have access to a car — with or without his parents' permission. Just after the war, when there were a lot of young men around, who had learned to drive in the forces but had no cars, there was a spate of unauthorised borrowings. The cars weren't "stolen". The Minch saw to that. But they were sometimes abandoned in inconvenient places.

Iain Campbell, the Art Organiser, who lived in a lonely spot on the Lochs road, told me, during this period, that he jacked up his car each evening, and took one of the wheels into the house, just to make sure that he had a car in the morning. Iain had a talent for embellishing a story, but there was an element of truth in it.

Just as there was an element of truth in his story of the night he was locked out of Duncraig Castle School. He arrived late, on purpose. He did not relish the prospect of being the only man in an exclusively female domain. But he found the place in darkness, and the door locked. He made a burglarious entry, through the pantry window, and was tip-toeing across the hall, in the darkness, when he heard a door open, and saw the matron coming down the stair, torch in hand, to let the dog out, before retiring for the night. Iain stood behind one of the pillars and held his breath. Just as the dog, descending the stair, was level with his face, Iain hiccupped. The dog barked. The matron screamed. Doors were flung open. Lights were switched on. Excited girls went running in all directions, in various states of night attire, or nudity. Or so he said!

The hey-day of the Lewis bus was during the war, when large numbers of servicemen and women were constantly on the move. The buses shuttled back and fore, late at night, or early in the morning, with those setting out reluctantly on long weary journeys, or arriving home, after an ordeal by train and steamer, sustained by the thought of the welcome that awaited them.

Buses were so essential to the life of the island that, when some of the bus drivers were called up as naval reservists, the villagers petitioned the Admiralty for their release. And in some cases the Admiralty agreed. John Macdonald, Sheshader, was working in a naval dockyard when he was unexpectedly told to pack his bag and go home. Arnol retrieved Malcolm Maclennan from a naval vessel somewhere off the coast of South Africa. His shipmates were as sorry to lose him as his passengers were glad to have him back. There were well over a dozen Lewismen on the ship, and Malcolm was the bard. One of his most popular poems was a description of his shipmates, listing their occupations — and their eccentricities.

The best-known knight of the road at that time, and later, was undoubtedly Calum Soda. He was not a bus driver, however. His chariot was a lorry. A historic lorry. It must have been the last T-model Ford in commercial use. The story was that Calum couldn't be bothered with a new-fangled gear lever, and his employers — Murdo Maclean & Sons — were too tolerant to coerce him. And so the kenspeckle lorry remained on the road, long after the last of the locally built buses had disappeared, becoming more and more conspicuous, as each new advance in mechanical sophistication overtook it, and left it behind. The stories about it were legion, and most of them apocryphal, but it was celebrated in an English parody on "Young Lochinvar", and a Gaelic song which may still be echoing round the island, for all I know.

The lorry featured in a famous court case, arising out of a minor accident in Bayhead. The other vehicle was driven by Miss Beamish, a formidable lady from Soval Lodge. The confrontation between a local worthy and one of the visiting "gentry" — self styled! — gave piquancy to the situation.

Much to Calum's annoyance, the Crown took the view that he had swerved out in front of Miss Beamish while she was overtaking him, without signalling his intention of turning into New Street, where he had to deliver some goods. Calum reduced the Court to a state bordering on hysteria by his stubborn insistence that there was no need for him to signal his intention of turning into New Street — a right hand turn, across the traffic, on the busiest street in town. It was purely by chance it emerged, some time later, that Calum was on his way home for lunch when the accident occurred. He had no intention of turning into New Street until he came back, a good hour later, travelling in the opposite direction, with the corner on his left.

"He would indeed be a prudent driver," commented the Sheriff drily, "who signalled before lunch his intention of turning a corner after lunch!"

I cannot recall the outcome of the case, but I do remember vividly Calum's glee, a few weeks later, when he told me Miss Beamish had been arrested as a German spy. I don't know whether the rumour had been started specially for Calum's benefit, but I do know that, as it traversed the town, it gathered precision and detail. "George Stewart read it in the papers," I was told. When I went into his draper's shop, and asked him, he was a good deal more surprised by my question than I was by his answer. Then "Roddy Smith read it in the paper". When I went to the chemist's and asked him, he told me he had certainly seen the name Beamish in the papers some days before, but it had nothing to do with German spies, nothing to do with Lewis, and, above all, nothing to do with Soval Lodge.

That did not prevent another informant from telling me that Miss Beamish was related to Goering's wife, and had conducted a long correspondence with Goering himself about dogs. That information, I was assured, had come from an irrefutable source — the Post Office. How the Post Office knew what was in a sealed letter was not explained, but the story refused to die even when a local shopkeeper — Bertie Steven, I think — had a letter from Miss Beamish on some matter of business.

The island was alive with "German spies" at that time. The most dangerous were on a yacht which was anchored in one of the fiords of Parc, at the outbreak of war. The crew spent their time painting. It is difficult to imagine what military installations they might have been recording in the wilds of the Eishken Deer Forest, but, the good folk of Parc took the matter so seriously that a messenger was sent out to warn them that, if they did not stop, they would be reported to the police. The wisdom of this approach was confirmed when the whole party was arrested at Tarbert, and taken to the mainland, under armed guard. Or so I was told.

It was a good story. But it was rather spoiled, when the lady from whom the yachtsmen had bought their milk received a parcel of shortbread from the "spies", to send to her son, who had just been called up with the rest of the reservists.

One of the great advantages of a small community is that you can follow the progress of a rumour of that sort, watch it grow, and sometimes trace it back to the incident — or the joker — which gave it life.

26
When the Germans Invaded Point

The German spies had their short, brisk, Mayfly flutter in the early days of the war. The invasion of Norway brought its own scare. There were few radios in the island, and, when a cailleach in Parc heard, in a neighbour's house, that British naval vessels were in action at Narvik, she told the village there was a battle at Marvig.

With so many submarines around, it was not entirely impossible, and one worthy, who perhaps had sensed what happened, solemnly lay on the grass with his ear to the ground, and announced that he could hear the gunfire. In a short time everyone could hear the gunfire!

The invasion of Point, a short time later, was given a measure of credibility by the fact that the airport had just been bombed. At least, it was presumed the bombs were intended for the airport, although they missed their target, by a fair margin.

It was about 1 am on a Sunday in 1941. Edwin Aldred, the chief Air Raid Warden for the town, phoned me to say, "Stand by! There's something doing!" I could hear planes overhead, but assumed they were our own, because the "stand by" was not followed by a full alert. In the morning, Alastair Macleod, the Town Clerk, told me the RAF had phoned him to say there were hostile aircraft approaching from the direction of Ness. Later they reported that two bombs had been dropped, but had missed the airport, and fallen in the sea, near Tong.

Alastair, and Sergt Murdo Macphail, went down to Tong by car, but found the village peacefully asleep. Murdo Macfarlane, the Melbost bard, however, was reading late. He told me he heard the bombs explode, and the dishes on his dresser rattled.

All that seems to be certain is that bombs fell in the middle of the Arnol moor. Three exploded, leaving craters up to forty feet wide. Others failed to explode, and buried themselves deeply in the peat. They fell within three hundred yards of a shieling where a cailleach of eighty was sleeping alone. She heard the planes, and she heard the bombs, but she rolled over and went to sleep again. It was some days later she returned home, and told the neighbours.

The women of Garrabost — some of them anyway — were not quite so "coma co dhiubh", a few days later, when they saw a flotilla of unidentified vessels sneaking into Broad Bay, and dropping anchor, close inshore.

Davy Fraser, the Police Sergt at Garrabost, told me he was in the middle of his shave when a crowd of women came to the door shouting, "The

Germans are here! The Germans are here!" "I never heard such a commotion in my life before," he said. When he got them calmed down a bit, they told him there were five strange vessels anchored close to the village. Some of them asserted they saw men coming ashore.

Davy assumed they must be survivors from a bombed or torpedoed vessel. He interrupted his shave, and went outside to investigate. There were women at every door looking anxiously seaward. Eventually he found the only two men in the village who were not on active service, or busy building the airport. One was an octogenarian. The other had only one arm. They were down at the beach, sitting on a stone, smoking their pipes, and wrestling with the problem why five seaworthy motor boats, from Stornoway naval base, should be sheltering in Broad Bay, on a day when no self-respecting Rudhach would bother to reef a sail.

These wartime scares were quite spontaneous, arising from the tensions of the time, but many of the incidents involving Calum Soda and his lorry, were carefully contrived, at the morning parliament, in Bob Scott's garage on Kenneth Street, beside the County Hotel, and just opposite the rear entrance of the warehouse where Calum plied his trade. Bob Scott was an incomer, with a Lewis wife. A highly skilled mechanic who shared, or adopted, the Lewis philosophy that man should not be a slave to the clock. No job, however urgent, was allowed to interfere with a good conversation. Among his regular visitors was Angus Smith, the chairman of the District Council.

When Angus picked up a cheap badge, used for advertising dodgems at a city fairground, he took it along to the garage. As soon as Calum appeared, Bob Scott dropped a casual remark about the decoration Angus had been given for his excellent driving. Calum was scornful. He had been on the road for more years than anyone else in Lewis, and he could drive more quickly, but he had never been involved in an accident for which he was blameworthy, while Angus Smith . . .! Calum could hardly find words to express his contempt. Angus, he declared, had collided with a stationery vehicle, when travelling, in broad daylight, on a clear road, at five miles an hour!

At that point, Angus produced the badge, but kept it discreetly out of reach, so that Calum would not discover what it was. Faced with apparent evidence that discrimination and injustice had indeed taken place, Calum flared up again. When he was in full spate, Bob Scott suggested that he should complain to Inspector Campbell, the local chief of police. Calum did just that. At the police station, Campbell, who also frequented the garage, was waiting with an identical badge, and an apology, for overlooking Calum's merits in the first place.

A short time after that, Angus Smith really did get an award. Not for driving. But an OBE for his service on the Council. I told Dan MacGregor that I had had a phone call from the *Scotsman,* which indicated that Angus Smith's name would be in the Honours List due to be published next day. I told him what the honour was, but Donald saw no reason why he should not enhance it, for purposes of his own. He went out of his way to find Calum Soda, and told him Angus Smith was to be made a knight. "He'll have to go to Buckingham Palace, and kneel before the King," said Donald. "The King will tap him on the shoulder, and say 'Arise, Sir Angus!' "

Which explains why, when I met Calum later in the day, and asked him what he thought of his friend Angus Smith now, he replied, "I knew fine Angus Smith would catch yon. Do you know, he has the highest award for driving in Britain. And he'll have to go to London, on his hands and knees before the King, and the King will say to him, 'Angus Smith, you arrive!' "

While Bob Scott's little coterie thought they were taking a rise out of Calum, I was never quite sure that Calum was not having his own quiet fun at their expense. There was a good deal of shrewd commonsense concealed behind his idiosyncratic use of English, and, in Stornoway, you could never be sure just who was fooling whom.

When the news spread round the town, for instance, that Lightfoot, a handyman at the pier and the hotels, had inherited a fortune from a wealthy uncle in Australia, Stornoway made the most of it. The idea of Lightfoot as a man of substance was irresistible. But while Stornoway was laughing at Lightfoot, Lightfoot was laughing at Stornoway.

It was some considerable time later I discovered that Lightfoot had started the story himself, to see what the town would make of it. He not only started it, he gave it an air of authenticity by going into a bank, at a busy time in the morning, with a huge wad of banknotes, which he handed across the counter with the comment, "I haven't much for you today, boys. Just three thousand quid."

Lightfoot knew, and the teller knew, but the bystanders didn't, that the notes were German. Dating from the raging inflation of the 'twenties, when Lord Leverhulme, as an advertising gimmick, wrapped his soap in crisp new German banknotes. The German mark had sunk so far against the pound, he could buy the banknotes cheaper than the paper they were printed on.

27
The "Witch" Raised an Action for Slander

When the buses rolled out of Stornoway in the evening, laden with assorted dry goods and wet humanity, there was an inevitable wayside stop, by some bridge or peat-stack, for the convenience of the men, many of whom would have spent the evening drinking and reminiscing in one of the bars, while their womenfolk, such as did travel, gossiped in a friend's house in town.

One evening, in the early thirties, in the gloaming, when the Tolsta bus stopped at the Glen Bridge, disgorging a crew of slightly inebriated fishermen, returning home for the weekend, an old lady who had gone out for her cow, was frightened by the din. She tumbled into a peat-bank to hide. All the men saw was a shadowy figure on the moor, move swiftly through the gathering darkness, and disappear. They duly reported that they had seen a witch. Some of them might have believed it, most of them didn't, but, whether they did or not, it was a good story, and Tolsta made the most of it.

A young Tolsta teacher, home on holiday from Glasgow, wrote a letter about the incident, and the local reaction, for the *Gazette*. It was a lovely bit of work, sending up everyone within sight. It was also, although I did not know it at the time, the beginning of a remarkable series of contributions from one of the ablest satirists Scotland has produced this century. I will come back to him later, because he performed a valuable service for the island in a period of traumatic change.

One can learn a lot from the writings of "the Breve" about the complex attitude of Lewis people, of my generation, towards their cultural background. One can learn even more about the therapeutic function of satire, or rather of fun-making in the Gaelic tradition. The Breve's satire, although it was uninhibited, was never barbed or offensive. There is all the difference in the world between satire, written from within a community, out of love, and satire written from outside a community, because of hate, or in an arrogant assumption of superiority.

Anyway, while Lewis chuckled over the Breve's account of the witch, who had "terrified" his neighbours, the old lady was telling her own story to hers. She complained of the rowdiness of the men, who had poured out of the bus, and the fright they had given her. When the two stories met in the middle of the village, so to speak, the mixture was explosive. Everyone now knew who the "witch" had been. So far as I know, no one took it seriously, once they knew the woman involved, but there is nothing more difficult than to stop a good story in its tracks. The old lady decided that she must defend her character, and sent her son post haste to Stornoway to see a solicitor, and raise an action for slander against the nine men who had been in the bus.

The son consulted Colin Scott Mackenzie, who advised him to let the matter drop. He saw that a court case would only inflate the whole matter, and give the story longer life. But the son was adamant. His mother's character must be cleared.

"Thank goodness I haven't a character", Colin Scott said to me, when we discussed the matter. "It must be a terrible burden to carry through life!"

He had come to ask which of the nine men in the bus had written the letter. He didn't expect to be told, but he had to make the inquiry. I said I would not reveal my source of information, but I could assure him the letter had not been written by any of the nine. In fact the men who had seen the "witch" were the writer's target.

So far as I can recall, the matter ended there, but, in the course of our discussion, the fiscal said something which stayed with me. He told me that on several occasions he had been consulted professionally, by elderly crofters, who wanted to interdict a neighbour from bewitching their cattle.

Lewis people are not, in my experience, superstitious. Certainly not more superstitious than the inhabitants of other rural — or for that matter, urban — areas. But, just as some families retained a valuable oral and musical tradition long after most of their neighbours had lost it, so some families, and perhaps some districts, showed residual traces of old beliefs, long after they had disappeared from the island generally.

The elder who, around the same time, reproved the old lady in Tolsta Chaolais for being houseproud, when her dishes were destroyed by lightning (or a poltergeist!), no doubt thought he was speaking the language of religion, but he was obviously carrying forward some much more ancient and primitive view of life. There is still in the religious beliefs of the island a good deal of detritus, left behind by earlier cultures. But this is true of churches everywhere, and of politics, and all our systems of thought. They are never, thank goodness, pure and logical, but always layered, like a growing tree.

Superstition is not something which one has, and then, snap!, one hasn't. It disappears like a Hebridean summer evening, slowly, in a long twilight, with a lingering afterglow.

At the time of the Tolsta "witch", and indeed for some time later, belief in the power of the seventh son, or the seventh daughter, to cure King's Evil persisted in isolated pockets. May still do, for all I know. Shortly before I left Lewis, in the early sixties, one of the girls on the *Gazette* staff told me of a recent instance in her own village, where the old cure had been resorted to.

Norman Jamieson, who was surgeon superintendent at Lews Hospital for many years, once told me that he not only knew of the "touch" being used in cases of King's Evil, but that he knew of cases where it had been efficaceous. No doubt, he added, there were other causes at work, but the patient's belief in the magical cure had been important.

My wife's aunt, Mary, was a seventh daughter, and was quite frequently called on, as a young girl, for the "touch". She had to bathe her fingers in water and apply them to the patient. She also had to wear a sixpence, with a hole in it, round her neck until a cure was effected. The patient wore another. Even as a grown woman, when she had come back to Lewis from Canada, she was asked by a neighbour to treat her son, and did so.

Touching for the King's Evil was the last remnant of an elaborate apparatus of cures, in which superstition, religion, and real knowledge of the medicinal power of different herbs, were mixed together. Alexander Carmichael gathered a great number of charms for various diseases all over the Highlands, towards the end of last century. A crofter in Brora gave him a detailed account of the ritual he followed when treating King's Evil, and a crofter in Kinlochewe gave him the words of the charm he pronounced, "in the name of the Father, in the name of the Son, and in name of the spirit of virtue."

The Celtic Church, and the Catholic Church, had given a religious dress to pre-existing pagan beliefs. In the retreat of these beliefs before the "enlightenment" brought by the Presbyterian churches and the schools, the religious element seems to have disappeared first. The knowledge of herbs went next. The crude superstition survived longest of all.

In some respects the wheel has come full circle. Many modern churchmen believe in faith healing, and medical men, like Norman Jamieson, in the instance I have quoted, believe in the power of mind over matter. At least within limits.

In a way we have stood the old superstitions on their head. Even those who are sceptical about faith healing accept the idea of psychosomatic illness. We believe the mind can make us ill, but we are not quite so sure the mind can make us well again.

There has probably been a greater change in the words we use than in the attitudes of mind that lie beneath the words. There is no one more superstitious, in the sense of holding irrational beliefs, than the dedicated Marxist, who has an almost magical belief in the efficacy of political systems, or, at the other end of the spectrum, the monetarist, who believes there is a simple cure for a complex problem.

28
Is the Devil a Crow or a Cat?

Apart from the benign magic (or faith) involved in the cure of King's Evil by the laying on of hands, I have come across one or two fairly well authenticated examples of black magic: the making of a "corp creadh", or clay mannie, to injure someone.

On one occasion a well known worthy fell out with the local headmaster because he had been brought to court for not sending his son to school. He decided to get rid of the headmaster by ordering a "corp creadh" from a tinker wife. He boasted of what he had done in the Stornoway pubs, and when the headmaster was clearly seen to be unaffected, there was a good deal of lively banter. The gentleman who had resorted to magic was unabashed. His faith in magic undimmed. The fault was his own. The tinker wife had offered him different spells at different prices. Stupidly, he had taken the cheapest!

There are situations, of course, where it is difficult to know whether an element of superstition is present or not. When I was still at school, my father came home one day with a report which set us all chuckling. It was a lively account of the panic which seized the Free Church congregation of Crossbost, when a crow came pecking at the window, one dark night in 1925. Some old women went scurrying from the church thinking it was the devil. As they went out, the crow flew in. It alighted on the head of the preacher, Rev William Cameron, Resolis, and, when he dislodged it, it flapped around and extinguished one of the pulpit lamps. By this time pandemonium prevailed, according to the report, and the service ended prematurely, with the congregation streaming out of the building.

The minister of the congregation, Rev Malcolm Maciver, an old classmate of my mother's, of whom she spoke with some affection, repudiated the allegation that there had been panic, or any fear of the supernatural, or that the service had ended prematurely, although there was, he admitted, a certain amount of not-unnatural excitement, when the crow flew in.

But how did the crow fly in, asks the cynic, if no one ran out, and left an open door? My guess would be that there was an element of panic, and an element of superstition too, but that they did not apply to the congregation as a whole. The *Gazette* reporter almost certainly played the incident up. The minister probably played it down.

And why should a few old ladies, two generations ago, not think they had seen the devil, in the shape of a crow, given the circumstances of the manifestation? After all it is on the record, as I have mentioned elsewhere, that a future Lord Chancellor of Britain once shot the landlord's cat, in a Stornoway hotel, because he thought it was the devil!

The one thing certain in the Crossbost incident is that there was no element of the supernatural, in the actual event, no matter what people thought, or were alleged to have thought. As soon as the report appeared in the *Gazette*, an explanation was forthcoming.

Gilbert Holmes, a great piping enthusiast, who had a fishing let of Gress Lodge, disclosed that he had a tame hoodie crow, which tapped at the window for food, and alighted on the head of anyone who would tolerate it. On the night of the Crossbost affair, the bird was missing from Gress.

As a boy I was only interested in the humour of the situation, but there was more to it than that. Something a little more disconcerting, if not more sinister, than a little residual tinge of superstition. The original report, if my guess is right, came from a Church of Scotland minister. There was an element of needle in it. A little bit of human malice. Gloating over the "enemies'" discomfiture.

Both the writer, whom I suspect, and Rev Malcolm Maciver, were good and tolerant men, by any reckoning, but they were old enough to carry with them scars from the traumatic years, at the beginning of the century, when the old Free Church of the Disruption was divided over the union with the United Presbyterian Church to form the United Free Church, which, a quarter of a century later, entered another union to form the present Church of Scotland. While nationally the great majority of the Disruption Church went into the union, in Lewis the majority rejected the union, remaining in what is the Free Church as we know it today. There was a good deal of controversy everywhere, but in Lewis the gulf was wide, and the argument bitter.

It is ironic that the last occasion on which armed police, and a warship, were sent to Lewis to keep the peace, was when Christians quarrelled over a church union!

It was a difficult time, with legal squabbles over possession of the property of the now divided (or united!) church. In Stornoway there was a surplus building, because the United Presbyterians had a substantial church at the foot of Lewis Street, which later became a tweed warehouse, and is now an electrical showroom. The first time I ever entered it, as a child, it was an empty shell, being used for rehearsals of a playlet for a Church of Scotland Sunday School Soiree. A playlet which appalled me by its banality, young though I was.

In other areas, congregations had to worship in borrowed or improvised buildings. The Free Church at Crossbost, having lost the church, had to build a temporary structure of timber and corrugated iron. It was rather more temporary than they envisaged. In a hurricane in 1905, it was almost completely demolished, and most of it blown out to sea. They had to start all over again.

While the Free Church congregation in Crossbost was surveying the ruins of their temporary church, the United Free congregation in Garrabost were holding their communion, attended by seven or eight hundred people, in a marquee, improvised with sails and timber, provided by Aeneas Mackenzie from the Patent Slip.

One of the interesting side effects of the row was that it seems to have added to the Communion Roll in both denominations. There must be something in the Lewis temperament which responds to an argument about principles.

Although the reason for their plight was novel, Lewis churches were not without prior experience of the state of homelessness. Many years before, the Free Church in Stornoway was destroyed by fire. The following Sunday the congregation worshipped in the open air, on the South Beach, "above the floodmark". Later they found a refuge in Sandy Morrison's ropeworks — or more properly rope-walk — which, by its structure, was reasonably suited to the purpose. It was from this old building Ropework Road took its name, preserving a little bit of Stornoway commercial and ecclesiastical history, until the residents decided that it wasn't grand enough for their letterheads, and petitioned the Town Council to call it Westview Terrace, a name without a pedigree, and of no distinction whatsoever.

Even when churches were available, it was customary, for many years, for communion services to be held in the open. It was the only way the large crowds attending could be accommodated.

One day, in the Library, Dan MacGregor drew my attention to an encyclopaedia of religion he had just got hold of. He directed my attention to a photograph, if I remember aright, of Moslems, turned towards Mecca, with their foreheads touching the ground. Then, with a dramatic flourish, he turned the page around. There, on the back, was a photograph of an open air communion service, on the Green at Stornoway, with a vast assemblage, the women elegantly dressed in black capes and white mutches.

That must have been one of the first photographs ever taken in Stornoway. It must have been a time exposure, and it interests me that the photographer was permitted to take it, at a time when Sunday, (and even the "little Sunday" of the Communion season) was so jealously guarded. It was not possible to reproduce the photograph, but a talented member of the *Gazette* office staff, Margaret Nicolson, made me an excellent copy in pen and ink.

But that communion service was long before the union which divided the Church, and the worshippers would have been very surprised if anyone had told them then that the day would come when armed police would be sent to the island, to keep them in order.

29
Why the "Polis" Went to Church

So far as Lewis is concerned, the epicentre of the disturbance over the formation of the United Free Church — if I can borrow a term from the science of seismology — appears to have been in Ness. It was there the armed police, and a warship, were sent when the Free Church congregation barricaded the building against those who had gone into the union, and refused to obey an interdict granted against them by the court.

The police force was drawn from the mainland of Ross-shire, from Inverness-shire, and from Lanarkshire. They crossed from Kyle of Lochalsh on a specially chartered steamer, and every one of them was seasick, or so I have been told. The smoothness of their reception, however, compensated for the roughness of the crossing. Their services were not required.

My informant, a reporter with the *Ross-shire Journal*, thumbed a lift, so to speak, from the police, and arrived with them, in Stornoway, late on a Friday night. The police spent the night in town, but the reporter, along with some colleagues, who were already on the scene, set off for Ness, in the darkness, in an open gig. They were feeling pretty miserable, by daylight, when Alex Macfarquhar, the miller at Dell, saw them, and asked them in for breakfast.

When they had been well fed, they were invited to join the family at worship. They were all kneeling in prayer, with their heads bowed, when the *Ross-shire Journal* reporter saw, out of the corner of his eye, the policemen marching past, in battle order, on their way to force the church door open. Without alerting his colleagues, he crept round the back of the worshipping company, on his hands and knees, and sneaked out. As a result he was the only reporter actually present, when the police forced their way into the church, and removed the barricade.

Sheriff Squair was in charge of the operation, accompanied by the Procurator Fiscal from Stornoway, Colin George Mackenzie, whose grandson now holds the post.

When Sunday came, the police were out in force, in case there was a clash at the church, between the warring factions. All was peace. The Free Church section of the divided congregation, had arranged to worship in a borrowed building elsewhere, and the police were told they could stand down for the day.

At that point something quite extraordinary happened. Something which, I think, could only happen in the Highlands. Instead of standing down, the Ross-shire detachment, having done their duty, and enforced the law, marched off, in a body, to join the "lawbreakers" in their temporary church.

The explanation is simple. The Ross-shire contingent was under the command of Deputy Chief Constable Cameron, a brother of Professor Kennedy Cameron, who was one of the leaders of the opposition to the union, and one of the founding fathers of the Free Church as we know it today. Rev Kenneth Macrae refers to him, in his diary, as one of the three men who most influenced his own career.

I don't know whether the Inverness-shire men went with their Ross-shire colleagues or not, but the Lanarkshire men did something equally surprising. They marched off to worship in the Parish church which had almost no congregation of its own.

The explanation for the Lanarkshire decision is also simple, but somewhat different. Having time on his hands on Saturday, Supt Gracie of Hamilton, who was in command, had gone for a walk. He got into conversation with the Parish Church minister, and was invited in for a tea of home baked scones. He had suffered more from seasickness than most of his colleagues, and these scones were the first bite of food he had been able to stomach since leaving Kyle, more than twenty four hours before. He felt he should repay the minister's hospitality by giving him a good congregation for once.

I think, on the whole, the police come out of the affair with more credit than the churches!

The events in Lewis, naturally, attracted a good deal of attention nationally. One, now vanished, organ of public opinion, *The World*, tried to encapsulate events in Ness in a little poem.

NEWS FROM NESS

Eagerly to church you press,
　(Holy Ness!)
To your minister's distress,
　(Wilful Ness!)
You the union would suppress;
　(Bitter Ness!)
Came *Bellona* HMS,
　(Lawless Ness!)
Soon your errors you confess;
　(Gentle Ness!)
And this comment we express —
　(Foolish Ness!)

This little rhyme, in my father's newspaper cutting book, which amused me as a child, was probably my first introduction to the theological controversy which has had such a long lasting effect on the religious life of

104

Lewis. Compared with many other cuttings in the book, from mainland newspapers commenting on island affairs, it is amusing and innocuous.

One of the first cuttings reports a public protest meeting in Stornoway, against an account of social and sanitary conditions in the island by Edgar Wallace, who later made his reputation as a writer of detective fiction. If the speakers at the protest meeting are to be believed, as I am sure they are, there was more fiction than detection in Edgar Wallace's account of his visit to Lewis.

In my own day, the worst offender was a Canadian journalist of the name of Halton, who spent a few days in the island, and then wrote an account of our local customs, based in large part on the writings of Martin Martin, two hundred and fifty years before. He went so far as to give an eye-witness account of the worship of the sea-god Shony, at Ness, although Martin Martin said the ceremony was extinct when he wrote, some time before 1700.

When Shony was worshipped, the Nessmen poured a libation of ale into the sea, with a prayer for a plentiful harvest of seaweed, then spent the night in Dionysian revels, round the old temple of St Molua, at Eoropie, which was built in the 14th and 15th century, possibly on the site of a pagan shrine associated with a Viking of the name of Olaf. Or so some of the authorities say. The one thing I am sure of is that the Nessmen of my own acquaintance were not in the habit of pouring ale into the sea, in honour of Shony or anyone else. They had other uses for it!

The temple at Eoropie was certainly one of the holy places of Lewis. More than half a century before Martin Martin, Capt Dymes, an Englishman, described how the Nessfolk celebrated Candlemas there. After "much dalliance together", and a good deal of eating and drinking, "they entered the church with lights in their hands; and continued at their devotions throughout the night."

Dymes also records that he saw arms and legs carved out of wood, with marks or gashes to represent wounds, laid on the altar to effect a cure. There was a sanctum sanctorum so holy that no woman was allowed to enter, and lunatics were taken from all parts of the West Highlands to be cured by the sprinkling of water from St Ronan's well nearby. So great was the fame of St Molua's, according to Dymes, the devout dropped on their knees while they were still five miles from the church.

Dymes wrote almost exactly three hundred years before Halton resurrected Shony for the delectation of his Canadian readers. I lambasted Halton in the *Gazette*, but the Lewis Society, in his home town of Toronto, went one better. They wrote a play about him, representing him, not as the new Munchausen (which he was), but as an Innocent Abroad, having his leg unmercifully pulled by the locals (as it may have been). When they staged the play, they invited Halton's editor to come and see it. I don't know whether he attended or not, but, even if he did, he would not have got the message. The play was in Gaelic!

30
Archangels Keep Out!

Perhaps I was a little unfair to Halton, the over-imaginative Canadian journalist, when I said so categorically that the worship of Shony had died out in Ness before Martin Martin wrote his account of the Western Isles at the end of the 17th century. That, certainly, is what Martin says but he had his information from a Protestant minister — a distant relative of mine — who no doubt had a vested interest in the suppression of what he would regard as Papist as well as pagan. He might have been tempted to claim that the custom had died out completely, even if it hadn't. Or he might not have known if some of his parishioners were still pouring a libation into the sea, surreptitiously, on the appropriate saint's day.

Alexander Carmichael, a substantial witness, says in *Carmina Gadelica* that the custom of pouring out a libation "of mead, ale or gruel" "to the god of the sea" continued in Lewis "till this century". The first edition of *Carmina Gadelica* was published in 1900, but the introduction is dated "St Michael's Day, 1899" so, presumably, "this century" means the 19th, not the 20th, which still leaves my Canadian friend a century adrift in his so-called contemporary account.

That Carmichael was writing of the early 1800s, not the early 1900s, is confirmed by his comment that in 1860 he met a middle-aged man in Iona whose father "when young" had taken part in the ceremony.

Customs of that sort linger on long after they have lost all religious, or actively superstitious, significance. I have taken part myself in pagan rituals connected with the celebration of Hallowe'en, and young people in Lewis may still do. I can see myself vividly, as a child, at a party in Davy Sime's, watching his mother pouring the yolk of an egg into a glass of water. The shape the yolk took in the water — if I understood the ritual aright — was to tell us something about the future.

The yolk or the white? At this point my recollection is vague. Not surprisingly. I can still feel the boredom and incredulity that part of the evening's proceedings induced in me, and my impatience to get back to dooking for apples which was a real boys' game.

It was a good party. It must have been when I remember it. Mention of it explains to me why, around that time, the location of my boyhood games shifted suddenly from Lewis Street to Keith Street, where I waged a war on three fronts with Eesa, Captain, and Ian Chuil as I have told in *The Hub of My Universe*. Until now I had assumed that the move was just the widening of my boyhood horizons as I wandered further from home. But no! I went in pursuit of a friendship. When the Hallowe'en party took place, Davy

Sime was my next door neighbour on Lewis Street, but shortly after that the Simes moved to Keith Street to a smaller house, right in the eye of the storm between Eesa, Captain and Ian Chuil. Thereafter Davy and I commuted between our respective bases.

In time that must have been almost midway between the visit to Lewis of Edgar Wallace which angered my father, and the visit by Halton which angered me. They, of course, were only two among the many, over the years, who wrote inaccurate and offensive articles about the Western Isles. Some may have thought of themselves as social reformers. Crusaders, trying to remedy the plight of the people. If so, they were lacking in sensitivity. What they did not realise — what many do-gooders do not realise — is that you can sometimes delay improvements by shouting too loud that they are needed. Especially if you are the wrong person to shout. A temperance fanatic lecturing a man with a drink problem is more likely to confirm him in his habits than to cure him. In fact, the more the advice is needed, the more it is likely to have the wrong effect.

If critics and commentators were sometimes lacking in sensitivity, we were perhaps at times too sensitive. Seeing offence where none was intended.

I well remember the uproar caused by Halliday Sutherland's book *The Arches of the Years*. His last chapter — *Ultima Thule* — about a visit he paid to the Western Isles with a medical colleague gave great offence. It was easy to criticise. It was a slovenly piece of writing, full of factual errors. But the offence was not in the errors. Most of them were of little importance. And, when I took the book down the other day, to refresh my memory, I wondered what all the fuss had been about. A fuss I no doubt helped to create.

I came to the conclusion that Sutherland was a sympathetic observer, trying to be helpful. The description of a black house he visited is precise and factual. There is no hint of superiority, or disapprobation. He noted that the cattle shared the same roof as the humans, and that there were hens scrabbling for what they could find on the living-room floor. But, he commented, "despite the smoke in the room, there was no dust or dirt on the white scrubbed wooden table, nor on the white crockery on the clean wooden shelves." And the box beds, he wrote, were "not the unwholesome closet beds of the Lowlands and Wales, built into the wall."

The black house he added, "might evolve into something better, although not, please God, into a white house. In the humblest black house there is nothing to suggest the cramped space of a doll's flat or the squalor of a slum".

As a doctor, he was particularly interested in the health of those who lived in thatched houses, which, at the time of his visit, not long after the end of the First World War, must have represented fifty per cent of the population.

"Now comes a most extraordinary fact," he writes. "Children are born in the black houses, and until they can walk — at nine months to a year —

107

they do not cross the threshold. Outside Stornoway there are no perambulators. And yet, in 1923, according to the registrar-general's report, the infantile mortality in Lewis was twenty-eight per one thousand births — one of the lowest in Europe. For the same year the rate in Edinburgh was eighty-two, in Glasgow ninety, and in Aberdeen one hundred and four. Rickets are unknown, and never have I seen healthier or more beautiful children."

Then he gives the reason: "The food of these people is rough, but pure and unadulterated: milk, potatoes, dried fish, salt herrings, oatmeal, butter, and, very occasionally meat." And, he adds, cod liver oil. Our diet today is much more varied. But is it better?

Why were people so angered by what was a sympathetic, and although inaccurate, not an untruthful account?

The mere fact that he mentioned black houses at all touched a raw nerve. The population of Lewis at that time could be divided into three groups. Those who had good white houses, and snobbishly wanted to pretend that black houses did not exist, or at any rate had nothing to do with them. The great majority, who were struggling as hard as they could to break free from poverty and the black house, but received very little help in their struggle from government, local or national. And the minority of, mainly elderly folk, who were content to remain in the homes they had been born in, provided they were left in peace. All three groups resented the pointing finger, even if it was the finger of a friend.

Sutherland also mentioned some other taboo topics such as lice and "caithris na h-oidhche." The latter he referred to, surprisingly, as a custom he had never heard of in any other country in the world. My surprise at the comment was heightened by the fact that he did not use the Gaelic name, but the common English term "bundling", which he is not likely to have heard on his visit, and which the OED relates to a custom "known in Wales and New England", with nary a word about the Western Isles.

Perhaps the "head and front of his offending", the thing that really lit the fuse was his attack on Calvinism in the first paragraph of his chapter. "For the youth of the island dancing, music, or gay dresses were taboo. These things were sinful. Many of the old women would sit in their chairs groaning aloud for hours. That was sanctity. Apart altogether from dogma, this attitude towards life is the antithesis of Catholicism. The Catholic church knows, and has named, every sin that the human heart can commit, and there is one sin defined as "Accidia" — taking a delight in being miserable."

That comment was resented equally, but for very different reasons, by the Calvinists and non-Calvinists in the community. It was over stated, especially when taken in conjunction with other comments of the same sort, which I have not quoted, but, as if to remind me that there was an element of truth in it, Cathie, not knowing what I was typing, interrupted me in the middle of the paragraph to read a letter from an old friend in California commenting on my description of a Lewis wedding.

"One item I remember was omitted", writes Donald Macleod from Oakland. "The dance on the wedding night was the original 'singles club'. To my knowledge, no married people ever attended the dance, no matter what their ages were. Once married you just did not qualify any more. Strange possibly, but that's the way it was."

Cathie recalls the sensation it caused when the rule that married women didn't dance was first breached in Back!

Halliday Sutherland's criticism of the island was relatively mild, and had an element of balance. Others were very different. The first article I ever wrote for the *Gazette* was a furious attack on Cutcliffe Hyne, the creator of Captain Kettle, for a really objectionable article about the Hebrides which he contributed to a national daily. If I remember aright, one of his mildest pleasantries was that Hebrideans were inveterate scroungers. We would beg the feathers out of an archangel's tail, if an archangel was misguided enough to venture among us!

I was still at school, and my brother, on vacation from Glasgow University, was running the *Gazette* while my father had a short holiday. When I gave him the article, my brother refused to publish it. It was too strong. He was afraid I had libelled Cutcliffe Hyne. When my father came home, he published my article without question. He made only one change. He deleted the adjective which my brother thought went over the score — and replaced it by something even stronger!

There was an amusing sequel. The *Gazette* must have found its way into Cutcliffe Hyne's hands. My father got a very peculiar letter from him, in which he sought to justify the article, on the ground that a friend of his, out of the goodness of his heart, found employment near his home — in Cumberland, I think — for two girls from a Scottish island (not Lewis). Their morals were so loose that, in a short time, both of them were pregnant.

My father replied, a little acidly that you cannot found a general accusation on an isolated incident. In any event, he added, the story told us a good deal more about the morals of Mr Hyne's friend's neighbours, than about the two young girls they had seduced.

31
He Might Have Been Soberer, Drunk!

Not long after I took over the *Gazette*, on my father's death, the *Daily Express* had a report about a row in Stornoway over the landing of herring by an East Coast boat, which had been netted on a Sunday. The first part of the report was factual, but, to emphasise the opposition of local fishermen to Sunday fishing, the sub-editor added a flourish of his own. A few years ago, readers were informed, an East Coast fisherman, who was reckless enough to land at Stornoway herring he had caught on a Sunday, disappeared mysteriously, and was never heard of again.

Clearly, the *Express* was not thinking of divine retribution. The inference was that the local fishermen had murdered him! The Town Council took the matter up, and sent a furious letter to the *Express*. Shortly after the letter reached Glasgow, I had a telegram, "Get from the Council what they want us to print, and bury it in a two thousand word article in praise of Stornoway." I readily complied. The apology was worthless. The feature article was of some help to the tourist trade.

On another occasion, when a national daily had a rather intemperate comment on the intemperance of Islanders, giving the impression that we are all inveterate topers, staggering to church on Sunday still nursing Saturday night's hangover, I challenged them to calculate the consumpt of alcohol per head, per annum, among their own editorial staff so that I could compare it with the consumpt per head, per annum, in the island of Lewis. Needless to say, the challenge was not accepted. I think the figures would have been interesting!

A well-known Scottish daily, whose blushes I will spare, sent one of their reporters to Lewis, in the early thirties, to write some travel articles on the lines of H. V. Morton's *In Search of Scotland*. He crossed the Minch on a Saturday night, and went to North Tolsta, with a casual acquaintance he had made on the boat. He survived the rigours of a Tolsta Sunday (as it was fifty years ago!) with some difficulty, and a certain degree of incredulity. The experience provided him with the only worthwhile material he got on his trip.

On Monday morning he sallied out to investigate "the natives", rather missing the point that he had already spent two nights in an island home, and found it not very different from his own, except that the shoes were brushed before midnight on Saturday, and Sunday's dishes were left unwashed until Monday morning.

He saw an old man working on the croft, and asked him, hopefully, if he had ever seen a fairy. The old man looked at him with some surprise, and

110

said "No!" The reporter asked if he had ever seen a witch, or been the victim of witchcraft. Again the answer was "No!" Trying another tack, the reporter asked if there was anything of historical interest he could have a look at. For instance, were there any Norwegian princesses buried anywhere around? The old man indicated that, in his experience, Norwegian princesses were scarcer in Tolsta than witches and fairies.

In exasperation the reporter suggested that his existence must be very dull and circumscribed. Perhaps the old man would like to see a bit of real life, in the outside world? The reporter would take him to the great city of Glasgow, and let him see the wonder of tramcars, and city shops, and a modern newspaper office. Provided he was permitted to record the old man's reaction to these marvels, for the delight of readers of his newspaper.

The old man thanked him. It was an idea worth thinking about. Would the reporter care to come across to the house and discuss it over a cup of tea? When the reporter was settled down in front of a blazing peat fire, with a cup of the thick black brew that passes for tea in rural Lewis (or did in those days, when the teapot never left the hob), and the inevitable pile of home-baked scones and oatcake, heaped high with crowdie, the old man went rummaging in a chest, in the corner of the room, and produced a little notebook. He handed it to the reporter without a word. It was a rough diary which he had kept as a seaman, recording his impressions of every major seaport in the world. He had seen a good deal more of city life than the reporter, and had not seen it with his eyes shut!

Of all the critical writings which have appeared about the Hebrides, none aroused so much resentment as Alasdair Alpin MacGregor's book, *The Western Isles*. It was by no means the worst, or the worst informed. MacGregor knew the Hebrides better than most people, but his judgments were erratic. Having earned his living by writing books about the islands which were nauseating because of their sickly romanticism — Compton Mackenzie guyed him as Hector Hamish Mackay in *Hunting The Fairies* — he had gone suddenly to the other extreme, and attacked the islanders, indiscriminately, for drunkenness, immorality, laziness, and for living as parasites on the rest of the country.

The Western Isles is a slovenly book, put together with scissors and paste. Much of it is plagiarised from an article I wrote for the *SMT Magazine*, but slanted to give a very different interpretation from mine to the borrowed facts. The allegation about drunkenness was vitiated by overstatement, and no evidence at all was adduced for the other allegations.

Whoever had written the book, it would have aroused indignation, but coming from MacGregor it was doubly objectionable. He was almost one of ourselves, and he had eaten our salt — in fact, a good deal more than our salt. When he came in search of copy, he was like an invading army, living off the countryside, as it was relatively easy for him to do in the island, where all the doors, and indeed all the hearts, were open — even if some of them must have sunk a little when they saw him coming up the croft to scrounge once more.

A few days after MacGregor's book was published, I was astonished to read in the *Editorial Diary* of the *Glasgow Herald*, a statement by the Chairman of the Lewis and Harris Association of Glasgow, that I would reply to the book, when I took the chair, a few days later, at the Association's Annual Gathering. It was true that I was due to speak at the gathering, but I hadn't even see the book, and, up until then, had no intention of mentioning it. I hastily got a copy, and read it in the Sheriff Court, while covering a tedious, long-drawn-out case.

It was easy to reply to MacGregor's allegations, but that would only publicise the book. I had to find some way of bringing home to the publishers the immensity of the damage they had done to the island's, and their own, reputation, by including a book, distinguished only by its spleen, in the County series, which was regarded as a collection of serious, perhaps even standard, works.

I finally decided to ask the audience at the Lewis and Harris to send telegrams of protest to the publishers. To make it easier for them, I distributed telegram forms, prepared by my partner Sam Longbotham, with the publisher's name and address ready printed in. Surely, I thought, some at least of those at the gathering would think it worth spending a bob or two to strike a blow for their native island.

I had no idea how well the ruse had succeeded, until I got a letter from MacGregor — seventeen years after the event! In it he complained bitterly that I had turned "half Scotland" against him by my speech, and antagonised his publishers, by flooding their office with more than two thousand telegrams of protest on a single Saturday morning.

The letter was followed by a series of abusive messages, written on postcards, and addressed to the Crofters Commission office, no doubt with the hope that they would be read by the staff, and I would be caused some embarrassment.

I began to understand the reason for the belated response to my attack, when I read a paragraph announcing that he had a new book coming out, in which he claimed to be unrepentant. Significantly, however, the only charge he repeated was that of drunkenness. The others were quietly dropped.

We do have a drink problem in the islands — as they have in many other places. But, as I said when *The Western Isles* was published, intemperance in argument is even more destructive than intemperance in the use of alcohol. MacGregor was so fanatical in all his views, he might have been soberer, drunk.

32
All Aboard for Gomorrah

Among the miscellaneous charges Alasdair Alpin directed at his father's fellow islanders were that they were notorious for wife-beating, for boisterous and irreverent funerals, for cruelty to animals, and sexual immorality. The only "fact" adduced in support of the charge of immorality was that in one of the islands a wedding had recently taken place which was attended by the couple's four-year-old twins.

"Better late than never!" I retorted. "It is a good deal less immoral for the four-year-old twins to be present at their parents' marriage than at their parents' divorce." At that time we had no experience in the islands of the effect on children of broken homes. If I were making the comment today, I would make it even more vehemently.

The Lewis Association published a booklet rebutting MacGregor's allegations point by point. Some people thought the Association over-reacted. I almost thought so myself a few years ago, when I visited Balquhidder, to see the memorial to Rob Roy, and found myself, quite unexpectedly, standing by the grave of the man who had been a regular visitor to my office for many years, until the controversy over *The Western Isles* brought his visits to an end. My life would have been poorer — less interesting anyway — without him, and without our row. I thought, a little nostalgically, of the headlines at the time, in the Scottish dailies: "Clean Up This Book", "Bury the Publishers in a Snowstorm of Protest", and "I Wrote the Truth — says Author."

The Lewis Association was influenced by the effect MacGregor's allegations, especially the allegations about laziness and immorality, might have on the hundreds of island girls seeking employment in hotels, or hospitals. I have no doubt that many were embarrassed by the comments of their acquaintances, if not prejudiced in the mind of prospective employers. But there was the dilemma, the inevitable dilemma, that the controversy gave wider publicity to the charges. Pursuing a smear is a hopeless task. It is like the bow wave of a ship: you push the lie in front of you, as you pursue it, and leave it behind you as a flurry on the water, which will only disappear in its own good time.

The Association was also influenced by the claims made by Alasdair Alpin's publishers. The book was described as the "synthesis of a lifetime's study", and the author as "the greatest living authority on the Highlands and Islands of Scotland."

The nature of his authority was revealed by his account of the seaweed industry in Uist, which he claimed to be factual, and "free from impressionism". He included an elaborate calculation to show that the Uist crofters were grossly overpaid for the work they did. In the course of the calculation he made an error in simple arithmetic, adding £400 and £350 to make £850. He then multiplied his error by fifty, in working out an annual rate. In addition, he failed to realise that the figure he started with represented the earnings of teams of three or four, not of individuals. He also assumed that the crofters were in regular full-time employment, despite the fact that the work was seasonal, intermittent and part-time, wholly dependent on favourable conditions of wind, tide and weather. Having compounded all these errors, he came up with the "fact" that 106 crofters in Uist earned between them, "on the side", £40,000 a year. Approximately half a million at current prices! The crofters were naturally astonished to discover how wealthy they were, without even knowing it. The man who paid their wages was even more astonished.

If the Association was a bit heavy-handed in dealing with the book, MacGregor was disposed of very neatly by a cousin, and namesake, of his own, who wrote a little poem for the *Gazette*. She made the point that MacGregor, having more or less claimed that he created the tourist industry in the north, by enveloping the area in a rosy, romantic haze, was now providing another bait for tourists lusting for the fleshpots. She pictured them in their thousands:

> "Streaming daily through the Kyles
> Heading for the new Gomorrah
> In MacGregor's Sinset Isles!"

And, of course, he fell a victim to the Breve, who made him the butt of many barbed allusions, over the years. So far as the Breve was concerned, MacGregor had the solace, if solace it was, of sharing the dock with many well-known figures in the life of the islands — Town Councillors, District Councillors, County Councillors, members of the Trust, David MacBrayne, successive Scottish Secretaries, ministers, tinkers, and dockers. Everyone in fact whose folly, or whose foibles, merited a reproving word. It was a bad patch in the public life of the island, and the Breve helped us through it, by saying under the cloak of humour, many things which needed saying, but which, said directly, would merely have produced resentment and resistance.

The other day, when someone, who should have known better, spoke of the islands as a place where the law was not held in high esteem, I reflected on the fact that, during the quarter of a century or so when I regularly attended the courts in Stornoway, we had seven different sheriffs-substitute. With two exceptions, they probably did more to diminish the respect in which the law was held than those who appeared before them in the dock.

During that period, the Sheriff-substitute was obliged to reside within his jurisdiction. A posting to the Hebrides did not attract the best candidates. It was the equivalent, for most Edinburgh lawyers, of a posting to Siberia. The Sheriff-Principal, fortunately, was a man of very different calibre, but we seldom saw the Sheriff-Principal in the Islands. Under the new system of "floating" sheriffs, the islands seem much better served than in the days when I had frequently (and most reluctantly) to blue pencil the Breve's strictures on the bench, to keep on the right side of the law. As he asked me on one occasion, "How can you be guilty of contempt of court by telling the truth about a court of contempt?" Unfortunately, you can.

While he disapproved of what sometimes happened in the official courtroom, the Breve, like the licensed jester of old, conducted a fantastical court of his own. His barbed, incisive wit was both dazzling and deadly, but it was thoroughly enjoyed, sometimes even by the victims. His pen-name defined his role for those who knew the history of Lewis. As a Morrison, he felt entitled to assume the mantle of the Breitheamh, or Breves, the hereditary law-givers of the island, of whom thirteen were said to have been Morisons.

The quality of George Morrison's work was never fully recognised either outside the island, or for that matter, within it. Because he wrote in Gaelic almost as frequently as English, and in a local paper on local themes, people outside the island community were largely unaware of his existence. Even those who read his column, and knew his victims, missed a good deal, because his articles were often spiced with classical allusions, which went over the heads of the readers, and sometimes of the editor as well.

His work was not all satirical. There was a strong strain of nostalgia for the Lewis of his boyhood running through it. He was in revolt against the hardships of the crofter-fisherman's life, the neglect and indifference of successive governments to the problems of the islands, and the narrow bigotry of some of the more vocal leaders of the local churches. He mocked the people of Stornoway, for mocking the people of rural Lewis. But he loved them all.

Occasionally, in a straight piece of prose, the Breve evoked, with brilliant clarity, a scene from his boyhood: the fishergirls returning from Yarmouth with gifts for the family; their gaiety in the face of hardship and discomfort; "Forty", the legendary bus-owner, to whom I have already referred; the hardihood of the skippers, launching their open boats from unprotected beaches; the cosy warmth of life in the old black house, centred on the peat fire, and embracing the whole village, animal and human, in one fellowship.

Sometimes it was simple uproarious fun, like his poem about the crofter who bought a sheep's head from an itinerant butcher, and found his own private mark on the ears. In real life, the incident gave rise to a prosaic court case. The Breve gave us the memorable, if apochryphal lament of the crofter, when he recognised his own ewe's head in the broth.

I often regretted that George did not write in a more permanent, and less localised way, about the rapidly changing Lewis which he knew, and which no one else could describe with the same insight and power. I was delighted that, shortly before I sold the *Gazette*, it was possible to publish a small anthology of his work, which Cathie selected and edited, and which I hope will be maintained in print, along with a selection of his Gaelic poems which she has also prepared.

33
The House that was Lit by a Teapot

It was always a problem to know how to sub-edit the Breve's contributions to the *Gazette*. There was a temptation to use the blue pencil, because he was dealing, irreverently, with the Lewis establishment, in the manner of *That Was The Week That Was*, thirty years before the BBC plucked up sufficient courage. Newspapers were much more cautious then than they are now with people's dignity and reputation, especially when dealing with the courts. I did make cuts, when I had to, but I sailed as close to the wind as I could. Sometimes closer than my legal adviser liked. Fortunately the Breve came to be accepted, in the bardic tradition of the Highlands, as specially privileged. He got away with things that would not have been tolerated from anyone else.

There were occasional squeals. I remember one irate gentleman coming into the office, holding a copy of the paper upside down, and thumping his fist on a passage he wanted me to read. It said simply, "In Lewis there are many sinners but only one Peacach."

Peacach is the Gaelic for sinner, but it was also the nickname of a crofter from Point, who was well-known throughout the island. I suspect that his anger was engendered by what his pals said to him about the paragraph, rather than what the paragraph itself said.

All was grist that came to the mill so far as the Breve was concerned, but much of his best material came from the Sheriff Court. Sometimes it required almost no embellishment. Like the rumpus at an RAF camp when the war was over, and the RAF pulled out suddenly on a Sunday afternoon. To all intents and purposes, they abandoned the place, leaving behind only a small quantity of rather indifferent furniture. A few of the locals thought it would be a pity to let it go to waste.

One group moved in shortly before midnight. Another group, having rather more regard for the fourth commandment than the seventh, held off until the Sabbath had run its course. Perhaps as a reward for their virtue, in that respect, they found most of the furniture neatly stacked for removal at the doors of the huts, while the first group were having a final rummage within. The new arrivals, presumably on the basis that it's not lost what a friend gets, took the furniture that was ready to hand, which caused a lot of heartburning when the first arrivals realised that it was gone.

When the police moved in, however, those who had been dispossessed by the later arrivals, sat back and laughed. They were in the clear! One unfortunate, who had acquired a rough wooden wardrobe in the second wave, quickly put it back, when he heard the police were making enquiries. He was too late. It was proved in court that he had taken it, and he was fined. Which was rather hard, because, when he put it hurriedly back, he failed to notice that his wife had hung his clothes in it, so that he lost the wardrobe, the fine, and his Sunday suit as well.

There were times when the Breve's social commentary was probing and sharp. One of the first questions he ever raised in the *Gazette* was addressed to the Education Committee of Ross and Cromarty. It was simply, "To what extent does relationship with the mighty improve the value of a poor degree?"

I am not close enough to affairs in the island now to know whether the question is still valid, but it may well be. It is always difficult, in a small community, to eradicate family, church and other influences, often unconsciously exercised, which may deprive the community of the service of its ablest sons.

Shortly after the outbreak of war, before he joined the Navy, the Breve was home on holiday in Lewis. Looking out from the croft one morning, he saw a cask, bobbing about in the Minch. All sorts of flotsam was coming ashore at the time, from vessels bombed or torpedoed off the Lewis coast — including a vast quantity of Chinese bank notes! The cask looked interesting. With a great deal of effort, George got it ashore, and discovered, to his dismay, that is was some sort of engine oil.

He reported it forthwith to the Receiver of Wreck, which he might not have done, had the contents been different. By return of post he got a complicated form to complete. He was so infuriated by its unnecessary complexity, he filled it up in a mixture of English, Gaelic, Greek and Latin, and left the Receiver of Wreck to make of it what he could.

The question which annoyed him most asked whether there were any "droits" "appertaining to the Lord of the Manor." He replied, "No Lord of the Manor in North Tolsta. Thank God!"

That night I met him in town where he had been meeting some friends. We went for a stroll, and a chat. On our way round the quays we bumped into the Receiver of Wreck. I introduced them, and stood back to listen to one of the liveliest discussions I have ever heard. The Receiver of Wreck, a young Englishman of the name of Broughton, fortunately had a sense of humour, and we all parted the best of friends.

The people of Lewis, as in most other seafaring communities, have always looked on anything the sea washes up as a gift from the gods. Murdo MacLean once told me that the first orange he ever saw was picked up on the beach at Brenish, following a wreck. I don't know whether he tasted it or not, or even if he knew what it was, at the time.

I have been told that when the first tea came to Lewis, from a wreck at Dalbeg, the crofters used it to manure the fields.

So far as I know there is no tradition in the Isles of "wrecking", in the Cornish sense of luring vessels to their doom for the sake of the cargo. On the contrary there is a well attested case of a farmer's wife at Mangursta, in

Uig, guiding a vessel to safety, in the darkness, with a burning peat. It was written up at the time in, I think, *The Strand Magazine*. When I mentioned the matter to an Uigeach of my acquaintance, Murdo "Policy", he indicated that, while the story was true, the farmer's wife had got the credit for an operation in which the local crofters had played the bigger part. And that would not surprise me.

In 1866 there was an official inquiry into allegations of "wrecking" in the Western Isles. It had been a particularly severe winter, and in three months, from December to February, 35 vessels had been wrecked on the coast of the Hebrides, most of them becoming a total loss. The estimated value of the cargoes was over £200,000, which would represent many millions today. What the loss of life was, I cannot say, but it must have been heavy, because many of the vessels were identified only from scraps of driftwood washed ashore, or markings on the cargo.

The inquiry was instructed, following a complaint from Lloyds. Mr Gray, of the Board of Trade, visited the Hebrides and prepared a report which was eventually laid before Parliament. He found plenty evidence of plundering. One wreck, the *Alfaretta*, was so extensively stripped that the copper bolts were hammered out of the hull. A cargo of paraffin from another vessel went into general circulation, once a local innkeeper discovered what the stuff was for. It must have been the first paraffin burnt in the Hebrides, at least in many of the poorer homes. Gray was astonished to find one house lit by a teapot, full of paraffin, with a wick through the spout.

It is many years since I last read the report but, as I recall, Gray found no evidence of "wrecking". He did express surprise at the extent of the plundering. But wrecks are plundered in most places, if they are left unattended, and it would have been unreasonable to expect Gaelic-speaking crofters, living meagrely off potatoes, herring, milk and porridge, to know that, in the great world of commerce, the law decrees that a wreck remains the property of the owner, if his identity can be established.

The crofters, in fact, come out of the matter very much better than the officials of the Board of Trade, or even Mr Gray himself.

Gray discovered that Mr Pithie, the Receiver of Wreck at Stornoway, was claiming fees for special duties, keeping watch on four different wrecks, in four different islands, simultaneously. He collected fees for watching each of them while actually he was skipping about, from island to island, leaving three wrecks unattended at any one time. He eventually put a watchman on the *Alfaretta*, but only after the copper bolts had gone!

As a result of the report, there were several transfers and dismissals in the Receiver of Wreck's Department, and Gray himself was threatened with an action for libel, by Alexander Macleod, the policeman in Barra, as a result of a colourful article he wrote for *Nature and Art*, on his adventures in *Ultima Thule*.

34
Ernie Bevin Lost His Cool

Some places are more favoured by the sea than others with flotsam. On a beach near Borve in Harris, every year, almost on the same day, logs of American timber used to be cast up by the tide. They still may be, for all I know.

When the motor fishing boat *Verbena* was making her way home to Stornoway, one night in 1942, in the face of a stiff breeze, the rudder broke loose and sank. The crew managed to keep the *Verbena* off the rocks with an improvised rudder and a jib. She drifted from Bayble up to Kebback. There she was sighted by the *Columbine* and taken in tow. To get wood for a new rudder in wartime was impossible. As the skipper said, he would have to fill a hundred forms and wait six months, and he might not get it in the end of the day. Instead he went to Uig. On the first beach he visited, he found a log of good red pine. He, and his companions, rolled it up the beach, got it on to a lorry. Four days later the *Verbena* had a new rudder which cost them next to nothing.

American seaweeds regularly make the journey across the Atlantic. John Campbell, who was headmaster at Barvas three quarters of a century ago, made a collection of unusual seaweeds he picked up on the beaches of the Taobh Siar. He sent them to Edinburgh to be identified. Every one of them came from America. The letter from Edinburgh conveying this news became flotsam itself, in a sense. It went, in error, to the Nicolson Institute, and lay there for years with the seaweed still in the package. Long after Mr Campbell had left Lewis, in fact after he was dead, the package came to light. In the interval his son, Iain Campbell, had become Supervisor of Art in the rural Lewis schools. It was he who got the answer to his father's query, thirty five years after it had been raised.

During the period of prohibition in America, a cargo of hooch was washed ashore, near the island of Scarp. Really foul stuff. A crofter from Uig, who got some at a friend's, failed to return home. His relatives were in a quandary. They could not call the police, or, too ostentatiously, organise a search, or their friends would be in trouble. Three days later, the missing man came home. He had been asleep for sixty hours, behind a pile of oats, in his own barn, while the family were surreptitiously searching the neighbouring bogs.

I never saw anything really valuable that floated across the Atlantic, but one day some fishermen from Point came into the office with a tin can they had picked up in the Minch. In it were some American coins, and a message to say that it had been thrown into the Gulf of Florida on a date some months before. I reckoned that it must have travelled, on average, four miles a day on its journey of well over three thousand miles.

The husk of a large nut found under five feet of peat at Barvas some years ago was said, by the experts, to have drifted across the Atlantic, thousands of years ago, before the peat was formed.

The flotsam that came ashore during the war did not have quite so far to travel. Many vessels were sunk quite close to the Hebrides. I may have occasion to mention some of them, specifically, later.

It was rumoured at one time that some of the Lewis buses were running on industrial alcohol, guided ashore by Providence, to relieve the petrol shortage. Of that I am not quite sure, but I do know that a vast quantity of timber came ashore in Uig — quite apart from a new rudder for the *Verbena*!

It was said that the crofters were salvaging it for their own purposes. When the Receiver of Wreck — Broughton's assistant — made a sudden descent, armed with a search warrant, the timber was mysteriously stored on the croft next door to the one for which he had the warrant. He tried to bluff his way into the barn where the timber was stored, but the crofter disputed his right of entry. "Do you realise that I am the Receiver of Wreck?" said the official, haughtily. The crofter, having leisurely surveyed the greasy raincoat, and battered hat, which was considered suitable for a journey to Uig, in a Lewis gale, replied, "Your wife may be!", and closed the door.

It was about that time rumours began to filter into Lewis about the wreck of the *Politician* off Eriskay with a fabulous cargo of whisky. The story could not be reported, because of the censorship, but the *Glasgow Herald* got round the difficulty. The Editorial Diary carried a cryptic statement that recent events in the Outer Hebrides were interpreted, by the natives, as fulfilment of the poet's promise, "The spirits of our fathers shall start from every wave".

I may be wrong, but I have always liked to believe that that inspired paragraph in the *Herald* was the work of Alastair Phillips, whose contributions to the Editorial Diary delighted me for so many years. At the time it appeared he was not writing the Diary, but he was nearer the source of the story. He was serving with the RAF at the camp where the crofter later lost his Sunday suit!

The first hard news I had about the *Politician* came from Broughton, the Receiver of Wreck. He told me thousands of cases of whisky had been looted, and a great deal of wanton damage done. Walnut and rosewood panels, he said, were smashed to matchwood, and the piano was so thoroughly demolished that the keys were in the engine room. "There was a motive for taking the whisky," he said, "But the destruction was the work of savages."

Later I got a fuller account from Rory Macleod (Bodach an Te) who had been night watchman on the *Politician* for five weeks. He had just recently returned home from Eriskay because of his wife's illness. As he told me, in his sailorly way, "Annie took a bad turn, so I goes to Mr Holden, my boss. He says 'My own wife was injured in the blitz on Glasgow, and I goes down every five weeks to see her. Away home you go and tell me how you get on.' " Rory added that he had just sent a telegram to say he would not be going back. The doctor had advised him that his wife might have a relapse at any time.

When I asked about the *Politician*, he said "There she was, sitting up — just like a supply ship at anchor". The local postmaster, he said was an old schoolmate of Norman Macarthur, Captain of the *Lochness*. Rory became friendly with him.

"He told me the owners tried to salve the cargo. Then they gave it up. It was too difficult. She was lying as far out as the Chicken is from Stornoway Harbour. The news spread in Eriskay that she was abandoned as a total loss. They were going to blow her up. So the Eriskay boys got busy. They took out the whisky in bottles. They took it in cases. They took it in hundreds of cases. Twelve year old Scotch. Then the Uisteachs joined in. Finally they were coming in motor boats and sailing boats — anything that would float — from Tarbert, Harris and even from Tobermory."

"They took the whisky," said Rory, "They took the bedding. They took the chairs. They stripped out the panels and took them too. They took everything moveable except the high explosives. They were going to Jamaica. And the cars. They were too heavy."

Rory thought an attempt might have been made even to shift the cars, if the wreckers had been left long enough on the job, but at that stage some of them began to sell the whisky. Benbecula was crammed with imported labour, building the airport. Much of it Irish. Money was plentiful. Twelve-year-old-Scotch was five bob a bottle! The sequel was inevitable.

"They drank themselves stiff," said Rory. "One day there was no one in the whole bloody place fit to lift a spade. Work was at a standstill. The Air Ministry asked the Ministry of Labour, 'What the hell is going on?' Ernie Bevin made enquiries. When they told him, he phoned the Ministry of Shipping, 'For God's sake blow her up, or take away your damned whisky' "

How Rory knew what the various Ministries had said to each other, I have no idea. I reckon it came from a lively imagination. I also reckon it was not far from the truth. But the Ministry of Shipping did not take decisive action as Bevin had asked. They temporised, as Ministries do. Having tried salvage, and abandoned the idea, they decided to have another look. An inspector was sent to Eriskay, and Rory was engaged as night watchman. But that was only the start of the story.

35
Harshly and Aggressively Treated

When Rory got aboard the *Politician* his first task was to cut away all the ladders, except one. "I wasn't sure the buggers wouldn't push me overboard, if they could get up behind me," he said. "I had nothing to defend myself with, and I wasn't taking chances."

He had another worry. "There she was, sitting up like a supply ship, asking any German plane that saw her to have a go. And me there alone, with a cargo of high explosives in the hold! I didn't even have a boat. I had to depend on the boat that came out every morning from the shore. In case it didn't come, I had two days' hard tack on board."

At night when boats came prowling round Rory would shout "Ship ahoy! What's your number?" If they cursed him in English, he would reply in English. If they cursed him in Gaelic, he would reply in Gaelic. Either way, the message was the same. "The game's up now! Away home, you buggers!"

"They could have knifed me!" he said. "A lot of damned papes!" and he spat in the gutter, where we were standing, just outside the Town Hall door.

That disconcerted me. I expected Rory, as a regular navy man, and the hired night-watchman on the wreck, to be on the side of authority, but I always thought of him as a man of the world, who had met all kinds, in all sorts of places, and who judged men on their individual merit; not in categories. There was only one thing certain, and he knew it as well as I did. If bad navigation, and the fortunes of war, had landed the *Politician* on a reef off Lewis the whisky would have been taken just the same. Religion had nothing to do with it.

I didn't discuss the matter with him. I was too anxious to get the rest of his tale. As well as putting a watchman on the wreck, the authorities had begun to search for the whisky. "When the crofters got drunk and quarrelled, they began to tell on each other," said Rory. "In a small patch of ground on one man's croft they found a hundred and thirty two bottles of whisky, cached in the ground, with the corn growing over them. Sometimes it was buried in no man's land, on the common grazings. If it was, they charged the man whose house was nearest to the spot."

According to Rory there had already been one round of prosecutions. Rory reckoned the fines worked out at about £1 per case. There was a second round of prosecutions in progress as we talked, he said. "I left for home the day the case was on. There were 32 Barra men, six police officers, and seven customs officials on the *Lochmor* with me. It took two hours to discharge the cargo of productions in the case. Whisky and God knows what."

It was after his adventure on the *Politician*, Rory was engaged to recruit island seamen for the salvage tugs. I saw him once or twice thereafter, and had letters from him occasionally. The last, not long before his death, ended with a flourish, "Your old friend, Rory. Still going strong."

The story of the *Politician* began to take a slightly different colour, when I discussed it, some days later, with Malcolm K. Macmillan MP. He handed me a sheaf of correspondence from island crofters, schoolmasters and government officials, from Alasdair Macdonald, the solicitor in Lochmaddy; Sir Alexander MacEwen, and Col Neil Macarthur, solicitors in Inverness, and from Tom Johnston, the Secretary of State for Scotland, all addressed to him as MP. for the Western Isles.

The first letter was from a crofter's wife in Garrynamoine. It was clear from it that those who had been charged had not escaped with Rory's fines of "£1 a case". A large number had been sent to prison for up to two months. "What is to become of their stock and crops?" asked the crofter's wife. "What about the boats that were seized? They can't go fishing."

The letter that interested me most was Alasdair Macdonald's. He was something of a legend in the South Isles when I took over the *Gazette* in the early thirties. I knew his name and reputation well, as one of the kingpins of the community. I met him only once or twice, but I well remember the first occasion, in my little two-roomed office on Kenneth Street, where, in order to get privacy, I had to interview him in the store, littered with bundles of ancient newspapers.

I cannot remember why he called, but I do remember the story he told me of a visit to Barra he made with W. S. Morrison, (a future speaker of the House of Commons) when he unsuccessfully contested the Western Isles as a Tory.

"When we got to North Bay I said to the ferryman, 'What's the fare?' " said Macdonald. " 'Five pounds,' he replied. 'That's ridiculous!' I said to him. 'I crossed with you last week, and it was only thirty bob!' 'That's right,' said the ferryman. 'But you were going to Barra. He wants to go to Westminster.' "

Alasdair Macdonald's letter was addressed to Sir Alexander Macewan, asking him to try to do something to help seven Uist crofters then in Inverness gaol. The men, he said, had been convicted of theft, but, in spite of the view taken by the Court, he would never agree that they were guilty. Salvage operations on the *Politician* had ceased. The vessel and her cargo had been abandoned. There was no one in charge, and the whisky was entirely unprotected in the ship's hold, which was full of sea water, with all sorts of rubbish floating around.

Even if the men had been guilty, the sentences were too severe. "A fine and not imprisonment would have been the appropriate penalty," said Mr Macdonald. "There was no previous conviction against any of the accused, and none of them was ever in a court of law before, and I know them myself to be thoroughly respectable, hard-working crofters."

He complained that the men had been removed from Uist before he had time to consult them on the question of an appeal. A later letter revealed that the Sheriff Clerk had refused to accept appeals on behalf of some of the men because they had not been lodged within the statutory five days.

Mr Macdonald asked that Sir Alexander, or one of his staff, should see the men in Inverness gaol, and suggested that an approach might be made to the Secretary of State for Scotland, for remission of the sentences. The men were all crofters. They were needed on the land, at that time of the year, and they had increased their cultivations substantially to meet the government's appeal for greater food production.

"My concern is not due to the fact that they were my clients, but that they are all my own countrymen, that I am certain they are not guilty of theft, and that, in any event, they have been harshly and aggressively treated."

A few days later, Col Macarthur, having interviewed the men, forwarded Mr Macdonald's letter to M. K. Macmillan, asking him to see Tom Johnston, the Scottish Secretary, and plead for some remission of the sentences.

"They are all crofters," he wrote. "Their main concern is that their crops will be ruined for want of attention, and that their sheep will have to remain unshorn with consequent serious loss of wool, as the womenfolk at home will not be able to do the work."

The appeal was backed by medical certificates in respect of five of the women involved, indicating that they suffered from serious complaints, ranging from tubercular glands, and cardiac disorders to pernicious anaemia and chronic rheumatism.

Details of the men's holdings, and stock, were given by John Warnock, the Agricultural Officer at Lochboisdale. It showed that all the men had substantial holdings which their womenfolk could not possibly cope with. One man had 3 horses, 13 cattle, 150 sheep, 2 acres potatoes, 7 acres oats and 3 acres hay. The other holdings were similar. One old woman, over seventy, was left alone to look after 2 horses, 6 cows, 4 calves, 3 stirks and 150 sheep.

In spite of Macmillan's plea, Tom Johnston was adamant. The offences, he said, were serious, and he could not feel justified in advising any interference with the sentences imposed.

One minor, almost derisory, concession was made. At the end of their sentences, the men were released from gaol early enough in the day to enable them catch the steamer home.

The trials had occupied four days in Lochmaddy Court, and there was a further batch of trials pending at the time I saw the correspondence.

A somewhat lighter note was introduced into the dossier by a JP from South Uist, who wrote asking Macmillan to intervene on behalf of one of his neighbours who had been gaoled. Eight men, he said, had gone out from the south end of South Uist to the *Politician*, his neighbour had gone "as owner of the boat, to ensure that it was not damaged, rather than to steal the whisky."

36
Aztecs in Todday

Compton Mackenzie used the incident of the *Politician* in his novel *Whisky Galore*, but the book fell far short of the reality. Not only was the truth stranger than fiction, there was a sombre side to it which only one of the great Russian novelists could have done justice to. That element was completely missing from Mackenzie's lighthearted and hilarious farce.

When I say "a sombre side" I am not thinking of the sentences imposed by the courts, but of the personal tragedies which are inevitable in any community where whisky flows as freely and as cheaply as water.

So far as the sentences are concerned, in spite of Broughton's complaint about "savages", and Rory's dislike of Catholics, I would agree with Alasdair Macdonald that they were harsh and unjustified. Rory himself went so far as to say that the salvage attempt had been abandoned, and the insurance paid, before the "looting" began. Even if he was mistaken in that, it is clear that that is what people in Uist honestly believed. They saw no point in leaving the Atlantic to devour an expensive and a scarce commodity.

When the authorities did eventually move it is probable that, as Alasdair Macdonald suggested, they got the wrong people. Not the ringleaders, or those who were making a commercial venture of it, by selling the whisky to the labourers at the airport, but normally law-abiding people, sucked into a vacuum the authorities themselves had created by their vacillation.

Although Compton Mackenzie dealt with only one side of the story, he did extract the elements of popular appeal, and, when the film version was released, shortly after the end of the war, it passed quickly into the folklore of Europe. It was more popular on the Continent even than in Britain. Here was the little man thumbing the nose at authority. Enjoying a riotous, uninhibited life of pleasure such as Europe had not known for a decade.

To the French, the Belgians, the Dutch, the Danes, and the Norwegians, who had suffered the privations and horrors of Nazi occupation, the inhabitants of Mackenzie's mythical island of Todday, were heroes. Larger than life. Mocking and humbling the oppressor. It meant even more to the many refugees there were in Western Europe at that time, fleeing from the oppression which continued, unabated, under Stalin, in the countries behind the Iron Curtain.

As soon as the film was released in Denmark, one of the leading journalists in Copenhagen — Palle Koch — was despatched to the Hebrides to write up "The Whisky Galore Islands". I became friendly with him, and, when I saw him in Copenhagen some years later, he was still chuckling over the film — and still thumbing his own nose at authority. There was some dispute at the time between little Denmark and mighty Russia. I forget what it was about, but the Russians tried to exert pressure by a threatening "popular" demonstration outside the Danish Embassy in Moscow. Palle Koch was unmoved. He published a vivid account of the demonstration, and then demolished it with the acid comment, "Another three rehearsals and it would have been spontaneous."

It was also shortly after the film *Whisky Galore* was released that Cathie and I visited Uppsala — the occasion on which we met the Swedish Macleod from Skye. We were on our way to the Annual Conference of the Liberal International, in company with Huntly Sinclair and his wife. Huntly was, and in fact still is, one of the leading figures in the Liberal International. A Canadian of Scottish extraction, and by training an economist, he contested the Western Isles, as a Liberal, in the same post-war election as Iain Macleod. It was a remarkable triumph for M. K. Macmillan to trounce two such formidable opponents.

For a young man, Macmillan was a shrewd campaigner — or had shrewd advisers, or both! When Sinclair challenged him to a public debate, on the eve of the poll, in Stornoway Town Hall, he made no reply. Sinclair made great play of the fact that Macmillan had shirked the issue. Then, at the end of Sinclair's meeting, when the audience was ready to disperse, Macmillan appeared dramatically at the Cromwell Street door of the Town Hall, and marched through the crowd to the front. There was nothing Sinclair could do but invite him up to the platform, and resume the meeting. To hold an audience once with a long political speech is difficult. To hold the same audience twice, in the same evening, is impossible. But Macmillan, although he had been campaigning elsewhere all day, was fresh and new, so far as the Town Hall audience was concerned. It was a superb piece of electioneering strategy, wrong-footing his opponent completely.

Elections were elections then. A form of entertainment which drew large, and enthusiastic crowds. The hecklers were just as important as the candidates, and better known. There would be a buzz of anticipation when Tartar, or Kady, or Warhorse, rose to make a point. It was the same in the rural areas. Large audiences would sit, late at night, in draughty and uncomfortable schools, waiting for a candidate to arrive from an earlier engagement.

Sinclair had a notable passage at arms in Shawbost with the redoubtable John Maciver. Even when John had exhausted all aspects of current controversy, relevant and irrelevant, he refused to sit down. Finally he demanded, "What did Gladstone say in 1891?" "In 1891," said Sinclair, "Gladstone predicted that, in years to come, a man would arise in the village of Shawbost, known as John Maciver, who would be a darned nuisance at meetings, and a menace to democracy." No one enjoyed the riposte better than John.

At Oslo, on the way to the conference, we were invited to dinner by a

Norwegian newspaper editor, a close friend of the Sinclairs. Although it was a private occasion, with only seven of us at the table, it was conducted with unusual formality. The host rose to make a speech of welcome for his guests, and then a speech of welcome for his own son, who had just arrived on holiday from Paris, where he was employed in the Norwegian embassy.

At the end of the meal, when we were all replete — more than replete — after unstinted Scandinavian hospitality, the host produced a bottle of whisky. When I declined a glass, he looked at me in amazement, and then exploded. "For the first time in my life, I meet a man from Todday, and by God, he will not drink my whisky!"

At the conference itself, we had just to mention where we came from to have delegates crowding round, many of them refugees from behind the Iron Curtain, saying "Mooch whisky!", with a wide grin, and asking to be told all about the wonderland in the west, where ordinary people still had a healthy disrespect for regimentation and control.

Compton Mackenzie had certainly put the Western Isles on the map, but that did not relieve my embarrassment — mixed, I must admit, with a certain element of pride — when I attended a special session of the conference for the members of the press, who were there to participate rather than report. I tucked myself into an inconspicuous seat at the back of the room to listen to my distinguished colleagues. To my dismay, the chairman called on us each to rise in turn, and introduce ourselves, and the paper we represented. It was like a roll call of the leading newspapers in Europe. The *Guardian*. The *News Chronicle*. National dailies from every capital city from Paris to Ankara. At the end of it all, I rose a little sheepishly, and said "Grant, *Stornoway Gazette*." At that moment I could have done with the dram I refused in Oslo!

Another session was devoted to Women's Lib. After it we all went off in coaches to inspect the castle at Skokloster. After the long bus ride, we found there was only one toilet, which was promptly occupied by the women delegates. A rather absent-minded professor, not noticing what had happened, strayed in after them. He retreated hastily, pursued by agitated females. He had the presence of mind to pause at the door before he made his exit, and ask, "You want equality, don't you?"

The dominating figure at the conference was Salvador de Madariaga, the Spanish writer and diplomat, exiled from his native country by the Franco dictatorship. A man of immense learning, with a delightful sense of humour. For years after that I kept my eyes open, when I was in a bookshop in Edinburgh or London, hoping to pick up some of his books in English. Without luck! Until one day I found what I wanted, unexpectedly, back in Todday!

In a small rack of books for sale in an hotel in Barra, I picked up *The Heart of Jade*, a historical novel by Madariaga about the Spanish invasion of Mexico in the time of the Aztecs. A story of the clash between two glittering civilisations, both riddled with greed, superstition and cruelty. A fascinating book.

And so I read a book about Mexico in Barra, because many years before I met a Spaniard in Sweden. It's odd the way we are nudged in this direction or that, by casual contacts which enrich our lives.

Madariaga, if he had ever visited it, would have been as fond of Barra as I am. It is his sort of island.

37
Do it Last Year! At Once!

Our rigidly compartmented, (or disintegrated) system of government, has never been able to cope effectively with the occupational pluralists of the Western Isles, generally referred to as crofters.

Frequently the system treats the crofter unfairly, as in the case of the *Politician* prosecutions. The Board of Trade, the Ministry of Shipping, the Ministry of Labour, and the Courts all took their own narrow look at the problem. None of them were interested in the fact that the crofters they gaoled were being pursued by the Department of Agriculture, at the same time, to increase food production in the national interest.

I remember dictating a furious leading article, when I was in bed with the flu, attacking the government because the Ministry of Labour was threatening island crofters (as labourers), with all sorts of penalties, if they did not take up work on the mainland, while the Department of Agriculture was threatening the same labourers (as crofters), if they did not stay at home and work their holdings. I don't know whether it was the flu, or the fury, that sent my temperature soaring, but I enjoyed writing the article.

Sometimes, of course, the rules work in the crofters' favour. I recall Bob Scott, standing at his garage door one morning, saying to me — I forgot what it was apropos — "They never drafted an act of Parliament yet which an old crofter in Cromore couldn't get his finger into, and work away until there was a hole big enough for the whole village to go through." It was an exaggeration, but there was an element of truth in it.

When the Dept of Agriculture decided to give a subsidy to farmers, prepared to help the war effort, by growing barley where it was not really economical to do so, the Agricultural Executive Committee in Lewis decided, quite properly, that every crofter who grew barley should get the subsidy, because no agriculturalist in his sane senses would try to grow barley anywhere in Lewis, unless he was compelled to by circumstances.

In order to keep within the terms of the scheme, the AEC had to serve compulsory orders on the crofters, instructing them to grow a specified acreage of barley, on land which was designated marginal. As a first step, they wrote the crofters, asking how much barley they intended to grow, so that they could specify the correct acreage in the compulsory orders.

The crofters said to themselves, "This is fine. We're going to get a subsidy," and stuck the letters in a drawer, or behind the clock, waiting for the money to arrive. All except one. An old lady in Ness, who could not read, took the letter to the schoolmaster. Under his direction, she went through the elaborate ritual prescribed by the Dept. and, in due course, got her cheque.

Then the fun began.

"Why didn't we get our subsidy?" her neighbours asked the Dept.

"You didn't comply with the regulations!" said the Dept.

"To hell with the regulations," retorted the crofters. "If a big farmer in Perthshire gets paid for growing barley on poor land, why should a small crofter in Lewis not get paid for growing barley on land that's ten times poorer?"

The logic was irresistible. After fighting a rearguard action, the Dept capitulated. But how could they get the crofters within their own regulations so late in the day?

They did it by issuing the crofters with notices, in 1944, threatening them with all sorts of penalties if they didn't grow barley, in 1943. Then, having made a hypothetical inspection of the little patches of barley stubble — or the ploughed land where the barley stubble had been — the Dept solemnly paid the crofters a grant, to enable them harvest the crop which they had already eaten.

Around the same time, I had another example of the inability of official bureaucratic machinery to adjust to the complexities of life in the Western Isles. A schoolmaster friend, who had just taken up a new appointment, bought a pet sheep for his children. He tethered it in the schoolhouse garden, and all went well for a week or so. Then one of his daughters came running into the house to say there were two men in the garden, examining the sheep.

When the Schoolmaster went out to investigate, one of the men said to him, "I hope it didn't eat too many of your cabbages?"

"It didn't have a chance," said the Schoolmaster. "It was tethered."

"You were quite right to tether it, if it was coming in at all," said the man.

At that stage the Schoolmaster realised that one of the men was claiming the sheep as his own. It had his ear marks.

The Schoolmaster told the man to take his sheep. He regretted the thirty shillings he had paid for it, but he had bought it from a man, at the other end of the parish, who, despite his sixty years, had the mentality of a ten-year-old.

Then he had second thoughts. "Suppose it gets round the parish that the new schoolmaster had a sheep tethered in his garden and another man claimed it as his?" he asked himself. "What would the neighbours think? What would the police think?" He finally decided that he should mention the incident to the police, to cover his own flank.

The Policeman immediately interviewed the Crofter who had sold the sheep. The Crofter went straight to the Schoolmaster and returned the thirty shillings. He didn't know what had happened. He thought the sheep was his. He had taken it as one of his own from a fank at which all the shepherds in the district had been present. When he sold it, he drove it, in broad daylight, along the main road through several villages. It was tethered in the garden for a week before anyone asked questions.

The Schoomaster's theory was that another sheep had been substituted for the one he bought from the crofter. Either by someone who stole the sheep, and put a stray on the tether to cover his tracks. Or, more likely, by the boys in the village as a prank on their new headmaster.

Anyway, at that stage, everyone was happy — until the blow fell. The Crofter was charged with sheep stealing. The law had been invoked, and the machinery was rumbling on.

As soon as I saw the Crofter in court I dubbed him "Tolas the Second". He reminded me irresistibly of one of the kenspeckle figures of Stornoway in my boyhood. The same diminutive frame. The same big dark staring eyes. The same look of bewilderment in face of a hostile world.

Before the case was called, he was terrified he would be locked up in a dark cell. He suffered from claustrophobia, although he had never heard of it.

"Are you guilty or not guilty?" asked the Sheriff.

"I am not guilty in a sort of a way," replied the accused.

"What do you mean by that?" asked the Sheriff.

"It was a very mistake", said the accused.

When further questions were put, he got completely flustered, and protested that he had no Gaelic, meaning that he had no English.

Fortunately the Sheriff realised what sort of person he was, and, although he found him guilty, dismissed him with an admonition, so that no serious harm was done. But I can think of several sheriffs, I knew in my time as a reporter, who would have been a good deal less understanding and humane.

Of course, it is not only the bureaucrats who tie themselves in knots with red tape. We are adepts at it ourselves, in our religious life. It was almost in the same week as that court case that the Lewis Youth Panel met for the first time, to discuss the lack of recreational facilities in the rural areas. A leading minister in the Free Church, who was appointed to the Panel, came to the meeting to say that he could not conscientiously serve on it. That was fair enough, if that was his view. I was astounded, however, when, at the end of the discussion, he flatly declined the chairman's invitation to close the proceedings with prayer.

Considering that Christ prayed from the Cross for those who crucified Him, I was puzzled to understand how there could be any circumstances in which it was inappropriate for a minister of religion to pray for his fellow creatures.

While the activities of the Youth Panel were being frustrated by the churches, there were 13 school districts in Lewis with no Sunday School of any description, and even more without a Bible class!

There is a better atmosphere in Lewis today where recreational facilities are concerned, but, in the thirties and forties, it was necessary to fight every inch of the way.

When the young men of Bayble decided to build a village hall, just before the outbreak of war, the elders sent a deputation to the Stornoway Trust, to make sure they could not get a site to build it on.

It was a memorable meeting. Bailie Mrs Fraser, a formidable lady, took the elders on. Mentioning several of them by name, she reminded them what their own behaviour had been like, when they were young. If they had had a hall in their own village, instead of the pubs in Stornoway, she would have felt a good deal safer going home along Sandwick Road in the dark!

As I sat writing my report, I could not resist the temptation to head it with the well known quatrain about "Crabbed age and youth", from *The Passionate Pilgrim.*

At the end of the meeting, one of the Trustees came to speak to me. His eye lighted on the four lines of poetry.

"Did you write that?" he asked.

"Yes!" I replied.

"Did you write it just now?"

"Yes!" I replied.

Which is an excellent example of how, with a blunt instrument like language, it is possible to tell a lie by speaking the truth.

At least it was the only time in my career I tried to impersonate Shakespeare.

38
Gratuitous Amputation

Although he lived for several years in Barra, and wrote books about the Western Isles, I never met Compton Mackenzie. At that time Barra was almost as remote from Lewis as Outer Mongolia. And Lewis, of course, was equally remote from Barra! Lewismen and Barramen met and mixed only at East Coast fishing ports, under the Highlanders' Umbrella in Glasgow, and in "suburbs" of the Western Isles like Hong Kong or Yokohama.

Some years ago, when the building of Eden Court theatre was under discussion, there was a lively argument as to the relative degree of support which should be given from local and from national funds. A party from the Scottish Office, including ministers as well as officials, took the line that Eden Court was a local amenity which should be supported by the County Council, but not by central government through HIDB.

At that point, I lost my cool. "Local?" I said. "If a crofter in Barra wants to go to the theatre it would be easier from him to go to Shaftesbury Avenue than to Eden Court, even if Inverness is the county town. Why should the people of Barra, rather than the people of London, be asked to pay for an amenity they will never use?"

The point was conceded by implication, although not during the discussion — face must be saved! — and I would reckon that, since the theatre was opened, more people have, in fact, visited it from London than from Castlebay.

Calling government "local" doesn't make it local, but governments have a great habit of dealing in notional categories, rather than in the realities of life.

Although I never met Compton Mackenze, I did correspond with him, in an intermittent sort of way. Shortly after I became editor of the *Gazette* I had a letter from him — threatening me with an action for libel!

His anger was aroused by a letter from a cantankerous Presbyterian which I had published. I don't think he ever really meant to take action, and I had little difficulty in smoothing down his ruffled feathers, but I learned a good deal about the art of sub-editing from the incident. In particular I learned the need to look for the hidden innuendo, whether intended or not. I also learned a lot about heredity, not immediately, but over the years. I did not know the writer of the letter personally, although I was familiar with him by name. I did, however, know his son, and I had the greatest difficulty, on many occasions, in preventing him from landing me in the same sort of trouble by his undisciplined comments on secular affairs. His subject was different from his father's. His inclination to make wild allegations against those who disagreed with him was the same.

My later contacts with Compton Mackenzie were in a field where we were in complete agreement. They arose from his involvement in the Sea League, along with J. L. Campbell of Canna, then resident in South Uist. They argued eloquently for the regional control of fisheries, to protect the interests of the littoral population. Something we are still arguing for, and which, if it had been granted then, would have saved central government a good slice of the special aid they have had to pump into the islands, to support the ailing economy.

Although Compton Mackenzie's stay in Barra was relatively short, he was a portent. I have always maintained that the turn of the tide for the Highlands and Islands was not signalled by the setting up of the Highland Board, but by the decision of Compton Mackenzie, Neil Gunn, Eric Linklater, and Naomi Mitchison, to live and work in the area. The Highland Board was a consequence as well as a cause. A fundamental change was taking place in the relationship between the Highlands and the rest of the country which the writers sensed before the politicians.

It was all related to, and part of, the revival of Scottish literature of which Hugh Macdiarmid, was the leader, or at least, the standard bearer. The outward and visible sign. Not the creator, perhaps, but the harbinger and the voice.

Similar signs of the same change were the decision of James Bridie to remain in Glasgow, and of Agnes Mure Mackenzie, the historian, to return to Edinburgh from the south. Signs, perhaps, simply of the decline of London as the cultural capital. A lessening of the magnetism which drew J. M. Barrie out of Thrums — and into what?

All of them had an influence on my own work, especially Agnes Mure Mackenzie. Her histories, especially her *Bruce*, aroused my interest in Scottish history, as distinct from British history, for the first time. More directly, she gave me considerable encouragement in many of the things I was trying to do.

Neil Gunn visited Lewis on several occasions and I met him in the home of a friend, as I have mentioned in another connection. He, too, encouraged me in many of the things I was engaged in, and he phoned me, not long before his death, to give his blessing to the proposals of the Crofters Commission, of which I was then chairman, in regard to owner occupation. It was a message I particularly valued because he had been an influential member of the Taylor Committee, as a result of whose recommendation the Commission was set up in 1955.

My first contact with Eric Linklater — apart from reading his books — came through our involvement in the *Matter of Opinion* programme which commanded a big listening audience in the days before television. At our first session together we were faced with the opinion that Orkney is prosperous agriculturally, because the inhabitants are industrious, while Lewis is an agricultural wilderness, because the people are lazy.

I replied that the difference is not in the people, but in the soil. "Give us Orkney," I said, "and we'll show you what can be made of it."

Loyal Orcadian though he was, Linklater agreed that the differences between the islands are geographical, not genetic. A few years later, although I did not foresee it, the crofters of Lewis demonstrated their energy in the great re-seeding drive of the sixties, when, it was put to me once, they "worked like coolies to reclaim the moor!"

Naomi Mitchison was more deeply involved in the parochial affairs of the Highlands and Islands than any of the others, and yet more detached from them, dividing her time between Carradale and London, between Britain and Botswana. She first got in touch with me because of her interest in the work of the Lewis Association, but later we were colleagues on the Highland Panel, and the Consultative Council of the HIDB. After Cathie and I moved to Inverness, she frequently spent the night with us when attending meetings.

These evening sessions were always stimulating, as were her interventions in Panel and Council affairs. I still chuckle over her protest when Lord Cameron suggested a Panel meeting for a date she thought a little close to Christmas for convenience.

"With respect, my Lord," she said, "that's a hell of a day to hold a meeting."

"I thought you might welcome an excuse to escape from the bosom of the family around that time!" said Lord Cameron, with a smile.

"It's well seen you don't cook the Christmas dinner!" she replied.

The date was changed.

I never met Macdiarmid, and only once corresponded with him, when he wrote asking whether there was an opening on the *Gazette* for his son who was going in for journalism. Unfortunately there was not, but the fact that I was asked reinforced my belief that the relationship between the islands and the rest of Britain was changing.

The assurance was needed, because, especially in the early years, I was very conscious of my isolation from all the exciting things that were happening elsewhere in Scotland. Running what was virtually a one-man business, it was impossible to afford the time consumed in travel by the means then available. Communication was by letter, or not at all.

That is why I value, perhaps even more than those who are involved in them, the contacts which now take place between the islands and the outside world. The global village has really arrived, and the Western Isles are an integral part of it.

Another of the key figures of the period was Sorley Maclean, giving a Gaelic dimension to the Scottish renaissance. I did not get to know him personally until after we had moved to Inverness, but I read his poems as soon as they were available to me — in translation!

They influenced me in two ways. For the first time the idea that Gaelic had a continuing usefulness was wholly credible, and I became even more acutely aware than I had previously been of the cultural amputation the

137

Scottish Education system had quite gratuitously inflicted on me. I always knew that without Gaelic I had lost a window on the past. I now realised that I might have lost a window on the future too.

39
They Crossed the Minch

Apart from the Scottish writers, who were, in a sense, part of the island scene, in that they had an influence on those of us who worked there, whether we realised it or not, there were a number of well-known writers from south of the border who drifted into Hebridean waters, like so much flotsam, and left again, sometimes without even a tide mark on the shore.

Louis Macneice, who, with Auden and Spender, was regarded as one of the outstanding poets of his generation, came to me shortly before the war, with an introduction from Hector MacIver. We had a long discussion, perhaps more than one, in my tiny office on Kenneth Street.

I cannot recall whether I felt flattered or annoyed — probably a bit of both — when his book *I Crossed the Minch* was published, and I discovered that both myself and the *Gazette* had been given a sort of evanescent immortality in its pages.

"The *Stornoway Gazette* is a paper which travels the world. In the Argentine there is a ranch of Lewismen who read it two months old and phone the contents to their friends in the backwoods. I found it odd to think of that presbyterian (Free Church probably) oasis among the pampas.

"It is to be regretted that the *Stornoway Gazette* which is the only paper published in the islands, should be almost entirely in English. The editor, a charming young man, believes in progress and no doubt thinks that an English paper is more progressive."

Macneice himself described his book as a pot-boiler. It is self-opinionated, a little bit supercilious, and riddled with hasty and inaccurate judgments. His suggestion that the *Gazette* was printed mainly in English because that was considered "more progressive" is a fair example.

By 1938, when the book was published, it was beginning to be considered progressive to encourage Gaelic, as the *Gazette* tried to do, within the limits of what was economically possible. Macneice missed the all-important point that an island newspaper had to be in English because Gaelic-speakers were being educated into illiteracy, so far as their native language was concerned. Surprisingly for a person with Marxist sympathies, as he had at that time, he also missed the point that there is inevitably an element of "cultural imperialism", whether intentional or not, when two languages are unequally yoked together.

I think it was Compton Mackenzie who commented that Macneice's title was a little arrogant, as if he were Columbus, voyaging perilously into the unknown. He seems to have tried to like the islands but found it difficult. When he fell ill in Uig — perhaps with an overdose of island hospitality — he wrote that he "lay like a corpse under a portly oil lamp", longing for his "flat in Hampstead, his curtains of peach-coloured chintz with white Victorian bows and his borzoi sleeping on the sofa."

He was a strange product for Belfast, but then he had been through Marlborough and Oxford, and regretted that he was not accompanied on his trip to the islands by his great friend, Anthony Blunt, whose name means a good deal more to me now than it did when I first came across it in Macneice's book.

There are some excellent things in the book, and Macneice was a good deal more sympathetic to the islands than many literary visitors I can name. He tried to make amends for any shortcomings in his dedication to Hector MacIver. "I do not suppose you will like this — the book of an outsider who has treated frivolously what he could not assess on its merits. May I thank you for the kindness of the islands."

Louis Macneice clearly felt out of place in the islands, just as many islanders I know would feel out of place in a flat in Hampstead with peach-coloured chintz curtains and white Victorian bows!

Hammond Innes raised no problems when he came. He was good company, and he was not writing a book about the islands in the normal sense. He was merely using the islands — and especially the island weather — as the backdrop for a dramatic adventure story, *Atlantic Fury*.

I missed Morris West altogether when he was in the islands gathering material for *Summer of the Red Wolf*. From the publication date, I would assume that he made his safari shortly after I moved to Inverness. That he did visit the islands is evident from his descriptions of island scenery, and of identifiable villages like Callanish, Rodil and Laxay.

His understanding of the people is a good deal less than his acquaintance with the superficial appearance of the landscape. He describes what he calls a ceilidh. It is in fact a private dinner party, with a few Gaelic songs thrown in. Among the guests at the ceilidh, (dinner, songs, drams and all) there was, believe it or not, a gentleman described as a Wee Free minister!

The ceilidh is contrived so that the author can confront the minister with a "schoolmistress from Dumfries, a pert redhead, salty of tongue, with a slightly scandalous humour." It makes for a lively discussion, but somehow it doesn't sound like Lewis — or Harris!

Morris West's view of Lewis, I would suspect, is based on conversations in a pub with a bunch of commercial travellers, or, perhaps, at a slightly more elevated level, with anglers in one of the fishing lodges. But read as caricature, with everything slightly heightened and distorted, one or two passages come uncomfortably close.

"We stand simple before God, free brothers in a free assembly. We keep the Sabbath holy because that's the Scriptural command. Our lot is harsh, our lives plain. We need a plain faith to sustain us," says the minister.

"That's only half the story," retorts the redhead. "You're a bunch of old line fundamentalists. Tyrants too, when you get a chance to be . . . If I want to drive my car on a Sunday, you scowl me off the road. If I want a drink — which I do — I'm the scarlet woman. Scriptural commands? You pick and choose the ones that suit you. Suppose I wanted to be like King David and dance naked before the Ark. Would you let me?"

The minister's reply is not recorded. In fact at that point the minister seems to disappear from the scene. He was there simply as an aunt Sally, and, once the coconuts had been thrown, the author had no more need of him.

Although it doesn't ring true as a picture of Lewis, *Summer of the Red Wolf* is a good yarn. The publisher describes it as "majestic" and "epic" but that is taking liberties with the English language.

Godfrey Winn did not stir it up on his visit like Morris West and Macneice. I cannot remember anything he said, or wrote about us. In fact I have great difficulty in visualising him at all, although I lunched with him. I might be inclined to doubt whether he ever did visit Lewis but for the fact that I have irrefutable proof, in the form of an autographed copy of his book, *This Fair Country*, "in memory of a happy visit to Stornoway."

Of all the casual literary visitors to Lewis I met in my work as a reporter, the one with whom I became most friendly, and whom I found most interesting, was Arthur Ransome, who located a popular children's story — *Great Northern* — in the moor around Ranish and Grimshader.

But then, Ransome's life was even more adventurous than his stories. He first met his wife-to-be while history was being made. In the Smolny Institute in Petrograd, during the Russian Revolution.

It is not every day, even in Stornoway, that you meet a man who has played chess with Lenin, and married Trotsky's secretary.

40
The Milk was Black and White

My introduction to Arthur Ransome came in a letter from A. S. Wallace, one time of the *Manchester Guardian* and a brother-in-law of James Dobson, who was tenant of Uig Lodge for many years.

"You will find him a very good fellow," Wallace wrote. "A tall chiel who looks strong but in later years has been cursed with duodenal trouble. He has a Russian wife, who has sailed the Baltic with him in a ten-tonner, in all sorts of weather."

The Russian wife, Evgenia, certainly seems to have been a woman of character. Hugh Brogan, in his splendid biography,* published in 1984, to mark the centenary of Ransome's birth, recalls an occasion when their little vessel was in imminent danger of sinking in a Baltic gale.

"Are we going to be drowned before morning?" she asked.

"Why?" said Ransome.

"Because I have two Thermos flasks full of hot coffee. If we are, we might as well drink both of them. If not, I will keep one till tomorrow."

They met when Ransome was correspondent of the *Daily News* during the Russian Revolution, and she was Trotsky's private secretary. Ransome was the first British journalist to realise that the change in Russia was permanent, and that Britain should try to make friends with the new regime. No one at home would believe him. "I feel I am shouting at a drunken man, asleep in the road, in front of a steam roller," he complained.

At that time he visited Trotsky's office almost every day. He was even given a pass entitling him to speak, but not to vote, at meetings of the Soviet, at the critical period when Russia was moving from the first revolution, led by Kerensky, to the October revolution, led by Lenin and Trotsky, and the grey figure in the wings whom everyone overlooked, or under-rated — Stalin.

Like a good journalist, Ransome attended the meetings of the Soviet, keeping his mouth shut and his ears open, recording the events, and the moods, of the chief participants as history bubbled in the crucible. Earlier he had been present at the Finland Station when Lenin returned dramatically from his long exile. Later, when the Soviet Government moved from Petrograd (Leningrad) to Moscow, Ransome helped to pack the Imperial archives for the journey. No journalist could have been closer to the events he recorded.

He first became friendly with Evgenia when he went one night to the

The Life of Arthur Ransome by Hugh Brogan, published by Jonathan Cape.

142

Soviet Foreign Office to get a telegram cleared by the censor. The building was practically deserted. He could find no one with authority to give him the clearance he wanted. Evgenia came to his aid, and finally ran the censor to earth. A high official of the new government of one of the most powerful nations on earth, he was cooking his own supper, consisting of three or four potatoes, in an old coffee pot, on a primus stove.

The telegram was duly stamped. Ransome raced with it to the post office, but came back, at Evgenia's request, to have a glass of tea with her and her sister. At that point he does not seem to have been sure which of the sisters he was really attracted by. His mind was made up when one day he looked on helplessly while Genia, as he called her, who had slipped while boarding a tram car, was dragged along the street, in imminent danger of being crushed beneath the wheels.

Unfortunately Evgenia was not with her husband on any of the occasions when I met him, over a period of three or four years, at the end of the war. If I had been asked, before I read Brogan's biography, I would have said she did not come to Lewis at all. Brogan, however, is quite specific. "He and Genia visited Lewis during the latter part of May to get local colour for the book." The book was *Great Northern*, a delightful children's story about the thwarting of an unscrupulous collector who tried to steal the eggs of a rare bird from a nest on the Lewis moor.

It may be that Evgenia was in Lewis but did not accompany him when he came round, almost daily, in the late afternoons, to my office for a chat, when his day's fishing and exploring and absorbing of local colour were at an end. Or it may be that she got her dates confused. Ransome was in Lewis on several occasions. According to Brogan, Evgenia told him Uig was her husband's favourite fishing resort "before the war". My guess is that it was his favourite fishing resort "after the war". Certainly it was in 1945 I met him first, and I know that he was back again in 1948, because I had a letter from him, from Uig, which I had quite forgotten until I stumbled on it the other day when looking for something entirely different.

"In spite of being here, I have read your beautiful *The Magic Rowan* and think you have got your hand on something entirely new and your own. It is a lovely thing. I should have written before but . . . you know what Uig is." He was at home among the Uigeachs — and the fish!

Clearly I had treasured the letter when I got it and I felt a twinge of nostalgia when I rediscovered it, for the heady days when the *Rowan* was produced at the Park Theatre in Glasgow, and went on to the Theatre Royal in the Hague, and Pasadena Playhouse, the experimental theatre in California, where at least one Lewisman, Percy Nicholson from Ness, took a special interest in it.

The Californians produced the play with what I can only describe as a Harry Lauder accent, which greatly annoyed one gentleman of Highland descent, rejoicing in the name of Roderick Dubh Macdonald. While he campaigned for a genuine Highland accent in a Highland play, the San Fransisco critics dismissed the play as "*Brigadoon* without the tune."

143

I was tempted, for a brief spell, to forsake journalism for play-writing. I like to persuade myself that I rejected the temptation, high-mindedly, to stay with the problems of an island to which I owed so much, but, when I am honest with myself, I know that prudence, and inertia, played a major part in my decision. Or, rather, in my lack of decision.

If I had known the details of Ransome's involvement with the Russian Revolution when I met him, I would have quizzed him more closely than I did. As it was we talked mostly of local affairs. "His aura was shaggy", Brogan quotes from a description of Ransome in his youth. It still was when I met him, and his moustache was still "a walrus affair on the grand scale", although by that time it was white. And his laugh was as hearty as the friends of his youth have set on record. I can almost hear, forty years on, the chortle of glee with which he told me of the mix-up which had taken place when he collected his picnic lunch, one morning, at the County Hotel.

Because of his duodenal, his lunch was simple — a packet of biscuits and a bottle of milk. That day, when he sat down by a lochside on the Ranish moor and opened up his luncheon bag, there were no biscuits. No milk! Just a bottle of Black and White. His one regret was that the mistake was discovered by the hotel staff in time to prevent Provost Mackenzie from setting off for a day's fishing, with Air Vice Marshall Sir Brian Baker and a bottle of milk!

Although the Air Vice Marshall went fishing with the Provost, he was in Lewis to make aviation history. He had come north to represent the RAF in welcoming the first jet planes which had ever crossed the Atlantic. Sixteen Shooting Stars of the US Air Force, which had flown into Stornoway in grand style with an escort of Flying Fortresses. The first British jets to fly the Atlantic took off from Stornoway about the same time.

Now that hundreds of jets fly the Atlantic non-stop every day, it is hard to believe that less than forty years ago they had to proceed in short hops, by way of Iceland and Greenland, and that their first crossing aroused almost as much interest as man's first landing on the moon.

It was not the first time Lewis had a little niche in aviation history.

41
Is It 'Awker?

When the Stornoway Trustees were earnestly debating whether a village hall in Bayble would be a recreational amenity or a den of iniquity, they were also, just as strangely, divided on the proposal that Lewis should have an airport.

Those who were against the airport were not opposed to flying. They were not fundamentalists like the County Councillor who refused to fly from Inverness to the Isles with Jock MacCallum, Rodil, protesting, "If the Lord intended me to fly he would have given me wings!"

"Yes!" said Jock. "And no doubt if he intended you to go by sea he would have given you a propellor!"

The opposition in the Trust was ideological. An air service was for the wealthy merchants of Stornoway. The ordinary people of rural Lewis would never use it. The Trust should have none of it! The opponents of the air service were the Trustees whom, on every other count, I would have regarded as the most progressive, or radical, in their opinions. It's odd what dogma can do to the mind.

On the first commercial flight into Stornoway the plane was chartered by an Inverness accountant — coming to audit the Trustees' own books. But not very long after that, in 1938, Lewis had its first air mail delivery, laid on by the Post Office in exasperation when the "incredible hulk" which MacBrayne had on the Stornoway run at that time — a single screw vessel, the *Lochgarry* — was too unmanageable to get out of the harbour in a sixty mile an hour wind.

A few months later, the ideological approach to air travel had another knock when Jessie Morrison and Effie Macleod, from Melbost, Galson; Johanna Mackenzie from High Borve; Katie Mary Macleod and Agnes Macleod from Bayble; and Mary Macaulay from Knock flew direct from Orkney to Lewis in a plane chartered by Duncan MacIver Ltd.

When war broke out the RAF took over and developed Stornoway airport. It was vital to Coastal Command. How many more Lewis seamen would have been lost on the North Atlantic convoys if Stornoway airport had not been there? Later it was used as a staging post by American fighters flying to Europe for the D-day landing.

Although we did not realise it at the time, the strategic importance of the Hebrides had been demonstrated twenty years before the war, at the very beginning of trans-Atlantic air travel, in May 1919, when a Danish steamer, the *Mary* of Copenhagen, hove-to opposite the Coastguard lookout at the Butt of Lewis, and ran up the international flag signal "saved hands". She must have been one of the last vessels on the Atlantic without wireless, and excitement grew in the Coastguard station as she spelt her message laboriously out in four hoists "S" "O" "P" "aeroplane".

Before another flag could be hoisted, Mr Ingham, the officer in charge of the Station, began signalling back his own impatient query, "Is it Hawker?", or as he put it to my father, "Is it 'Awker?" It was quick thinking on his part, and it brought the answer "Yes", just before the *Mary* passed out of signalling range.

No aircraft had ever crossed the Atlantic. The *Daily Mail* had just offered a prize of £10,000 for the first to do it. The American navy was planning a crossing. In hops. Via the Azores. Using seaplanes. With naval vessels strung along the route in case anything went wrong. They lost two seaplanes in the attempt, but saved the crews. Eventually the third seaplane reached Plymouth.

When the Americans were engaged in this carefully planned "fail safe" exercise two British aviators — Harry Hawker, an Englishman born in Australia, and Mackenzie Grieve, a Scot — tried to beat them to it, setting off from Newfoundland, in a tiny aeroplane, with no back-up, and a defective radio, to do it "in one".

I can still feel all the passionate excitement of a nine-year-old at the unequal contest between the organised might of the American navy, and the naked courage of two mad British aviators. But at that stage it was remote from Lewis. It was happening in another world. The world of the newspapers — arriving two days late! But it was still reflected in our conversation at meal-times and in our play.

Hawker and Grieve took off into an Atlantic gale, and disappeared. There was a false report that they had landed safely in Co Clare. Then a false report that they had ditched in the sea off the Irish Coast and British destroyers were racing from Loch Swilly to pick them up. Then silence. The days passed and they were given up for lost. There was talk of a memorial service in London, but Mrs Hawker refused to go. She still clung to a slender hope. Those who knew better pitied her. The *Daily Mail* announced that, if their fears were confirmed, the £10,000 would go to Hawker's "widow" and their child. We youngsters lost interest. Our team was out of the race.

Then out of the blue came this sluggish Danish steamer. The heroes were safe, though defeated, and my father was rushing between the Butt and the Post Office, on a Sunday at that, with telegrams that would blaze, next morning, in headlines around the world.

It is difficult now to understand the frenzy the news created. The News Editor of *The Times* was so impatient he instructed his Glasgow representative to proceed to the Butt of Lewis, immediately — by taxi! The navy sent the destroyer *Woolston* to meet the *Mary* off Loch Erribol. Hawker and Grieve were taken to Scapa where the Grand Fleet was still stationed guarding the German Navy which had not yet got round to scuttling itself. They were feasted that night on HMS *Revenge* as the Admiral's guests.

Next day at Scrabster they were met by the Provost of Thurso, and an enthusiastic crowd. They were given a civic lunch. At Brora, Golspie and Lairg there were crowds cheering and asking for autographs. At Bonar Bridge there was a Pipe Band playing "Happy we've been a- the -gither". At Invergordon a crowd of servicemen encouraged the aviators to try again. "Don't let the Yankees beat you!" At Alness there was another Pipe Band and at Dingwall another civic reception.

At Inverness every inch of platform space in the station was occupied and boys clambered on carriage roofs to get vantage points. The railway company charged a penny a head to get into the station. They were making a mint, until the pressure of the crowd proved too much for the doors, and the rest could walk in free. The aviators had dinner in the Station Hotel with Provost Macdonald, and came out on the balcony to bow, like royalty, to a vast crowd in Academy Street.

The *Inverness Courier* sent a reporter to Brora to join the train. He was probably the first reporter to get the full story straight from the horses' mouth. The aviators told him they had covered a thousand miles, flying at 15,000 feet, without oxygen, and without artificial heating. When they developed a choke in the water cooling system they knew they would never reach Ireland, and left the Great Circle route to fly diagonally across the shipping lanes. They sighted the *Mary* just in time, and ditched ahead of it. It was so stormy it took the *Mary's* crew an hour and a half, at the risk of their own lives, to get them aboard.

Despite the excitement their attempt to fly the Atlantic created at the time, Hawker and Grieve have disappeared from the history books, almost as completely as they disappeared into the Atlantic storm. The latest edition of the *Encyclopaedia Britannica* does not even mention them in a long article about early trans-Atlantic flights. The *Dictionary of National Biography* and the relevant issues of *Who's Who* are equally silent. Webster's *Dictionary of Biography*, which I always thought was a standard work, hadn't caught up with the *Mary's* rescue 23 years after the event. The edition I have, dated 1942, says Hawker attempted to fly the Atlantic in May 1919 and was never heard of again. Perhaps it was a ghost the crowds were cheering from Thurso to Inverness, and on to London!

The story of Harry Hawker has a link with Harris just as surely as with Lewis. The letters "Sop" gave the Coastguards the clue because Hawker was flying a Sopwith plane. In fact it was T. O. M. Sopwith, the great English pioneer of aviation who first taught Hawker to fly. For a number of years Sopwith owned the North Harris estate, and his yacht was manned almost entirely by Harrismen.

Fifteen years after Hawker's gallant failure, Harris came even more directly into the run-up to the space age. This time I covered the event myself, light-heartedly, as a bit of comedy, although it was serious enough for those involved, and I did not see the Sputniks at the end of the trail.

147

In 1934 a young German inventor of the name of Zucker was trying to interest the British Post Office in the idea that mails — and even medicine — could be delivered to remote islands by rocket. He was financed — and exploited — by a wide-boy named Dombrowski, who offered to send letters by Rocket Mail for 2/6 a time over and above the normal postal charge. He found five thousand suckers for his Harris experiment — including me! The Post Office was sufficiently interested to ask for a demonstration delivery, across the Sound of Scarp, from the island to the mainland. It was watched by photographers and reporters from the national press, and by the head postmaster from Kilmarnock, who I think was an official observer, but may have been there out of curiosity. He belonged to Stornoway.

I have a vague feeling that I first met Dombrowski and Zucker on the pier at Stornoway. I certainly saw them, and had a long talk with them, in the Hotel at Tarbert, on the way to Scarp. Their launching platform was made in a joiner's shed near the hotel. A flimsy wooden structure of laths nailed together.

I was accompanied to Hushinish by my friend Stephen MacLean. I think there was another old schoolmate there as well. Probably Ian MacLean, but through the haze of half a century, I cannot be sure. Anyway, my friends stayed at Husinish while I went across to Scarp with the rest of the pressmen. There was no pier at Husinish. We were carried out to an open boat, on the backs of thigh-booted fishermen, one by one, and dumped on the thwarts, like so many sacks of potatoes. It was a strange introduction to the space age, and a journey by rocket to the moon!

Husinish Pier, like the pier at Stroma, was not built when there was a living community to serve with the vitality to survive. It was built, by a procrastinating government, just in time to make it easier for the last survivors to get out. Some day the National Trust should get round to preserving, with suitable cynicism, as part of our heritage, the piers, dotted all over the Highlands, which served only as expensive tombstones, marking the places where fishing communities died, because the piers were built too late, in the wrong place, or to the wrong design, by a distant and uncomprehending government. Memorials to the twin failings of the Scottish system of administration. The unwillingness to move decisively when the need is there. The inability to resist a back-log of political pressure, when the chance of doing something useful has passed.

When we got to Scarp; Zucker set up his apparatus on the beach. We all retired to a safe distance. Zucker crouched behind a boulder, and pressed the plunger on his firing box. There was a spurt of fire, a puff of smoke. The rocket rose ten or fifteen feet into the air, and then exploded. Hundreds, thousands, of letters came fluttering down on the sand, like snowflakes incongruously charred along the edge. I picked one up addressed to the King. I was tempted to keep it as a memento of the occasion, but resisted and dutifully handed it back to Dombrowski. Later I received, through ordinary postal channels, despite the Rocket Mail stamp on the cover, and a singe mark on one edge a letter addressed to myself, from T. B. Wilson

148

Ramsay, then MP for the Western Isles. I still treasure it for its message. "The invention is full of possibilities for the delivery of messages, medical supplies and foodstuffs, in time of peace and war."

It sounded ironical at the time, when I thought of the fiasco at Scarp, enshrined for all time in a photograph the *Daily Record* cameraman got, just as the rocket was exploding, and the can of mail was opening like a rose.

I thought it ironic in another sense, when, sometime after the end of the war, I was leafing through *Time* magazine, and came on a report on the development of rocketry in Germany, under Werner Von Braun. The article mentioned Zucker as one of those who had been engaged on the development of the V1 and V2 rockets, which caused so much death and destruction in the latter part of the war. It added that he fell out with Hitler and was "liquidated". That's why I described him as a gallant loser, although in rather a different category from Harry Hawker.

It never occurred to Wilson Ramsay, or myself, that the experiment that failed at Scarp, could succeed elsewhere, and if it did, that a rocket which could carry messages and medicines could carry warheads too.

There is a definite, if tenuous, link through a long chain of espionage, and international rivalry, between the fiasco on the beach at Scarp and the achievement of Soviet Russia when Yuri Gagarin became the first man to travel in space.

Another link with Russia of a different sort was forged just after the Second World War when the Russian Revolution caught up with Arthur Ransome on North Beach Quay, at the Lazy Corner.

But that's another story.

42
Astrid at the Lazy Corner

The wry footnote to Arthur Ransome's involvement in the Russian Revolution was written during one of his visits to Lewis, when the tiny motor boat *Astrid* put into Stornoway Harbour and tied up in the Lazy Corner. It had come from Sweden, and on board were 29 Esthonian refugees, including ten women and seven children, attempting to cross the Atlantic, to escape from Stalin's tyranny, in a boat considerably smaller than most of the vessels in the Stornoway inshore fishing fleet.

When I told Ransome of the *Astrid*'s arrival, he was tremendously interested. He had been the go-between, when Esthonia gained its freedom from Russia, under a peace treaty signed by the Soviet government. Now, thirty years later, in a Hebridean harbour, he was to meet up again with Esthonians, fleeing from a new Russian conquest, and a new terror, imposed by the Bolsheviks, who had freed them in the first place.

Ransome had been on his way back to Russia from Britain when he was asked by the Esthonians to carry a message to Lenin, seeking terms for peace. The Esthonians were fighting along with the White Russians under Judenich, whose army was threatening Petrograd. They reckoned, wisely, that they had more chance of getting freedom by negotiating with the beleagured Red Army than by helping the Whites to restore the old Imperial regime.

The Bolshevik government, however, refused to have Ransome back. In his absence they had come to the conclusion that he had been a British spy. He told the Esthonians to pretend that he had left before they had received the telegram from Petrograd refusing him a visa: to give him a short start; and then reply to the Russians that it was too late to call him back.

The Esthonians agreed, and Ransome set out by himself, across no-man's-land, between the armies, with a portable typewriter in his hand, and a huge pipe in his mouth. He smoked furiously all the way, in the hope that the smoke would be noticed, and the Russians would decide that a man who was placidly smoking a pipe could be no danger to anyone. He began to change his mind when he saw a dozen Russian rifles aimed in his direction.

Hugh Brogan tells the story dramatically in his biography of Ransome. The Russians held their fire, but seized Ransome when he reached their lines. He was able to persuade them they would be well advised to consult a senior officer, before shooting him as a spy. In that way he argued up the chain of command, until he found himself in Petrograd, in the office of

Litvinov, the Foreign Minister. When he entered, Litvinov, who knew him well, was reading a telegram he had just received, from Esthonia, to say the authorities there had got the first Russian message too late to hold him back.

Ransome handed Litvinov the Esthonian terms for peace, and went off to celebrate his return to Russia with his girl friend, Evgenia. They feasted on the best fare they could muster — potato cakes and Horlicks Malted Milk!

The Russians agreed to negotiate, and entrusted Ransome with their reply. His return journey to Esthonia was even more hazardous than his journey out. Although he aimed to get through the front line where it was held by the peace-seeking Esthonians, there was always the risk that he would fall into the hands of Judenich's Whites, and be shot as a Bolshevik agent. Evgenia, even more at risk, and more courageous than himself, went with him. As Trotsky's secretary she could not hope for mercy if she were caught.

When they sought shelter in a farmhouse between the opposing armies, the farmer threatened to hang them. Evgenia purchased their freedom with their most treasured possession — a travelling kettle. Then they were surrounded by a troop of Lettish irregulars. Ransome, who, by chance, was wearing an old Tzarist army greatcoat, demanded to know who was in command. They had no officer with them, so he took command himself, and sent them packing.

The third challenge came from a long column of White cavalry. It looked like the end when they were surrounded, but Ransome recognised the commanding officer as an old friend from pre-revolution days. More importantly, the friend recognised him, and greeted him with the shout, "We never finished that game of chess!"

The last time they had met, on the war front in Galicia, before the revolution, they had been interrupted in a close game of chess, just when the Russian seemed to be winning. And so, as Brogan says, while the soldiers had their soup, Arthur and the officer resumed their unfinished business at the chessboard. The officer won, and, unsuspecting, let them go. Arthur and Evgenia got safely to Reval with their vital message of peace from the Soviet Government. After that they lived in newly freed Esthonia for several years.

It is not surprising that he hurried to the harbour, when I told him there was a boatload of Esthonians there, fleeing from the new Russian tyranny. He greeted the first of the party he met, in her native Esthonian. She beamed, and replied to him volubly. He couldn't continue the conversation in Esthonian, and, when he lapsed into Russian, she turned and fled. She must have thought the KGB were on their tail, even in Stornoway.

Fortunately that was the only contretemps during the *Astrid*'s stay. 'Fine peoples here! Very fine peoples here!" Capt Vilu said to me before his vessel sailed. He was acknowledging the gifts of food, clothes and money which had been showered on them by the townsfolk. When they made their landfall safely in Newfoundland, he sent me a telegram, so that their friends in Stornoway would know that they were safe. And that greatly puzzled the news editor of the *Times*, successor to the man who wanted his Glasgow correspondent to go to the Butt of Lewis by taxi. He demanded to know how the devil a story about refugees from Esthonia, landing in Canada, could be date-lined from Stornoway.

When Ransome heard that the refugees had landed safely in Canada, he commented to me that it was unlikely that any vessel as small as the *Astrid*, had crossed the Atlantic safely, from east to west, so late in the season, since the days of the Vikings.

Shortly before the war, Stornoway harboured a Russian refugee of another sort. Vera Marisoff was the daughter of a Russian aristocrat, who fled abroad at the time of the revolution. Vera must then have been a child. She became a nurse in Shanghai, but, in 1938, made her way to Britain to visit a married sister. There she found herself in deep trouble. Because of the Sino-Japanese war she could not return to Shanghai. She had no valid passport for a permanent stay in Britain. She was a stateless person, living on a three months' visa.

She got a job for two months in Lewis Sanatorium, and endeared herself to the patients. Although her stay was so short, the patients presented her with an oak inkstand inscribed with all their names.

"Before I came to Stornoway" Sister Vera told me when she left, 'I was warned that the Lewis people were difficult. That they were very clannish. But, when I came here, I found they were the nicest people I had ever met."

As we shall see, these were not the first, or only, occasions on which Russian and Esthonian refugees had reason to thank the people of Lewis.

43
The Story of Isidor Bass

The *Norge* disaster occurred six years before I was born, but I heard so much about it in my youth, and read my father's account so often in his scrap-book, I could almost swear I was present and reported it myself.

It was one of the greatest disasters in the history of the sea. Although there were survivors, the loss of life was greater even than when the Atlantic liner, *City of Glasgow* disappeared without trace, in circumstances I have already described.

The *Norge*, a Danish steamer, of only 2,000 tons, carried a crew of 71. When she sailed from Copenhagen, her last port of call, on her last disastrous voyage, she had nearly 700 passengers, bound for New York. There were 79 Danes, 68 Swedes, 296 Norwegians, 15 Finns, and 236 Russians. The so-called Russians were mainly Jews, Poles, Esthonians and Letts, fleeing from poverty and Russian oppression.

On the 28th of June, 1904, the *Norge* struck a reef near Rockall, and sank within 27 minutes. Just before she disappeared, there was a tremendous explosion in the boiler room, and sparks cascaded from the funnel. A moment later the sea was empty, apart from a black scum of coal dust, the heads of hundreds of men, women and children, bobbing about among the wreckage, for a few minutes until they disappeared, and five overcrowded lifeboats, rowing frantically from the spot, on voyages which took them to destinations hundreds of miles apart.

Altogether 602 men, women and children lost their lives. The 163 who survived were landed eventually by five different vessels in Stornoway, Grimsby, Aberdeen and the Faroes.

The impact of the disaster on the public imagination, as my father wrote at the time, was heightened by the loneliness of the spot where it occurred, "more than 240 miles west of the Butt of Lewis, and 184 miles from 'lone St Kilda', the nearest inhabited island. There is a sand bank extending some 25 miles by 15 miles, but the only visible part is a granite rock, 100 yards in circumference, rising sheer out of the sea to a height of 75 feet . . . whitened during the ages by the droppings of successive generations of sea fowl: a solitary sentinel in the waste of waters, situated at a greater distance from the mainland than any other rock or islet of the same diminutive size in any part of the world."

The *Norge* had no radio, nor had any of the vessels which picked the survivors up. It was a week after the disaster before anyone knew of it, apart from the survivors themselves and those who rescued them.

The great majority of the survivors — more than a hundred — were landed and cared for in Stornoway. The first arrivals were on the Dundee steamer *Cervona*, which dropped anchor off Arnish Light, and hailed a passing fishing boat, asking the crew to report that she had thirty survivors on board picked up from an open boat in the Atlantic.

The steamer *Bonawe*, which was discharging coal in Stornoway, went out immediately with John Mackenzie, the Norwegian and Russian consul, to take the survivors ashore. He found that many of them could not be moved without medical supervision. The *Bonawe* went out a second time with Dr Murray, who was the local MOH, and later became the first member of Parliament for the Western Isles.

By this time a crowd had gathered on the pier. Cabs had been procured, and there were plenty of willing helpers to carry the survivors to them. "Several of them clearly had the hand of death on them," my father wrote, and as they "were carried up the gangway there were tears in many eyes among the crowd, and, as the corpse of a little boy, who had perished before the *Cervona* fell in with the boat, was carried up, wrapped in his winding sheet, all heads were bared.

"Altogether thirty-two survivors were landed from the *Cervona*, including seven children. They were picked up ninety miles westward from the Butt after being six days on the open sea, during four of which they had nothing to eat, and for three days no fresh water. Most of them were driven by the agonies of thirst to drink salt water, which only aggravated their suffering. Hardly any were decently clad, and all were in a most pitiful state physically, having endured great hardships from hunger, thirst and exposure. Were it not that the weather on the whole was good, all but the strongest would have perished during that terrible week."

Communication was a major problem. Few of the survivors could speak any English. A Mr and Mrs Ritchie, who lived on Plantation Road, interpreted for the Scandinavians. Ritchie had worked in Sweden for a number of years, and his wife was a Swede. Mrs Robertson, wife of Ossian Robertson, a local banker, belonged to Germany, and was able to speak to some of the Poles. My father found a Russian Jew, Isidor Bass, who had worked for some years in Dundee, and had fluent English. He was with the fittest of the survivors in the Sailors' Home. The others had been taken to Lewis Hospital, then a tiny building, without resident medical or surgical staff, to the Poor House, or to private homes.

"We had a fine passage until the time of the accident," Bass told my father. "It was about 7.30, I judge, when I heard a rumbling noise like thunder and the ship began to roll. I had been reading late, and fell asleep partly dressed. Jumping up, I got my jacket on and rushed on deck.

"I asked some of the crew what was the matter. 'Nothing! We don't know', they told me. I could see something serious was wrong and went below for my lifebelt. When I got on deck again the crew were getting the boats launched. The first was overcrowded, and, as she was being launched off the davits, the ropes broke, and they were all drowned, except a

154

Norwegian and a young Russian. I saw them scramble into one of the boats that were launched later."

The boat in which Bass got away had no officer, or even a member of the crew on board. There was no mast or sail. No provisions and no water. A Norwegian passenger, Jorgen Hansen, who had been a sailor, took command. He rigged a jury mast with a boathook and an oar, and improvised a sail from a blanket and strips of canvas, torn from the lifebelts and tied together with string.

On the first day they tried to keep company with the lifeboat commanded by the second mate. He gave them a small keg of water and a few biscuits. Then he left them. His boat was much speedier. He thought it best that he should go in search of help.

On three successive days, Bass told my father, they saw steamers passing but could not attract their attention. Hansen was certain some of the vessels had sighted them, but paid no heed. He counted on finding land to the east, and sailed all day by the sun, in lieu of a compass. At night he hove-to and waited for the sun to guide him again.

They knew that the *Oscar II*, belonging to the same line as the *Norge*, was due to pass along the same course on Sunday, six days after the shipwreck. They kept close watch for her, and eventually spotted her, but their signals were not seen.

Their spirits were low by then, but Hansen succeeded in capturing an injured seabird. He gave the blood and mouthfuls of flesh to the women and children. Then, in the afternoon, the *Cervona* sighted them, and took them on board. At first Capt Stokes thought he would continue his voyage and land them at Montreal. When he realised how ill they were, he put about and raced for Stornoway.

I always thought, as a child, that the arrival of the *Cervona* at Arnish Light brought the first news to the outside world of the *Norge* disaster. Fifty years later I learned that the trawler *Salvia*, with 27 survivors, had got to Grimsby a few hours before the *Cervona* got to Stornoway. This new information came to me from an article in the *Straits Times*, picked up by a Lewis seaman in Singapore. Just as, a few years earlier, I had received a series of artist's impressions of the Aignish Riots of 1888, from a seaman from Aird, who found an ancient tattered copy of a London newspaper in one of the lesser known ports of the Pacific, of which I have forgotten even the name.

44
How Much Panic Do You Need?

Shortly after the first survivors from the emigrant ship *Norge* were landed at Stornoway by the *Cervona*, there was a telegram from the Butt of Lewis to say that the *Energie* of Geestemunde was steaming to the port with more. The largest single group saved from the wreck. Seventy men, women and children. Among them the Captain of the *Norge*, Valdemar Gundel, a Dane.

The women and children from the *Energie* were taken ashore first. None of them could walk up the gangplank unaided. They were taken to the Fish Mart, the old pagoda-shaped building, which was a feature of the harbour during all the years I lived in Lewis. There they were laid on the benches until transport could be organised.

One woman was weeping bitterly and could not be comforted. She was a Pole and no one could speak to her. Then it was realised she must have lost her child. There were several unaccompanied children among the survivors. They were brought to her one by one, but she waved them aside until the very last. "To see that mother's fond embrace touched every heart. How she stroked and fondled him!" my father wrote.

When the second boatload from the *Energie* arrived, the scene was very different. They were able-bodied men. There was a waving of hands and shouting as they recognised friends among those already landed from the *Cervona*.

The *Cervona* survivors could not believe their eyes when they saw Capt Gundel. They had reported that he went down with his ship. As indeed he had. He was still on the bridge, having said goodbye to his officers, when the vessel took the final plunge. The rail buckled and closed on his leg like a rat trap. He was dragged down and down, until some movement of the disintegrating wreck loosened the rail and released him. He came to the surface, badly injured but still able to swim. When he got to one of the boats, the survivors there refused to let him in. The lifeboat was already overcrowded, they said. And so, in a sense it was. Designed for 30, it was carrying nearly 70.

"You better take me", he said. "I'm the Capt and you may need my help."

They did. There wasn't a single seaman among them.

Capt Gundel took command. Got the sail up, and set a course for St Kilda. He was within sight of the island when the *Energie* picked them up.

She was bound from Philadelphia to Stettin with a cargo of oil, and altered course to pick them up as soon as she saw their signal. Earlier, several boats had passed without seeing them, or responding to their signal.

There is one sharp difference between my father's contemporary account of the disaster, and the report which appeared, more than fifty years later, in the *Straits Times*. The *Times* gives a vivid account of "a fighting screaming mob struggling for the lifeboats." "Above the shouting rose the hysterical screams of the women, and the wails of children torn from their mothers in the confusion. On the deck itself the scene beggared description. As each lifeboat swung to deck level, a mob stormed forward kicking and panicking, stumbling over rigging and flinging themselves into the overladen boats.

"Many of the women refused to jump. They knelt on the deck with their shawls over their heads, weeping and praying, while their terrified children clung to their skirts. All around them the frantic battle for the lifeboats surged across the tilting deck."

My father, on the other hand, was struck by the unanimity with which the survivors assured him there had been no general panic. He commented that that appeared to be borne out by the fact that, of the 101 who were landed at Stornoway, 91 were passengers, and more than fifty women or children. Among the ten members of the crew landed at Stornoway there wasn't a single officer or seaman, apart from the Capt, who, in effect, came back from the dead. The crew members who survived were cooks and stewards.

Some panic there must have been, and, no doubt, wailing and praying women, and jostling. One Swedish lady complained to my father that, in the lifeboat, another survivor had stolen the blanket she had taken with her for her baby. On the other hand there seems to have been a surprising degree of discipline and self-sacrifice. Against what standard does one measure human behaviour in a catastrophe like that? How much panic is panic, on a sinking ship?

Ironically, perhaps significantly, the *Straits Times* account of the "battle for the lifeboats" seems to be based on the statement of one man, presumably in an interview given to a Grimsby newspaper at the time. The man was the sole survivor of his family. His wife and five children drowned. He gave a very circumstantial account of how he got separated from them, and it may be true. On the other hand there is the suspicion that, as so often happens with those who feel guilty, he may have been attributing to all the others a selfish panic he succumbed to himself.

Whatever happened on the ship, we know what happened in Stornoway. Everyone rallied round with food, money and clothes, including the tourists who were in town at the time on the *Claymore*, and on visiting yachts. At the Poorhouse the governor, black-bearded Robert Drummond, went without any sleep for two successive nights. A Lewis nurse, on holiday from the Western Infirmary, worked with him for twelve consecutive hours attending to the injured. Conditions were even more difficult at Lews

157

Hospital where the most serious cases were dealt with by the five local doctors.

Although there was no formal organisation then for dealing with emergencies, volunteers went unsought to the Poorhouse and Hospital to help out at meal times. A group of young girls made a house to house collection of clothes. A concert was hastily organised to raise funds for the survivors. Some of them were almost naked when they arrived, but, when they left, they were all "well dressed and comfortably found in every way." There was a large crowd on the pier to see them off, and much waving of handkerchiefs, hand-shaking and cheering, as if they had been long-term residents well known to everyone in town. Fifty four of them travelled to Liverpool where the Danish Government had organised passages for them by the Cunard Line to New York. The rest returned to the homes they had left so recently with high hopes of fortune in the New World.

"The children and sick have been nursed as carefully by your ladies as if they were children of their own," said Capt Gundel in a written statement before he left. "I think no other place in the world would have done what you have done."

Although he does not seem to have been superstitious he did tell my father it was the third time he had been shipwrecked on the 28th day of the month.

Despite all that was done for the survivors, nine of them died in Stornoway, eight of them children. In the old cemetery at Sandwick, almost against the sea wall, there is a handsome tombstone to mark their resting place. On it are the names of Alfield Natalia Hindersen, of Christiana, Norway (now known as Oslo), aged five; Max and Rebecca Posansky of Sloman, in Russia, aged 4 and 11; Ingride and Haral Jorgensen, of Wisconsin USA, aged 4 and 1½; Andrea M Hansen, of Sweden aged 4; Salman and Sara Reisman of Shorsky in Russia aged 11 months and 5 years; and Joseph Simmco, a 38 year old blacksmith from Finland, who lost all his family, and went mad before he died.

A reminder, if I can adapt the poet's oft-quoted phrase, that no island is an island, complete in itself, but part of the main. Especially an island like Lewis, in one of the stormiest regions of the world, and close to one of the great Atlantic seaways.

45
Scalpay Herring in Red Square

A few years ago we went to Russia for a short visit. It was a package tour of the Art Treasures of the Kremlin, the Hermitage and other famous galleries, and of some of the great churches in Vladimir and Novgorod, as well as Moscow and Leningrad, with a little ballet, opera, music and the circus thrown in for good measure.

The group we travelled with was, in some ways, as interesting as the tour itself. Our art expert was the widow of a Scottish professor, but she was Russian, a member of one of the old princely families of pre-revolution days. She escaped from Russia, after the revolution, at the age of ten. When I asked her how, she said, "I cannot tell you here, but I might when we get back to Britain. We thought it was a great adventure. It wasn't so funny for our parents." When we visited one of the extravagant Tzarist palaces near Leningrad, destroyed by Nazi gunfire, and now, ironically, rebuilt for the second time by the blood and sweat of Russian working men, she recalled a party she had attended there as a child, with the Tzar's children, and an enormous Christmas tree in one corner of the room.

One of the members of the party was a grandson of Sir Arthur Nicolson, as he then was, who was British ambassador in St Petersburg in 1907, when the Triple Entente was entered into by Britain, France and Russia, setting the stage for much that happened afterwards. There was also an American couple whose grandparents had fled from Tzarist tyranny around the time of the *Norge* disaster. They were perhaps the most interesting of all. The husband was an expert on music, the wife on art. They squabbled vociferously, but, in a curious way, quite amicably, throughout the tour, as if that was the natural mode of life. Descendants of Russian Jews, they had repudiated both Judaism and Russia, but still were anxious to dig back to the family roots.

It was unusual to find on a package tour so many people who had not only come to see and stare, like ourselves, but had a contribution to make, from their own family history, which gave a new dimension to the whole experience for the rest of us. That set me thinking about my own background, and led to the conclusion that, although I spent my life cooped up in a small Atlantic island, which many people regard as one of the world's backwaters, I had direct points of contact with almost everything we saw during the trip.

I have already mentioned the Russian aristocrat whose daughter was a nurse in Lewis Sanatorium; the refugees from Tzarist tyranny cast on our shores by the shipwreck at Rockall; the Esthonians who sought shelter at Stornoway as they fled from the latter-day Russian tyranny of Stalin; and my friendship with a writer who knew Lenin, Trotsky, Litvinov, and Kerensky, in fact all the leading figures in one of the great upheavals in world history, whose names reverberated through my reading, over the greater part of my life.

Behind them I could visualise the brightly coloured wooden bowls in my granny's parlour, brought home by my grandfather from the Baltic. We saw them in every tourist shop we visited in Russia, and it was there I learned, for the first time, that they were generally known in Scotland as Rigaware because it was through that port they had been, at one time, imported in bulk.

And now the question occurs to me for the first time: why was there a shop in Stornoway when I was a child, known as The Baltic Boot Shop, and referred to in every village in rural Lewis as Buth nam Baltic?

It was of "the Baltic" we used to tell the story of the man who came through a doorway festooned with boots into a shop where every shelf was crammed with them, and asked a rather astonished shop assistant, "Have you got boots?"

"Yes," said the assistant.

"Well, I'll take two," said the man.

My recollection is that the owner of the shop was a man called Louis Bittner, but I cannot visualise him, or remember anything about him. The name could well have come from one of the Baltic states. Is there a little bit of Lewis history congealed in the name?

Although the locally-owned fleet which traded to the Baltic had disappeared before I was born, the names of the Baltic seaports were as familiar in my childhood as the names of the rural Lewis villages, which I never saw until my father bought our first motor car, when I was almost ready to leave the Nicolson and go to Glasgow university.

There were other memories too, on that Russian tour. Cecil Braithwaite, for instance. The somewhat eccentric London stockbroker, who was for many years a member of the Grimersta syndicate, and wrote a book called *Fishing Here and There*, about which I will have something to say in quite another context. He used to send me cuttings from the more rabid anti-communist newspapers, with furious little notes exhorting me to "tell the truth!" His ire was aroused by a series of articles on Russia I published from the pen of my old headmaster, W. J. Gibson, described by Principal Taylor of Aberdeen University as "one of the greatest headmasters in all Scotland", a phrase which was almost exactly the same as that used by Prof Fisher when Edinburgh University conferred an honorary doctorate on Gibson's most distinguished pupil, Robert Maciver. Having spent all his holidays in Lewis during his long headmastership, Gibson, after his retirement, began to travel abroad, at a time when foreign travel was too slow, difficult and expensive for most people to contemplate. In that, as in his teaching, he was a trail-blazer for the rest of us.

No doubt Gibson, in the euphoria of the time, missed the growing tyranny under Stalin's rule, and concentrated on the social improvements which were taking place, an error into which Bernard Shaw, the Webbs, and many others, were falling at the same time. But if, in the light of later events, there was some reason for Braithwaite's acerbity, he was right for the wrong reasons, and in quite the wrong way. Something not at all unusual in human affairs.

The old Russian bayonet picked up on the field of Balaclava by my grandfather, during the Crimean War, and which my granny used as a poker in my childhood, provided a link with an earlier period, when Russia and Britain were at war with each other, while the many seamen I knew who helped to keep the route to Murmansk open during the Second World War, often at the cost of their lives, provided a link with the period when Britain and Russia were closely allied. An alliance rather mocked at by the insistence we observed in Russia, whenever the war was mentioned, that it was the Great Patriotic War, fought by Russia against the Nazis, as if no one else had taken part, and of which the memory was deliberately kept alive by the goose-stepping guard at the national memorial in Red Square, and by school children mounting an eternal vigil over smaller memorials in rural places.

We even encountered a link with the island of Scarp, when we were invited to a free film show in a Moscow cinema. Although most of the party opted out, Cathie and I attended, along with the ambassador's grandson, and a biologist from New Zealand. We all wanted to see what it was Russian propaganda was trying to do to us. Visitors were bussed from hotels all over Moscow to one of the largest cinemas in the city, but we were not taken to the main auditorium where the Russians were pouring in. We were taken to a beautifully equipped little auditorium at the back, where we were shown a film in English: an exciting story about the development of space travel. It was fiction in more ways than one.

The plot centred on the conflict between a brilliant Russian scientist, who was the hero, and the dull-witted boorish bureaucrats whose incomprehension threatened to frustrate him. The satire on the bureaucrats cleverly disguised the propaganda message that space travel was developed by Russian scientists, through their own unaided efforts, for peaceful purposes, until they were blown off course by the wicked Americans, perverting the Russian invention for imperialistic ends. There was no hint of what the Russians had learned, or borrowed, or stolen from the Germans, or for that matter from the Americans themselves.

There was no mention of Werner von Braun, or of poor dejected Gerhard Zucker with his snowstorm of letters on the beach at Scarp. Although ostensibly a failure, Zucker was in the space game before the Russians, and that cinema in Moscow is inextricably mixed in my memory with the slightly singed souvenir envelope which hangs on my wall, with its "Western Isles Rocket Post" stamp, and the cancellation: "Trial Firing. Scarp Harris. 28 VII 34."

And with two Scalpay herring, which went up in the same rocket, in a parcel addressed to Sir Godfrey Collins, Secretary of State for Scotland, with an exhortation that he should encourage people to eat more fish. Herring were plentiful, then!

And with the parcel of patent medicine, also in the rocket, addressed to the Scarp twins, who made medical history when they were born in different islands, in different counties, and in different weeks.

46
Twins from Different Counties

The twins, to whom the bottle of patent medicine was consigned in Zucker's ill-fated rocket, had been born just a few months earlier, in circumstances which focused the attention of the world on Scarp.

The first of the twins was born on a Saturday in 1934, in the home of the parents, Christina and James Maclennan. On the previous day the father had tried to get a doctor across from Tarbert, but there was a heavy sea running and it was not possible for him to cross the Sound. The birth was supervised by an 85-year-old midwife.

The midwife realised that there was a second child to come. So on Sunday morning, when the weather had moderated, the father went across to Husinish to phone for help. The phone was out of order. The postman's son set off by car for Tarbert, seventeen miles away to call the doctor.

As soon as he got to Scarp, the doctor decided he must move the patient to the little Rest Room at Tarbert where he could have her under close surveillance. A stretcher was improvised from a mattress and blankets. Mrs Maclennan was carried down to the open beach, and through the breakers to the waiting boat. There she was laid across the seats, and the journey to Husinish began.

At Husinish she had to be carried through the breakers again, and across a strip of land, half moor half machair, to the road end where the postman's bus was waiting. She was laid on the floor. The bumpy, winding journey to Tarbert took more than three hours.

At Tarbert the doctor decided that he must get his patient urgently into Lews Hospital, where there was a surgeon and an operating theatre. This time the conveyance was an ordinary saloon car. Throughout the whole journey Mrs Maclennan carried her first child with her, wrapped in a shawl. The second of the twins was born on Monday morning, nearly two days after the first, and the birth was registered in a different county.

Mrs Maclennan was none the worse of her ordeal. She left Lews Hospital after the normal period for a straightforward confinement, and returned to Scarp with two fine, and famous, daughters.

Shortly after the birth, T. B. Wilson Ramsay, the MP for the Western Isles, asked questions in the House of Commons about the inadequacy of communications and medical services in his constituency. He got the usual bland reply from Sir Godfrey Collins, Secretary of State for Scotland. Perhaps a better indication of the manner in which the House of Commons regarded the matter was provided by the Prime Minister, Ramsay

Macdonald. As Collins rose to reply, Macdonald whispered to him, "Tell him it's as well they didn't take her on to Glasgow or there might have been triplets!"

There may have been an ironic symbolism in the fact that when the package of medicine for the twins was despatched by rocket it was heading in the wrong direction. A cynic suggested, at the time, that it was decided to fire the rocket from Scarp rather than to Scarp because there was less chance of missing Harris than of missing Scarp. Actually the decision was quite sensible. It would have been difficult to aim at Scarp without some risk of hitting the houses in the village. Firing in the opposite direction they had the man-made wilderness of the Harris deer forest. But the rocket didn't get that far!

Following Wilson Ramsay's questions, the *News Chronicle* asked me to go to Scarp and interview the mother. I couldn't. It was a fine morning in Stornoway with a little rain. There was some snow on the Harris hills, but it was so calm there was quite a lot of mist. But, when I got to Husinish, the Sound of Scarp was like a cauldron. No boat could be launched in it and live. The Husinish postman went through the motions of summoning a boat from Scarp. He ran up the appropriate signal on the little flagpole by the beach. A gloomy black flag, without the skull and crossbones.

I waited but nothing happened. When I returned to Stornoway, I sent off my report to the *Chronicle*. It began, "If a man lies dying on the island of Scarp today for want of medical attention, he will just have to die." Life in Scarp was as stark as that.

There was no telephone to Scarp. No pier or landing stage at Scarp or Husinish. It was just about a decade earlier that they even got a road to Husinish, and they owed that to Lord Leverhulme more than to central government or local authority. Prior to that, the road stopped at Amhuinnsuidhe.

When J. M. Barrie was in Amhuinnsuidhe gathering some of the material for *Mary Rose*, like the legend of "the island that likes to be visited," and the other legend of the erudite Harris gillies who carry Euripides, in the original Greek, in their pockets, when they go out on the loch, and who speak as fluently in French as in English, or even Gaelic, he was able to travel in comparative comfort from Tarbert by car. But the crofters of Scarp had still to take everything from Tarbert by sea, and, when it was too rough to venture round Husinish Point, they had to lug their household goods on their backs, for seven or eight miles across the hills, and hope that the Sound was passable.

There was no ambulance service in Lewis or Harris, and although there was a surgeon at Lews Hospital, the facilities were restricted, and he worked under conditions that would not be tolerated today. Norman Jamieson, when he was surgeon, gave me a graphic account of an operation he carried out, in a black house, by the light of an oil lamp, with hens flying round him as he worked. When my father required an operation, a few years earlier, before the first surgeon was appointed, it was carried out by the family doctor, Jack Tolmie, in our own house, and, as soon as my father had recovered from the anaesthetic, the doctor went off to attend to his surgery, leaving my mother to nurse the patient single-handed.

When I became editor of the *Gazette* in 1932 there was no telephonic communication with the mainland. Even when we got the phone it was almost impossible to make oneself understood on a long distance call. When Amhuinnsuidhe Castle caught fire I spent forty minutes spelling the name to an incredulous sub-editor in Manchester. Even when he had it right, he refused to believe it.

Once the link with the mainland was established, the service throughout the islands was extended fairly rapidly. Scarp got a phone — a few years before the island was abandoned! One of the last villages to be linked up was Rhenigidale. The last time I saw Donald Macdonald, who was District Clerk at the time, he reminded me of the circumstances.

Harris District Council was a small friendly body, meeting cosily in arm chairs, round the lounge fire, in the Tarbert Hotel. The meetings were civilised even when there was a clash of opinion, and I enjoyed going to them as a relief from the uproar that used to prevail in the larger Lewis Council, in the heyday of John Maciver, Shawbost, and Donald Mackay, Kershader.

At one meeting the question of a telephone for Rhenigidale cropped up. The members agreed that they would make representations to the Post Office, but they had little hope of success, and did not treat the matter with urgency.

Reporters at Council meetings are like Victorian children, they are supposed to be seen but not heard. However, I asked if I could chip in. The Chairman said "Yes". I said, "If you're going to move, move quickly, and address your letter direct to Marples, the Postmaster General. It hasn't been announced yet, but I hear on the grapevine he's coming to Harris on a fishery cruiser."

"You know," said Donald, relishing the recollection, "We did just that, and the first words Marples spoke to me when he came down the gangway were, 'Where's this place Rhenigidale?' "

When Rhenigidale got the phone, it was the best twopence worth in Britain. A call to Tarbert was still "local", although the message travelled over a hundred miles to get there. It crossed the Minch twice by radio, and then travelled by landline from Bennadrobh to Tarbert via the Stornoway Exchange.

Now we have satellites, sending our conversations on even longer journeys, when we ring up friends in USA or Australia.

47
Boots for a Chinese Murderer

Although I lived through the revolution in communications, and in medical services, in Lewis over the past seventy years or so, it requires a real effort of recollection to think back to the conditions in which a great many Lewis families lived in the twenties and early thirties.

No hot water on tap! For that matter, no cold water on tap! No drainage! No electricity! No radio! No TV! No telephone! No private cars! No calor gas! No central heating! No hoover! No washing machine! No fridge! No freezer!

How would children today react to the daily journey to a distant well with a cearcall and two buckets for water? And a two mile tramp to school in the wind and rain, with nothing solid to eat between breakfast and the evening meal?

As I write there comes floating into my memory, from very early childhood, a letter my father read to us one day, from a crofter on the West Side, complaining that one of his neighbours had started keeping ducks, and they were polluting the local water supply. It was an eloquent letter with a vivid description of a duck and a dozen ducklings in line astern, waddling down the village street, leading to the punch line. "And all them dirty duck give bath to themselves in the clean water of the well."

Infectious diseases were more common, and more dangerous, than they are today. Diphtheria was almost endemic in some areas, and tuberculosis a scourge. It claimed several of my closest friends at school and university.

Although there is much less drudgery, and much less disease, in Lewis now than there was in my childhood, I doubt if there is any more real happiness, or even contentment. There is certainly a good deal more drunkenness, and a good deal more crime.

Infectious diseases apart, people might even have been basically healthier in the past. In the forties I reported the deaths of two notable centenarians within a few months of each other. Mrs Margaret Macleod of Rodil was in her 106th year when she died. Mrs Isabella Macleod of Vatisker was in her 108th. The *New York Times* devoted a leaderette to Isabella, when she died, referring to her as "the oldest human of whose age there is an authentic record." Claims to greater longevity have, I think, been established elsewhere since, but Isabella Macleod, in her day, was unique.

An official who visited Margaret Macleod from time to time, in the course of his duties, told me that he asked her, not very long before her death, whether there had been any change in the family circumstances since his last visit. "Yes" she said. "My son is working now!" Her son, who was in his middle seventies, had been a self-employed crofter-fisherman all his life, but now, for the first time, he had a real job — working on the roads.

Behind all the changes of the period one thing has remained constant — the sea, and the island's relationship to it, as a refuge for mariners. The only real difference is that we now take the ill or the injured ashore by helicopter.

When Lews Hospital was built in the 1890s it was intended to serve the local community. Although it was both a medical and a surgical hospital from the start it had a very modest beginning. There was no resident doctor or surgeon. Surgical cases were dealt with by one of the local GPs, Dr Murdoch Mackenzie, father of Agnes Mure Mackenzie the historian. At the very outset there was a staff of two, a nurse and a housekeeper — both part-time. The nurse also acted as district nurse for the burgh, while the housekeeper was also a "Biblewoman". I don't know precisely what duties being a "Biblewoman" entailed.

Of the first hundred patients treated in this little local hospital more than one in four came from ships at sea. That was more than twice as many as from the whole burgh of Stornoway. Only one of the hundred came from Harris.

At that time Lews Hospital was a self-contained local institution, maintained by the voluntary donations of a poor community. The service it gave freely to seamen of all nations never entered into the calculation when representatives of central government totted up, as they did from time to time, the various grants paid to the islands, and groaned at the burden on the taxpayers' back. The assessment of government support to the peripheral areas is a highly selective and misleading operation.

Circumstances at Lews Hospital changed radically even before the introduction of the National Health Service, thanks to the operations of the Highlands and Islands Medical Service, but, right up to nationalisation, there was a remarkable input of local funds. It was still largely a voluntary institution during the Second World War when it was called on to cope with a flow of ill and injured seamen of many nations such as the island had never seen before, even at the time of the *Norge* disaster.

When the *Rotaroa* was torpedoed 180 miles north west of the Butt more survivors were landed than from the *Norge*, and with rather less warning. It was an even more cosmopolitan mixture, including a Chinaman charged with murder.

The survivors were on three Admiralty trawlers. Although the naval base at Stornoway must have known they were on their way while they were still well north of the Butt, they did not inform the civil authorities until about twenty minutes before the trawlers arrived. Playing up the role of the silent service, perhaps!

When the survivors did come ashore, they were huddled in a group at the end of the pier, in the open. Nothing seemed to be happening. At last the Sergeant of Police, Murdo Macphail, remonstrated with the senior naval

167

officer on the spot. "You're O.C. this bloody show!" was the reply. "I've got nothing to do with it."

Once the ball was clearly in the local court, everyone got busy. The WVS prepared meals. The Home Guard provided blankets. Volunteers from the RAF helped to distribute the blankets and get folk bedded down. A dance being held that night stopped early so that a hot meal could be prepared for those who were able to travel, before the boat sailed, in the small hours of the morning.

The Inspector of Police was in a real tizzy. A Chinese murderer was the hottest property he had ever handled. His anxiety increased when he learned that all the papers relating to the incident had gone down with the ship. Having got the Chinaman on his hands, he had a problem getting rid of him.

The story, which is no doubt true, was that the Chinaman had knifed another member of the crew following a dispute at cards. He was locked up on board ship until the torpedo struck. Then he was taken to one of the lifeboats under guard. He jumped overboard from the lifeboat to rescue one of the officers.

When he was handed over to the police at Stornoway, he said to Bill Urquhart the constable, "London? Hang me?", and drew his hand across his throat as if to signify a rope tightening.

When the rest of the survivors left, the Chinaman remained in gaol. Thirty days later Inspector Fraser breathed a sigh of relief. That was the maximum period for which a prisoner could be held in Stornoway. The Chinaman was shipped across to Inverness till things were sorted out. In the meantime the news on the grapevine was that the authorities were taking the sensible course and sending him back to the shipping pool to get on with the war.

He had almost no clothes, so Macinnes, the gaoler, approached the Shipwrecked Mariners Society. They hummed and hawed. "You know, we have no authority to equip a criminal."

"He's not a criminal," replied Macinnes. "He hasn't been convicted yet. He hasn't even been formally charged. He's a shipwrecked mariner, and should be treated as such."

Somewhat reluctantly, the Society provided a pair of boots. For the rest, the Chinese "murderer" was protected from the cold of a January journey in wartime by a coat and jacket given him by his gaoler.

48
The Bang That Shook Up Kyle

A few weeks after the *Rotoroa* was torpedoed another convoy was attacked 230 miles from the Butt. A tanker, with a great hole in her side, came limping into Stornoway. The hole was so big you could see it with the naked eye from the pier although the vessel was in Glumaig.

Three vessels in the convoy were sunk and two damaged. Altogether 67 survivors were landed at Stornoway. Lagely (Dugald Kennedy), who was providing transport with his taxi, told me that when the Sergt of Police was sorting out the survivors he called for those from the first ship on his list to step forward. One solitary figure staggered to his feet. A young man badly burned about the legs. Everyone else on board, including his father, had been lost.

A few days earlier the crew of a Faroese fishing smack were landed at Stornoway. They were on their way from Iceland to the East Coast, with a cargo of salt fish, when a submarine surfaced. She sank the smack with shell fire, and machine-gunned the crew. They were two days in an open boat before they landed at the Flannans. They were on one of the uninhabited islands when the lighthouse-keepers spotted them, and signalled them across to the lighthouse. By the time they were picked up from there, the lighthouse was running out of tobacco.

A little later the crew of a torpedoed tanker was landed at Stornoway. The tanker blew up and the sea caught fire. That was how they described it. Those who jumped overboard died in an inferno. The four survivors had crouched in the bottom of a boat until it drifted clear of the blaze.

One of the crew of the destroyer which picked them up was a Lewisman resident in London. I have forgotten his name, if in fact I ever knew it. But I was told that, when he asked for a few hours leave to see his mother, the captain gave him nine days. When he got home, his wife was there before him. She had been bombed out of their London home. Had gone to Swansea, and was bombed out there, as well.

When a Grimsby trawler put in with the crew of a sister ship which had been machine-gunned, the Hospital was warned to stand-by for casualties. Dr Doig, as MOH, went down to organise their removal to hospital. One of the crew of the rescue ship was leaning on the rail.

"Have you any casualties on board?" asked Doig.

"Dunno!" said the trawl-hand.

"I'm a doctor. I was told there were casualties."

"Tell you what, Jack," said the trawl-hand. "I'll go below and find out."

A few minutes later he returned to report that there was a man below with a sore foot. When Doig went down, he found a trawlhand sitting on the edge of a bunk. He had wounds in his head, hand and foot. He was cursing vociferously because he couldn't get his boots on, his feet were so swollen. He wanted to go ashore with his pals.

It was around that time Kyle of Lochalsh was almost obliterated. Not by enemy action but by accident. Kyle was a very busy naval base. The Stornoway mail steamer still went there nightly, but the Sound of Sleat was closed to shipping and the *Lochness* could no longer go on to Mallaig, as she used to do.

One day as she lay at Kyle, Capt Macarthur told me, she was ordered suddenly to put to sea. A six thousand ton vessel had caught fire with a cargo of 550 mines on board. When it proved impossible to control the fire, the vessel was scuttled, and the crew jumped overboard.

Capt Macarthur told me there were seven tremendous explosions. He heard the first explosion as he hurried out to sea. A column of flame shot two hundred feet into the air. The plates of the vessel, he said, were "playing likkan lokkan" for a mile across the loch.

That recollection presents me with a puzzle. I didn't see the scene, but it was so vividly described for me by Capt Macarthur I feel that I can visualise it. The key word in my recollection is "likkan lokkan," which conjures up a vision of myself as a child at Sandwick Beach spending hours, if not days, searching for flat slate-like stones which I could throw into the water so that they bounced across the surface five, six or even seven times. But did Capt Macarthur actually use that word when he described the scene, or did I translate his description into the language of my childhood? I don't know. And I don't know where the word itself comes from. Is "likkan lokkan" Gaelic, old Norse, or just Stornoway slang? Wherever it comes from, it is highly descriptive — the visual equivalent of onomatopoeia.

Fortunately there were no casualties from the Kyle explosion, although there was a risk for a time that the whole village might vanish. Some of the survivors swam across to Skye and landed near Broadford. Nine of them were seen clambering up the beach by a Stornoway lady, Margaret Morrison (Mrs MacGregor), who took them home, dried them out, and fed them. Then sat them down to an impromptu ceilidh, provided by another Stornoway lady, Margaret Graham, who was staying with her at the time.

It was Margaret Graham — or her sister — who had played the heroine in *Campbell of Kilmhor*, the play which helped to arouse my interest in the theatre as a boy, and who lay sobbing on the stage as the curtain fell, while we sat sobbing in the audience, moved beyond endurance by the shot, off stage, which signified the final tragedy, and the plaintive voice of Hugh Matheson, the baker, singing in the wings, as if his own heart would break, "No more we'll see such deeds again . . ."

In these wartime days, we saw many deeds that make the Jacobite rebellion, and the fugitive Prince look very tinselly.

It was just around that time, for instance, I heard of an incident involving several reservists from Point when three British vessels sailed into a minefield, which might have been one of our own! As I was told the story, although I cannot now recall who my informant was, HMS *Express* was the first of the three to strike. Immediately she signalled to the other two vessels — HMS *Esk* and HMS *Ivanhoe* — not to come to her aid. It was too dangerous. But they steamed in, and both struck mines.

The *Esk* sank quickly. The *Ivanhoe* limped from the scene, badly holed, and had to be abandoned. The only vessel to make port was the *Express* to whose aid the other two had gone.

When the *Express* struck the mine some of the Point lads swam to the *Ivanhoe*. She blew up almost as soon as they got on board. One of the Point lads was blown into the sea by the second explosion, and swam back to the *Express*. He came out of it safely.

There were only two survivors from the *Esk*, one of them Donald Mackenzie from Sheshader. About thirty got away in a lifeboat when she struck the mine. They rowed for eight hours before they met up with the *Ivanhoe*, limping homewards. As they passed under her stern to come alongside, the lifeboat overturned. Lines were thrown from the deck, but only Mackenzie and an Englishman were able to grab them. The Englishman was hauled on board. Mackenzie's line snapped just as he came to the rail. Back in the water he swam around for some time. Then he saw a light. He swam towards it. It was the *Ivanhoe*'s launch looking for the men from the upturned lifeboat. Mackenzie was the only one still afloat. A short time after he was picked up he was transferred, with the rest of the men on the *Ivanhoe*, to another ship, just as the *Ivanhoe* sank.

It was against a background of almost daily reports of incidents of that sort, involving Island seamen in many parts of the world, and reports, almost as frequent, of murderous attacks on convoys going north round the Butt from Loch Ewe, that the people of Lewis welcomed the expansion of Stornoway airport, then taking place, and the arrival of the RAF in strength to provide cover for the ships.

Even with the added air cover, attacks on the convoys continued, as I realised one morning when I met Bob Steven, who had been librarian in the old Town Hall, but opened a tobacconist's shop when the Hall was destroyed by fire while in naval occupation at the end of an earlier war. He told me he had been talking to Angus Smith, who had just received word from the Ministry of Food to release all stocks of meat available in the Slaughterhouse immediately, because a Norwegian vessel was racing to Stornoway with nearly three hundred survivors from a British ship. There would be many mouths to feed.

49
Chinese Lady in the Snow

Some hours after Bob Steven told me a large number of survivors were expected in port, a big Norwegian cargo vessel came alongside Number One Quay. Her decks were crowded. Norwegian sailors, lascars, women, children, airmen, sailors, soldiers, marines, whites, Indians, Burmese, and Chinese. I never saw such a cosmopolitan crowd in Stornoway before or since. Three ambulances were drawn up on the quay to take the injured to hospital. There were two buses for the women and children. The men were to march to the halls prepared for them.

One of the lascars got left behind as they came ashore. He came round the end of the Maritime Buildings alone, clearly expecting to see his pals ahead of him. He looked this way and that, for all the world like a startled rabbit. Then dashed for one of the buses. It was full of women. Looking puzzled, he darted to the other bus. It was also full of women. He took a quick glance at the crowd of sightseers on the pier. Then saw his pals marching along South Beach and raced after them. As I turned back towards the ship, I saw a lady in brightly coloured Oriental dress, and with oily black hair done in the Chinese style, come round the end of the Maritime Buildings, and walk through the snow to one of the buses with a stately grace.

At that time we did not know the name of the ship or what had happened to her. I was discussing the cosmopolitan group of survivors with Ian Maclean, John Morrison, Barvas, and my old classmate, Ian Mor. Then a local shopkeeper came over to me, the Cando. "There's a man in the Town Hall asking for you," he said. "One of the survivors. He says he knows you."

I hurried along to the Town Hall. It was crowded with wet, bedraggled, unshaven men and shivering women some of them still wearing lifebelts. Local women were serving tea. The Sergt of Police was making announcements. The Immigration Officer was sitting at a table in the corner taking particulars. I walked round the hall several times but could see no one remotely familiar. Then I saw a man catch the Sergt by the sleeve and say something to him. I heard the Sergt say, "Jim Grant? Yes, I saw him here." I had never set eyes on the man in my life before, but I went over to introduce myself. "I'm Nat," he said urgently. "Nat Tait! Nat Tait!" he added when he saw the look of incomprehension on my face. Then I knew. Sheila Morrison, whose brother Ian had been one of my closest friends when they lived in the Schoolhouse at Back, had married an Indian tea-planter, named Tait. His brother was a well-known cartoonist on the staff of the *Bulletin*.

Before I could respond, a man, two places ahead of Nat in the queue at the Immigration Officer's table, turned and said, "You're not Tait of Calcutta?" "Yes!" said Nat. "Good Lord!" said the man. "I had dinner with you once, but that's a long time ago."

I told Nat he must come and stay with us, once he got through the formalities. In the meantime I would go and get the car. "I'll tell you what you can do for me," he said "I've lost my glasses and I'm helpless without them, can you arrange something with an oculist?"

On the way home in the car, Nat told me what had happened. "It was the Bibby liner *Staffordshire*", he said. "We were bombed, about two hundred miles north of the Butt. It's an extraordinary thing. A Sunderland flying boat had just passed over, most of us were still looking after it, when a Nazi came out of the sun before anyone noticed, and we got a packet. Then he came back and machine-gunned us in the boats."

"Sheila always told me I should visit Stornoway!" he said, with a forced smile, when my mother opened the door. It wasn't easy. He was stiff and sore and wet. He had sticking plaster on his face and hands. He had been rowing for four hours, exercise he was not used to. And he was soaked in oil. Most of them were soaked in oil. The lifeboats had to pass under a broken oil pipe as they left the ship, and everyone got sprayed with it. Never in the history of Lewis have there been so many hot baths simultaneously.

We kitted him out as best we could. A suit of mine fitted not badly, with the legs turned up, but I had to go off on my bike to my uncle's manse to borrow a pair of long johns. He needed them for the cold.

"The passengers in our boat were splendid," he told us over a meal. "Especially the women. There were two young women there going out to join their husbands in India. They had just married in the summer. Mrs Bell and Mrs Saunders. Mrs Bell had a knapsack with a first-aid outfit. She attended to the wounded in the boat. When we got to the Norwegian she took her slacks off and gave them to a seaman. She went about in her knickers. Then she gave her stockings to someone else. I wish I could say the same about some of the men. There was a young army officer there in a very posh British Warm. He came into the lifeboat looking like Bond Street. He sat there wrapped to the neck. He didn't even give his coat to the young child lying beside him in the boat, dying of wounds. He made no effort to help with the rowing, but when we got to the Norwegian he was the second up the ladder, before the women and children."

There had been no ship's officers in Nat's boat. They had difficulty in casting off. It was Mrs Bell who finally cut the ropes with a sheath knife. Although they rowed as best they could, they had no direction. They could not keep the lifeboat's head into the sea, and shipped a lot of water.

After our meal I took Nat to the Royal Hotel where his friends Mrs Bell and Mrs Saunders had been billeted. "As they were in my boat, I feel a responsibility for them!" he said. Mrs Bell, I discovered, needed no one to look after her. She was tall, dark skinned, mannishly pretty, competent, and full of energy. Mrs Saunders, however, needed cosseting, and I felt that Nat enjoyed the role of comforter.

I told the ladies that our next door neighbours, May and Duggie Maclean, had a bed prepared for them. Mrs Saunders was tempted, but first she consulted Mrs Bell. "No!" was the decisive answer. "The staff have been too good to us here. We really cannot go now. Two Air Force Officers have given up their beds for us, and the chambermaids have changed the sheets." Mrs Saunders agreed. "The maids have been very good to us. One of them gave me this skirt and blouse." As she spoke a maid came over, whispered to her a little shyly, and took her apart. Mrs Saunders came back laughing, and showed us a pink silky nightdress. "I've just been given this as well" she said. A few minutes later another maid came along with a nightdress for Mrs Bell. She took it gratefully, but passed it on to someone else. She didn't sleep in a nightdress, she told us. Eventually she slept in a pair of men's pyjamas, borrowed from my near neighbour Walter Lees.

"I've had a bath!" said Mrs Saunders, as if she were describing the most luxurious experience on earth. "I've got rid of the oil. It has left my skin all smooth and soft. Feel my arm!"

"I've still to get it out of my hair," responded Mrs Bell. "It's all matted, but there's so much to do. There's poor Mrs Breadmore. Her husband's death has left her prostrate. And there's Peggy Chicken. She was marvellous in the boat, but she's cracked up completely."

"That's another of the girls I told you of," said Nat. "She's quite a young thing, but she fairly showed up some of the men."

Peggy Chicken, I was told, had been on her way to the Mission field in China, but the sudden traumatic interruption of her journey had left her confused. Wondering whether the real mission field for her was not with the ageing parents she was leaving behind in a Welsh valley.

It was only then I realised that Mrs Bell was still without stockings, having given hers away on the Norwegian steamer. And Mrs Saunders had no coat for the journey south. I went rummaging again, and got some warm ladies' stockings, and a coat of my mother's, roughly hemmed to suit Mrs Saunders' diminutive figure. She was quite pleased when she put it on. "When is early Communion?" she asked. "I would like to attend now that I have a coat to go in."

I told her the time, and gave her directions to St Peter's. Later she told me she was the only person present. "It's the first time I ever had a service all to myself!"

But there was another service, in the crowded Town Hall. The most unusual service I have ever attended.

174

50
My Head With Oil . . .

The survivors from the *Staffordshire* arrived in Stornoway on a Saturday afternoon. On Sunday morning I went to the Royal Hotel to see how my new friends were faring, as many other Stornoway men and women were doing around the same time.

Just outside the Royal I met Ara Macaulay, coming from the Town Hall, where she had been busy with the other helpers. She told me another of the survivors had died in hospital, and one of the women was to have a leg amputated. Then she added, much to my surprise, "The *Staffordshire* is in Loch Ewe. They got the fire out and she came in under her own steam. They're going to send the lascars back in one of the patrol boats." Later I heard that, at first, the lascars refused to return to the ship. They were eventually marched to the pier by a naval escort with bayonets fixed. Nat told me that, after the bombing, the lascars had made off with two of the ship's lifeboats. They had to be threatened with machine-gun fire to bring them back so that the women and children could be accommodated.

When we told Mrs Bell about the amputation, she flung her scarf across the room. "It's all my fault!" she said. "I attended to that man with cuts in his head thinking he was more serious, and left poor Mrs Bradley without splints."

"What will you have to drink?" asked Nat. Mrs Bell refused the offer emphatically. Her mind was on other things. Mrs Saunders refused, a little half-heartedly, I thought. Then suggested, "Why not have one yourself?" "You want one after all," said Nat triumphantly, and went off to order two brandies with ginger ale.

"Col Breadmore is to be buried in Stornoway. Probably on Tuesday. It's not decided yet," said Mrs Bell. "I've persuaded Peggy Chicken to stay with Mrs Breadmore and look after their son, Jonathan. I'm going to help with her business arrangements. As far as I can see I'll be here for some days yet."

"Brandy and ginger ale is an excellant pick me up," said Nat, as the drinks arrived. "Three and five pence isn't bad. It's usually a very expensive drink." Mrs Bell's reply was a question to me about banks and travellers cheques. It was as if the conversation was running on two divergent sets of rails. Then Nat brought everyone together again by striking a mannequin pose, and claiming to be the best dressed refugee in Stornoway — in an old blue suit of mine that didn't fit him. Mrs Saunders showed us how she had dressed for early Communion in my mother's coat and a skirt given her by one of the maids. Mrs Bell produced the trump card. A Red Cross waterproof she had been given. A gent's outsize. It looked it, on her spare frame. "And" she added, "I've the most wonderful salmon pink body belt you ever saw. I got it from the WVS. It keeps me warm where I'm sore with sitting on a coil of rope."

Just then another of the survivors came into the room. A tall languid lady who stood in the door, looking rather like a slightly straightened question mark. "We're having a party," said Nat cheerily, waving his glass of brandy. "I wonder have you got any iodine, my dear," said the Question Mark, almost as if she were speaking in her sleep. Mrs Bell went purposefully to her knapsack and produced a bottle of iodine. The talk about clothes continued. "My stablemate has a lovely shine on her shoes. She did them with face cream", said the Question Mark, whose name I never discovered. "Lucky devil to have face cream," said Mrs Bell. "I had to wash my hair last night without a shampoo, trying to get rid of that oil. Look at it now. All over the place."

In the afternoon we all went to a service of thanksgiving which had been arranged in the Town Hall.

Five clergymen took part. All survivors from the *Staffordshire*. The Archbishop Designate of Rangoon presided. A jovial, fresh complexioned man, for all the world like an advertisement for Four Square or Bells Three Nuns. There was a thin dark Methodist Missionary with a squeaky voice. Tall, swarthy, skinny. In fact he had the thinnest neck I have ever seen. I couldn't make up my mind whether he was British or Indian. Later Ian Carmichael, my own minister, told me he was a representative of the London Missionary Society on the borders of Tibet, and was engaged in translating the *New Testament* into a dialect which has not yet been reduced to writing.

Then there was a very boyish fair-haired man who turned out to be the Professor of Modern History at Canton Theological Seminary. There was an inconspicuous Church of England Missionary at the piano. As I recall, the fifth (whom I cannot now visualise) was an American. Every Christian denomination was represented in the congregation from Quakers to Catholics, and there were many non-Christians as well. Indians, Burmese, Chinese. I couldn't take my eyes off a little Chinese boy, sitting near me, with jet black hair, sticking out at right angles from his head, for all the world like a golliwog. I wonder what he made of it all?

At the beginning, and even, in some measure, in retrospect, the service was deeply moving. The multi-racial congregation. The circumstances which had brought them all together. The pent-up emotion of people who had lost dear ones, or of those who had come through an ordeal unscathed. Even the Stornoway coat of arms above the preacher's heads. "God's Providence is Our Inheritance". Then, unfortunately, the Archbishop announced the 23rd Psalm. It was a natural, almost an inevitable, choice for such an occasion. But, with my sub-editorial instinct for the hidden pitfall, I could see it coming. "My head with oil Thou dost anoint . . ."

Glances were exchanged. There was a suppressed titter. The spell was broken.

Probably it would have been broken anyway. A short, simple devotional exercise would have sufficed, such as I was sometimes engaged in as a child, when I had a meal in my uncle's manse, and we all knelt in front of the dining-room chairs for family worship. But this had to be an ecumenical occasion. Ecumenical in the wrong way. All the denominations had to get in on the act.

The squeaky little Methodist prayed interminably and repetitively, thanking God for saving his life, but finding it difficult to know what to say about those who perished. Then the boyish Professor prayed briefly, but grasped the nettle in his opening words. "Father, forgive them. They know not what they do!" Unless the congregation could find it in their hearts to forgive the people who had bombed the ship, and then machine-gunned them in their lifeboats, their faith was valueless. True, no doubt, but you could feel the shock wave passing through the congregation. I thought of the Shelley family, a mother and daughter, lying dead in the mortuary, and a lovely boy of nine, whose name I never knew, riddled with machine-gun bullets.

The American was more Presbyterian in his approach. Aggressively so, I thought, having regard to the cosmopolitan nature of the congregation. The man at the piano said a few innocuous words, and then the Archbishop gave us an address based mainly on trifling personal reminiscences of which it was difficult to see the relevance.

As we left the hall, Mrs Bell came over to me. "What did you think of that?" she demanded. "Too long!" I said, non-committally. "They all had to say their little piece!" she replied. "I'm afraid I hadn't a very high opinion of the way the clergy behaved on the boat, and it isn't any higher now. Just fancy, when Mrs Ballard was lying with a fractured thigh the padre insisted on passing her texts. She didn't need texts. She needed splints. It was too bad rubbing it in about anointing our heads with oil. It took me hours to get mine clean."

She was much too sweeping in her condemnation. I know, from other sources, that the frail Methodist laboured manfully at the oars in his lifeboat. But he fell from grace, by his own standard, and was still regretting it when he left.

"I was never so miserable in my life," he confessed to Carmichael. "I was cold and wet, and, although I was trying to row, I was very sick. There was I pulling at the oar, and gloop, gloop it would come, every now and then. Do you know, I was so bad, I actually took a swig out of a whisky bottle!"

He spoke as if hell had gaped because he accepted the proferred dram.

51
Light from a Norwegian's Torso

The *Lochness* was always overcrowded in war-time. Grossly overcrowded. Eventually it became infested with cockroaches and rats. There were continual complaints, but no one listened. Never was it so overcrowded as on the Sunday night when the survivors from the *Staffordshire* sailed.

When I looked into the Smoking Room I saw a Chinese general playing bridge with three Indians. The pack of cards they used had bright, intricate Oriental patterns on the back. The general was in civvies. A burly man with horn-rimmed glasses. Practically the whole of the room was occupied by Indians and other Orientals. The lounge was equally crammed, with women and parsons.

As I stood outside the bar door talking to Nat I heard angry voices from within. "Forgive the buggers! What a bloody cheek!" There was an animated, and one-sided, discussion of the Professor's prayer in progress. It was interrupted when a drunk came along. Not a local. Not one of the survivors, as far as I know. But someone thoroughly objectionable, as only a drunk man can be.

An elderly man passed saying he was going to get a berth for his wife. "You won't get a berth on this bloody ship tonight!" said the Drunk. Stupidly, the man replied, "It was booked hours ago." "Moneybags," growled the drunk. "I hope the bloody stuff'll choke you!" The Drunk was right in saying there were no berths, but wrong about the moneybags. The berths had been set aside that night for the elderly women among the survivors, and those with children.

Then the Drunk saw someone in an airman's leather coat. "That's my coat!" he said. "The airman gave it to me. I gave it over for a lady, not for a bloody swine like you." "Your coat wouldn't fit me," replied the man. I don't think he was an airman, and I don't know how he came by the coat. "You want to make money out of it," said the Drunk, still on about the coat. "You'll pawn it for five quid. I would give you thirty bob myself." Having started by claiming the coat as his own, he was now offering to buy it!

We couldn't shake him off, and I was glad when the ship sailed. It was ironic that my last conversation with a small group of people I had never seen before and would never see again but who, for two crowded days, had become integrated into my life, should have been disrupted in this way by another complete stranger, thrusting himself in, unasked. And, yet, his irrelevant talk remains with me more vividly than much else that happened over that weekend.

Oddly, too, I remember the big Norwegian mate who took care of Mrs Saunders when she was passed up from the lifeboat almost in a state of collapse. He came round to the *Lochness* to say goodbye to her. Conversation was difficult. Apart from the language difficulty, they had little to say to each other, but it was a friendly gesture. In desperation for a topic, Mrs Saunders pointed to the flashlight he was carrying to guide him through the blackout, in which we were all enveloped as soon as we stepped out of the saloon. "That's a fine big torch you have!" she said. The Norwegian looked puzzled. Then, with a smile, he drew his hand across his chest. "Oh no!" he said. "It is just the many clothes I am wearing." I came to the conclusion that he thought she said "torso", and was surprised that he knew the word. Although I would suspect, "that's a fine big torso you've got", must be rather an unusual opening gambit for a conversation between a man and woman, who have met in the middle of a shipwreck, even in Norway.

I don't know how many casualties there were on the *Staffordshire*. There must have been quite a number because several of the lifeboats were said to have overturned as they were being launched from the burning ship. Twenty-three of the survivors were taken to Lews Hospital. One of them with appendicitis! Five at least of the passengers were buried in Sandwick, in a series of funerals which ran rather counter to the egalitarian traditions of the island.

Col Breadmore's funeral was arranged by the Navy, with all due ceremony. There was a bearer party from the Home Guard. A firing party from the Navy and the RAF. There were at least three senior naval officers at the service in St Peters. Mrs Ballard, who died in hospital, had a small family funeral attended by some relatives who came north for the occasion, by some of her friends among the other passengers, and some of the friends they had made in Stornoway during their brief stay. Those who had been dead on arrival were almost forgotten. They were buried, decently enough, but almost anonymously, with services organised by the police.

Some of us were more than a little shocked by the brother of one of the victims who arrived for the funeral wearing a gaudy red and white tie. "See what I've brought her!" he said, holding up a silk nightdress. 'It'll be the purest thing she's ever worn."

The nightdress was unnecessary. She had already been shrouded decently for burial. And the strangers to whom he insisted on retailing slightly scandalous stories about his sister had no wish to hear them. They saw her rather as a heroine. She had sustained a compound fracture of the thigh when the ship was bombed. She was lowered into a lifeboat, on a door, in lieu of a stretcher. The door overturned, and then three people, clambering into the lifeboat, fell heavily on top of her. A Chinese woman doctor in the lifeboat tried to give her morphia but the syringe broke and it had to be administered orally. She was still in great pain when the

179

Norwegian vessel docked. Dr Doig was rushed to her to give her an injection. "She was very brave," he told me. "I'm sorry I didn't have a chance to visit her in hospital before she died."

While everyone tried to do as much as possible for all the survivors, the lascars proved a handful. "I gave one poor miserable shivering devil a sweet," Dr Doig told me. "The rest were round me like bees demanding sweets. I gave another an aspirin. They all had to get aspirins. At last I had to go across to Bella Bovril to get sweets to pacify them". Bella gave him practically the whole of her stock, which was doubly generous. Not only were sweets expensive, they were rationed. Issuing them without coupons was illegal, and might have been reflected later in her replacement stocks. But no one at that time paused to count the cost.

A similar difficulty arose when the lascars were being kitted out before their departure. Local stocks of clothes could not provide identical garments for all of them, but, like children, each insisted on getting precisely what his neighbour had. Some of them walked barefoot through the snow rather than accept a different pair of boots from their pals. And when Hughie Matheson, the baker, sent them round forty dozen meat pies they refused to eat them. Presumably on religious grounds.

There were many groups of survivors landed at Stornoway around that time, when the war at sea was being waged very close to the Scottish coast. So far as I can recall the group from the *Staffordshire* was the largest, but it would be interesting to know just how many casualties of war, from how many different nationalities, were treated in Lews Hospital during these years.

The Hospital was still a voluntary institution, giving a free service to all who needed help, irrespective of race, religion or means. Fortunately it had been extended just before the war, thanks to a tremendous effort by the people of the island in the late thirties. They not only undertook to raise a large capital sum, in order to qualify for a roughly equivalent grant from the Department of Health, they also shouldered the additional maintenance costs, inevitably arising from the extension. The sums involved seem small as we look back on them today, but, in real terms, the people of Lewis and Harris, although very much poorer than they are today, undertook to raise, each year, the equivalent of £150,000 at today's prices.

Every week — not every year, but every week ! — a collection for the Hospital was made in every village from the Butt to Rodil. Every pay-day fishworkers, weavers, dockers, shop assistants, roadmen and others, handed over part of their wages for the Hospital. In addition to the village collections, every congregation had a Hospital collection. In addition to money, every village contributed potatoes, eggs, fleeces of wool and fowls, at least once a year. Every sample of herring sold in Stornoway Fish Mart was gifted to the Hospital, and every fishing boat which came into the harbour paid a Hospital levy.

In addition to the direct fund-raising, concerts were regularly held for the

Hospital in many districts of the island, much as the elders frowned, and a large part of the capital cost of the extension was raised in three fantastic carnivals in which the whole island participated, in a way which has never been equalled since. The Hospital Carnivals were a real high point in the social life of the island. Short sunny carefree festivals of fun and fellowship, as the island clambered out of the grim years of poverty and emigration which followed the First World War and hovered on the brink of the Second.

52
Poser for the Preacher

The three pre-war Hospital carnivals were unique. Not only for Lewis. Few places can have enjoyed precisely the same experience.

They were not unique in form or content. It was not the carnivals themselves but the background against which they were held which gave them their special quality. They had all the innocent wonder of first love, or the discovery of a great new book. Keats's "wild surmise". A springtime promise like Shakespeare's daffodils "that come before the swallows dare".

The carnivals had been preceded by a series of visits to the rural areas by a Hospital concert party from Stornoway. Visits to some areas that is. It is strange to think that in an island that is now bubbling with life there were "no go" areas, where it was not possible to hold a concert, even for the Hospital, because of the opposition of the church. Not any particular denomination. "Nay-saying" to youth and fun was common to them all. It was around that time a child in a rural school replied to the minister's question at a Bible examination, "What is the First Commandment?" "Please, sir, thou shalt not live!" "Out of the mouths of babes . . ."

There were areas in which concerts could be held. In some of them there was an input of local talent which presaged the thaw which came with the carnivals. I still recall the account I got from Ena Macleod of the Hospital concert in Pairc at which took place the first appearance — manifestation might be a better word — of the redoubtable Cailleach an Deacoin, complete with a potato apple lashed to "her" neck by layers of sticking plaster — the boil round which the evening's hilarity revolved.

It was then, too, I got an unsolicited report from a village which shall be nameless of a little local show. One of the early stirrings of the Phoenix. It read: "A small conscert was held on halwin night at miss Macphail Cottage on the south side. As the amusement were announsed threw out the villiage which were Murdo Matheson Peter Chistholm and John Matheson and the waiters were Effie and Johanna MacPhail. The cottage were opened at 7 oclock and the start was given by Annie Macaulay which kept the dance going for the members and acting as an actor all night."

The innocence. The complete lack of sophistication. The honest natural pleasure, untrammelled and unabashed by comparison with other places, or other media, is something we can never recapture. Television has killed that sort of joy in one's own achievement. The report also reminds us that at that time, on the brink of the Second World War, Lewis was still basically a Gaelic-speaking rather than a truly bilingual island.

Alexander Carmichael records in *Carmina Gadelica* a conversation he had at the end of last century with a cailleach in Ness about the suppression of music and dancing by the elders. She approved of the elders' actions and assured Carmichael that the people of Ness had put "foolishness" behind them, but, at the same time, she revealed that singing and dancing by the young still went on, illicitly, with her connivance, "in the culaist".

One might argue that there was an element of hypocrisy in the old lady's attitude. It was not the mean, corrosive hypocrisy of those who use the trappings of religion to cover their own wrong-doing — a form of hypocrisy known in Lewis, as everywhere else on earth. In fact I came across some prime examples of it in my work as a reporter.

The old lady's hypocrisy was different — an essential ingredient in civilised living. The grass bending before the gale so that it does not break! The flexibility which enables the human spirit to survive under any dogma, religious or political, which, in contradiction of its own essential truth, tries to impose a drab uniformity on a whole community. A flexibility which is the counterpart, and sometimes the more successful counterpart, of the dogged courage which resists.

The situation in the middle thirties, when the first carnival was planned, was very different from that encountered by Carmichael half a century before. The social life of the island was no longer suppressed by a rampant church driving underground the natural ebullience of youth. The social life of the island had collapsed from within. Lewis, as I have said before in other contexts, had become a hollow shell. An island of the old. A surprising number of them unmarried. Dry spinsters and crusty bachelors. Some of them anyway. Black had become the prevailing colour, and not only on Sundays. Even twenty years later, though things were changing by then, when a motorist was charged with careless driving because he bumped into some old ladies coming from church, in the dark, on an unlit road, and he pled that he could not see them as they were dressed in black, the Sheriff brushed the excuse aside. "Did you expect them to be dressed like flamingoes?" For some time after, among the irreverent, church-goers were spoken of as flamingoes.

Our thoughts as well as our clothes were black in those days. Hodden grey at least. It was a surprise to me — almost a shock — to come on a report by my father of a concert at Barvas on behalf of the Hospital around 1905. It was described as the fifth annual concert for Hospital funds, implying a well-established tradition. The programme included several playlets, some of them locally written. When I mentioned it to John Macrae, the Rector of the Nicolson, he told me how he had travelled once from Aberdeen, when he was a student, to keep a promise that he would play in a football match against a local side at Barvas. He injured his ankle in the course of the game and missed a term at University. When he told me the story he was chuckling over the mishap, although it must have been serious enough for him at the time. He thought it not too great a price to pay for encouraging sport in the rural areas.

183

It was then I realised that Lewis had survived the onslaught of gloom which Carmichael wrote of, and that the bleak depression in which I grew up myself was something new, creeping up on the island like an insidious frost from social and economic causes. The nadir was reached when the *Metagama*, the *Marloch* and the *Canada* sailed with their hundreds of young emigrants to enrich the life of Canada and USA. By the time of the first carnival there were signs that the irrepressible gregarious gaiety of the island was reasserting itself.

Organised football was being played again in rural Lewis. There was an annual sports day at Barvas. One of the active figures in the movement was Murdo Macleod, later headmaster at Bayble, who at that time was an invalid, lying in bed in his home at Brue, recovering from the illness which interrupted his career at Aberdeen University, and brought an end to his career as one of the island's outstanding athletes. Others, of course, contributed, but Murdo's input was symbolic. He used to send me reports of football matches he had helped to organise but hadn't seen. He reconstructed them from the conversation of the players when they gathered round his sick-bed after the game. And, when he helped to organise the Barvas Sports, he attended on a stretcher, lying on the floor of his father's bus.

In that dreary decade, in an island emptied almost of youth, one could truly say of those who remained, their heads were "bloody but unbowed". They had compensations. The Barvas Sports, a simple football match, and then the carnivals, were not events.They were adventures. Causes. Crusades. Surrounding the ordinary fun of the ploy itself there was a halo of achievement. We were hitting back at fate.

The carnivals did not escape criticism, but by then we had recovered sufficiently for the criticism to be part of the fun.

When the fancy dress parade at the first carnival was preached against from the text in Deuteronomy, "The woman shall not wear that which pertaineth unto a man, neither shall a man put on a woman's garment", Stephen MacLean drew attention to the verse in the same chapter, "Thou shalt not wear a garment of divers sorts as of woollen and linen together."

He posed the question, "Which is the reverend gentleman going to do without, his dog collar or his drawers? Clearly he cannot have both."

It might not be good theology but it caught the mood of the moment.

53
Haile Selassie in Lewis

On the eve of the first Carnival there was a Fancy Dress Dance in the Town Hall. More than five hundred people attended. The costumes were judged by Madame Schiaparelli, a famous Parisian fashion designer. She said she had seen many parades in provincial towns but nothing to equal Stornoway. She was astonished.

Also at the dance were Lady Portarlington from Lews Castle, and Lady Dorothy D'Oyly Carte from Soval Lodge. The latter was a regular visitor to Lewis for many years which explains why football clubs in a Hebridean island played for a trophy named after a famous opera company which none of us had ever seen, and many of us had never even heard of.

Lord Portarlington was also there. An ungainly figure with a paunch like a herring barrel. I watched him from the balcony as he danced the "Boomps a Daisy" on the crowded dance floor, with great abandon, like a berserk tug-boat amok in a harbour basin crowded with graceful yachts.

The Portarlingtons may have had a happy married life — I have no reason to believe the contrary — but, to outsiders, they seemed an ill-assorted pair.

He spent much of his time hanging around the piers and the boats, as I used to do myself as a child. The only apparent difference was that, while I got to the pier on foot in company with other smudgy gamins like myself, he arrived and departed in a chauffeur-driven Rolls.

One of his great delights was letting off fireworks from the Castle lawn. A Lewisman who worked for him gave me a hilarious description of how he used to set the fireworks up in little iron tubes. He would tip-toe forward in his ungainly manner to apply the match, then lumber back to safety like an agitated hippopotamus while the burnt-out sticks rained down on Kenneth Street as the Free Church midweek prayer meeting was slowly skailing.

On one occasion when his Lordship went shooting, my friend and a gamekeeper were stowed in a trailer behind the Rolls along with the gun dogs. As they climbed the brae at the County Hospital they peeped out from beneath the canvas cover, and saw a familiar figure approaching. Jessie Herbert, handsome and unwashed. The daughter of Herbert Jennings: "chimney sweep and licensed portificer". Herbert was one of the landmarks of my childhood with his sweep's brushes and coal-black face. For nearly seventy years I have been striving in vain to discover what a portificer was and how one acquired a licence to be one.

Jessie was a product of her environment. Rightly or wrongly she had the sort of reputation her squalor and her handsome figure might inspire.

When my friend and his companion spotted her, they snuggled out of sight and gave her a loud "Coooeee".

Jessie assumed the greeting came from the Rolls. She waved and smiled to his Lordship. In his amiable way Lord Portarlington acknowledged the greeting, while the two in the back chuckled quietly over the implications for anyone who witnessed the scene.

Her Ladyship, I suspect, would not have acknowledged a greeting from Jessie Herbert in any circumstances. Still less a greeting from Herbert Jennings himself if he were still around. Her friends came from the top echelon of Mayfair. She had a photograph of the Prince of Wales in her bedroom inscribed "With Love from Teddy". On the table nearby was a book entitled "Fun in Bed".

If you wonder how I know the lay-out of her Ladyship's bedroom, the answer is simple. I saw it with my ears, as I saw the incident on the County Hospital brae.

Lady Portarlington's guests — and I assume they were her guests rather than his — included people like the Duff Coopers whose visit to Stornoway aroused a good deal of interest, although not perhaps the sort of interest pillars of the establishment would have appreciated.

The Lewis attitude is neatly encapsulated in the fact that for us Jessie Herbert and the Duff Coopers can be found cheek by jowl (figuratively speaking) in the same story.

The visiting aristocrats we invited to the Carnival dance were there, as independent outsiders, to do a job as judges. The real guests of the carnival were Haile Selassie, Emperor of Ethiopia, and his glamorous daughter. They had come to Lewis specially for the occasion!

Ethiopia was in the news then, as it has been recently, but for very different reasons. Haile Selassie was a refugee from the invading Italians, who were trying to bomb his country into submission. He was a hero with us. One might almost say an immaculate hero.

It came as a great shock, years later, when he was driven out again by his own people, turned Marxist, denouncing him as an oppressor, and seizing control of the country. Presiding over one of the worst famines in their troubled country's history they may now be learning that it takes more than ideology to fill the bellies of the poor.

There may have been a few who believed that Haile Selassie had really come to Lewis, but even those who knew it was a joke kept up the pretence, and crowded to the quay to greet him. Long before the crowd began to gather, Haile Selassie and his daughter — good Lewismen, both of them! — had been smuggled on board a launch and taken to a rendezvous with the *Lochness*, well out of sight of the quay. And so they were standing on the bridge, smiling and bowing, as the vessel docked, looking none the worse for their presumptive crossing of the Minch. The vessel was decked with flags from stem to stern, as befitted the occasion, and fired rockets as she approached the pier to herald the presence of royalty.

The parts of Haile Selassie and his daughter were played with great

186

distinction by Iain Brown from Marybank, and Ian Macmillan, the dentist, who was then a slender rosy-cheeked schoolboy. We little realised when we saw him play the part of a princess that a few years later he would be parachuted into Normandy on D-day in the first wave of the attack.

Not long ago Iain Brown gave me a lively account of Haile Selassie's arrival as seen by the "monarch" himself.

His evening began in a room in the Town Hall where he was dressed in a white robe — a surgical coat borrowed from E. Norman Jamieson the Surgeon-superintendent at the Hospital. And a pith helmet provided by Norrie MacIver. His make-up was applied by Dr Peter Aulay Macleod, Carloway, who deftly gave him Haile Selassie's beard, correct to the last hair. Iain needed no colouring on his cheeks. A rich open-air tan gave him a sufficiently Oriental look.

He enjoyed being smuggled out from the mouth of the Creed in the Trust's launch, to rendezvous with the *Lochness* near Arnish Light. As the vessel entered the harbour he and his "daughter" stood beside Capt Macarthur surveying with delight the huge crowd gathered on the pier to greet them.

Then there was a moment of panic. So many people expected the real Emperor he was afraid some hotheads in the crowd might take it out on him for having fooled them.

In a photograph the two "imposters" could well have been mistaken for the real thing. The giveaway was the carriage which awaited them. It was the best that Stornoway could produce in the way of horse-drawn vehicles but hardly a state coach. It was in fact a humble float. The equerry was Tolas, spruced up and sober, resplendent in a sash and golden headgear.

That perhaps was the measure of the Carnival. All sections of the community were involved, from Tolas, a "character" best known for his addiction to the four and a halfs* when Stornoway was dry, to leading figures in the public life of the town, like Norrie MacIver, the fish curer, who led the Carnival procession, dressed like a policeman out of some crazy nightmare, and wielding, as his marshal's baton, his wife's punt roller — a device like a rubber rolling pin with "octopus" suckers much favoured at the time as a means of melting the "too too solid flesh" without the inconvenience of reducing the dietary intake. Also in the procession were professional men like Dr P. J. Macleod, and John MacSween, officials like Alastair Macleod the Town Clerk, and on a later occasion, one of the tweed barons, James Macdonald, gorgeously arrayed as an Indian maharajah.

The most effective entry in any of the Hospital carnivals was a slice of Lewis life. I think it was the second carnival in 1937. Charlie Alexander entered the firm's lorry in the procession. Seated on it were a group of fisher-girls straight from the farlins, in their working garb. Bloody to the elbows. They laughed and sang and held up their oilskin aprons to collect the shower of coins — tuiltean na Drobh in solid copper. When the procession was over, they handed in their hoard and went back to the job.

*See *The Hub of My Universe.*

54
Divine Retribution on a Very Modest Scale

The first of the pre-war carnivals raised £500. The second £1,000. And the third over £2,000. That seems small beer today, but in modern terms it represents: £10,000, £20,000 and £40,000, each time raised in a single week, in an island immeasurably poorer than it is today.

The country districts participated just as fully as the town. Perhaps more fully. Most of them had their own carnival collections mid-week and then came into town on Saturday to swell the main parade and join in the general jamboree.

In the first carnival one of the entrants that took the eye was a sgoth from Point, with a crew who insisted on putting about with a great flutter of sails whenever they had a corner to negotiate.

Many of the entries had a topical significance, like the Monster from Loch Mor a Starr — a centipede of Boy Scouts marshalled by Billy Grant, and described at the time as 75 feet of multi-coloured measles. The monster was much appreciated by the crowd. Stornoway was still having teething troubles with its new water scheme. The fortunate few found miniscule trout in the bath. The less fortunate got bigger fish which jammed the pipes, requiring a Caesarean delivery by plumber.

The Town Council made heavy weather with the problem and had some curious debates at which remedies were suggested which set at nought all the laws of hydraulics. Stephen MacLean eventually celebrated the Council's wisdom in a satirical little ode which ended with a delightful reference to local topography, and Stornoway's class distinctions, such as they were. He described the water from Loch Mor a Starr coming to the great divide at Mitchell's garage where it had to choose between Matheson Road and Bayhead, or as the poet put it:

> The left branch climbs to villas high
> With baths and chromium faucets,
> The right goes on through Ceann a bhaigh
> To goks and water closets.

The participation of the whole island in the carnival was very simply organised. A succession of meetings was held in Stornoway open to anyone who cared to come, and plenty did. All ideas were welcomed, and tossed around, and left for any willing worker to pick up and develop. The meetings were fully reported so that everyone knew what was going on, and the rest was left to spontaneous combustion.

Only the financial administration — the issue and retrieval of collecting boxes — was tightly organised from the centre, and even there Lewis, characteristically, defied regimentation. In the 1937 carnival 61 collecting boxes were issued in Ness, but 63 were returned, duly filled. The extras proved to be Foreign Mission boxes pressed into service for the day, presumably by someone who subscribed to the adage that charity begins at home.

Many of the entries to the carnival procession were very elaborate. Bain & Morrison produced a huge and lifelike whale, while Henderson's garage transformed a car into the *Girl Pat*, an English fishing boat then very much in the news because it had been hi-jacked. The Siarachs produced a splendid airidh on wheels, anticipating by a generation the advent of the mobile home. Kemp and Co had a skit on the Town Council's tardiness in dealing with the burgh's housing problem tracing by stages the progress from a few loose bricks in 1936 to a doll's house (maybe) by 1950!

There were innumerable sideshows before and during the carnival. People were invited to guess the weight of the baby placidly sucking a teat in his pram. It was 12 stone 7 lbs! The very lifelike granny in another pram sometimes barked like a dog — because it was a dog.

There was a wedding in Perceval Square at which the happy couple solicited, and got, innumerable wedding presents — for the hospital. It was all so realistic I kept my fingers crossed that no one had got married inadvertently under Scots law as it then was.

In the evening, after the procession, Messrs Rack and Ruin, faintly recognisable as two well known fish salesmen, held an auction at which they sold everything from live sheep to white mice and a venerable "doosh" all with appropriate patter. They also sold everyone rash enough to make a bid, but the purchasers didn't mind, they were seeking fun rather than bargains. In fact one of the problems was getting rid of the stock, so many people insisted on handing their purchases back to be auctioned all over again.

There was a balloon race at each carnival. The winning balloon generally made it to Aberdeen on the prevailing wind, but once the winner was in Norway. The Push Ball game involved the strong men of the island. I was going to say "From Cailean Neilly up and down" but, considering his height, it could only be down! Push Ball was a sort of tug-of-war in reverse in which the opposing teams tried to push a football eight feet high which was liable to shoot off at a tangent leaving the participants prostrate in the mud.

And there was real football but not with real teams. The police, the lawyers, the doctors and the ministers took part. Yes, the ministers! Some of them anyway. When Rev Lachlan Macleod, in a bright new football strip, borrowed for the occasion, vaulted lightly over the rail at Goathill Park, he wrenched his ankle in the process and missed the game. Wiseacres in other denominations — perhaps even in his own! — shook their heads and said it was a judgment!

A similar sentiment was expressed a decade or so later when John Skinner, the young minister of Martin's Memorial, shocked at how little the churches at that time were doing for the youth of the island, tried to establish contact, and give a lead, by participating in the annual sports at Willowglen. When he soared over the bar at the pole vault, at quite a presentable height, a by-stander, not particularly renowned for his piety or good works, turned away in disgust, muttering, "It's as high as ever he'll get!"

Some months after the first carnival a torrential fall of rain swept away some of the Creed bridges, and flooded part of the Castle Grounds, providing a pond where the youngsters, for a few days, had fun with rafts of floating logs.

Yan Morison, Major's brother, told me how he crossed the Creed Bridge at the foot of Beinn a Bhuine with his car when the river was beginning to lap across the timbers of the decking. He drove to safety a few yards up the hill, then parked his car and went back to have a look. In the interval the bridge had vanished!

Following the deluge — which one of our leading councillors insisted on calling "the delooge" — a minister of one of the smaller Presbyterian denominations wrote a letter to the *Gazette* declaring that the flood was Divine retribution for the wickedness of the Carnival.

I thought it a bit rough that anyone should condemn the efforts of those who were trying to help the Hospital, and arrogant that anyone should presume to read the mind of the Almighty on the matter, as if a few drops of rain in a wet and windy climate could rank with the judgment that befell the Cities of the Plain.

I doubt if the letter did the cause of true religion any good. It certainly did the carnival no harm, as the success of later carnivals showed.

But there were real shadows on the horizon, as we were soon to discover.

190

55
The Island's Mayfly Dance

It was the repressive attitude of so many of the leaders of the churches which made the pre-war carnivals seem such a great break-through to the young folk of my generation.

Village halls were frowned on. Dances were frowned on. Concerts were frowned on. One had the feeling that there were people around, in places of influence and authority, who wanted to squeeze all the laughter out of life and remake the world in their own black and gloomy image.

Some villages were no-go areas even for the Hospital concert party. Some years later even than the time I am talking about one of my own plays was banned in Ness. An innocent little frolic I had written for the Stornoway Girl Guides. There were no village halls in Lewis, except in the immediate vicinity of the town, until Dr P. J. Macleod established one in his native Bernera. Except at weddings, dances had to be held clandestinely, in the open air — if that is not a contradiction in terms!

Lewis had been much more liberal in these matters in the past. There was a lively social club in Barvas, for example, at the beginning of the century. In the middle thirties, however, the repressive element in the churches was still reinforced by the social catastrophe of the two preceding decades, when war and emigration had drained the island of its youth.

It is not so much active opposition the young folk of my generation had to contend with. Active repression tends to produce an active revolt. It was rather a general ennui and despair. A loss almost of the will to live. Or at least the will to be seen enjoying life. That is a problem young folk don't have today, although, God knows, they have problems of their own that may be even worse.

Today young folk tend to run on the accelerator without brakes. In the thirties it was all brakes and no accelerator. That is why the carnivals meant so much to us.

If we thought the first carnival in 1936 heralded a new springtime for the island, we knew, by 1939, it was but a mayfly dance. War was already close. In fact there were times when we wondered whether the carnival would take place at all. We were dancing on a plank on the lip of the Niagara Falls! If anything, that heightened the mood of gay abandon. There were several other reasons why the 1939 carnival was the most successful of them all.

It was, for one thing, the summer of the red-haired poacher, a story I have told elsewhere. That gave the proceedings a tart flavour of social anger and what we saw as a sweet revenge. It was also the first occasion on which

191

we had a carnival queen. That was a real innovation. The idea had been briefly discussed on earlier occasions, and then abandoned. It was too risky. The island wasn't ready for it. But by 1939 the mood was right. The earlier carnivals had done their work.

There was just one difficulty. We were conscious of a feeling in the rural areas that the whole thing would be rigged to put some well-connected Stornoway girl in the seat of honour. It was difficult to convince folk otherwise.

The Committee gave an assurance that the final choice would be made by someone from outwith the island with no Stornoway connections whatever. That was where the war began to catch up with us. We assumed there would have been plenty of suitable visitors at the fishing lodges, and, if not, that one of the newspapers — the *Bulletin* perhaps, Scotland's lively picture paper, still flourishing then in Glasgow — would send us a judge for the sake of the story.

In that expectation the preliminary rounds went ahead. Every rural area had a dance, or a series of dances, at which eliminating contests were held. The main problem resolved itself when Stornoway chose as its representative Murdina Macleod from Tong, who qualified because she worked in town. There were no "well connected" Stornoway girls left in the race! It was a popular choice and a very profitable one for the hospital.

The approach was unashamedly commercial. The Stornoway contest was held in the Playhouse, and the committee decided that there should be a ballot. Not one man, one vote. The voting papers were on sale. Sixpence a time I think it was. You could buy as many as you liked. Some folk may have bought a few extra to hedge their bets, so that whoever was chosen they could claim as theirs. But others plunged to back the beauty of their choice. "Give me a quid's worth of voting papers!" A quid was big money in 1939.

Although the town was out of the contest, the promise to produce an independent judge had still to be redeemed. People were leaving the fishing lodges early because of the international news. Those who remained were determined to spend what time they had on the river. The newspapers also had more important things on hand than carnivals in remote provincial towns.

There was an emergency meeting in P.J.'s home on the Friday morning. The choice was to be made that night at a dance in the Town Hall. At last someone said, a little tentatively, that they had seen a total stranger going into the County Hotel. We clutched at the straw. Mrs Macleod hurried to the phone and spoke to David Mackenzie the manager of the hotel. She came back glumly. "It's a Swedish archaeologist come to study the Callanish stones!"

Almost together P.J. and I said, "Just what we want!" It seemed hilariously funny, and certainly it met our criterion of complete independence. A deputation was sent to the hotel, and that is how Prof Ake Campbell of Uppsala University came to choose the first carnival queen ever crowned in Lewis. Not surprisingly he chose Murdina, a handsome "Scandinavian" blonde.

Actually he hadn't come to see the Callanish Stones, but the little beehive sheiling at Garynahine which he regarded as an important historical monument, but which we have since vandalised. He gave a new dimension to the whole carnival by relating the choice of a queen to a picturesque Swedish folk-custom which still survives, or did in 1939.

By a happy coincidence when Queen Murdina presided at another dance in the Town Hall on the following night, just after the procession, the local dance band — the Rhythm Boys — was reinforced by a group of Swedish accordionists from the mackerel vessels in the bay.

The mackerel vessels were not the huge factory ships from Iron Curtain countries which have visited Ullapool in recent years. Mackerel was not fished for deliberately before the war. The only mackerel brought to port were a by-catch with the herring. No one really wanted them except a few small Swedish fishing boats attracted by their cheapness. They anchored each year in Glumaig and pickled their purchases on board ship.

The Queen was crowned by the hospital matron, Miss Anderson, during the procession on Saturday. She and her attendants drove through the streets in an elaborate carriage with a throne fashioned like butterfly wings. It was designed by R. R. Macdonald from Borve and built by Frank Macintyre from Sandwick.

"R.R." had not trained as an artist but he was an excellent natural painter — and cartoonist. He designed the cover for the school magazine Hector MacIver and I produced, with a few others, to end the long hiatus which had followed the First World War. The early, intermittent, school magazines, which appeared before and during the war, had come from the top down, so to speak. Pupils contributed, but the staff organised. Ours was a proletarian revolution. The initiative came from the classroom. I was deputed to see the Rector, the redoubtable Johnnie Macrae, and tell him we wanted a magazine.

"Can you produce one?" he asked, in his dry probing manner.

"It is already written, sir!" I replied.

"In that case," he said, "I have funds to print it for you".

I saw "R.R." not long ago, at a Lewis and Harris dinner in Glasgow. We had a long talk about these old days and wandered on to other things. He told me of some articles which appeared in a Canadian newspaper in the early twenties about a Lewisman, a relative of his, who played an important part in suppressing the Riel Rebellion. That set me rummaging (by proxy) in the archives of a Canadian library, and gave me a lively tale, which I will pick up when I come back to the part played by Hebrideans in the pioneering days in the Canadian west.

In the meantime, however, I must follow the spoor of another Lewisman whose life was spent in Australia and Rhodesia, and whose unexpected visit home helped to make the 1939 carnival the liveliest of them all.

56
A Lorry Load of Social History

Murdo Macaulay once told me that, when he left Ness, he hadn't a penny in his pocket, and hardly a word of English in his head. He left Lewis long before I was born, and, by the time I met him, he was a man of substance, as they used to say, with property and gold-mining interests in Rhodesia, and a long adventurous career behind him.

I heard of him from my father when I was a youngster during the First World War. He volunteered to serve in the British Army, but they didn't want him. He was over age. So he offered his services to the French, bought and equipped an ambulance, and won the Croix du Guerre for his courage in saving the wounded when his ambulance came under shell fire.

After the First World War he returned to Rhodesia and I heard little of him until he arrived in Lewis to visit his relatives, in 1939, and became the biggest single contributor to that year's carnival. Not content with boosting the funds, he took part in the fun.

On the day of the Ness Carnival he went out in fancy dress with a friend, collecting round the villages. He was chuckling when he told me his friend's sister had almost fainted when she saw them walking up to her door. "She thought her brother was her mother back from the dead!" He was wearing the old lady's Sunday clothes, carefully preserved in the kist as things were in Lewis then.

When the Second World War broke out he was too old even to run an ambulance, but he took a job in a munitions factory in East Anglia. After that he disappeared from my horizon again, until one day, some years after the war, my banker, Calum Smith, asked me to call and see him at what was then the British Linen Bank. He told me that Murdo Macaulay had died and, under his will, had left something like £100,000 for charitable purposes in Lewis to be administered by the Trustees of Barclay's Bank.

"The bank," said Calum, "Is setting up an advisory committee in Lewis. Norrie Maciver has agreed to chair it and we would like you to be a member."

The other members were Murdo Macleod, the merchant in Eoropie, and John Smith, my old classmate, who had been headmaster in Lionel at one time. Later John Morrison, Barvas, joined us.

We were faced with a problem right away. Macaulay had been thinking of the Lewis he knew in his youth when he wrote the will. Many of the worthy objects on which money could be spent were now taken over by the state. An input of Macaulay money would merely have relieved the Treasury.

I remember an early discussion we had with the representative of Barclay's Bank. He wanted us to set up bursaries to enable Lewis children go to university. We said, "No! That's quite unnecessary. Any Lewis child who wants to go to university can do so. We should spend the money on encouraging people who have already qualified to take a higher degree."

Barclay's man pooh-poohed the idea. "A small island like Lewis will never produce sufficient graduates looking for higher degrees."

"Try it and see!" we suggested.

The Bank finally agreed to offer two post-graduate bursaries each year for a period to see what happened. Much to my delight — but not to my surprise — in almost every year for which the scheme continued they had to offer extra bursaries because there were too many applicants too good to turn away.

Those who are familiar with the graduation photographs which appear almost weekly in the *Gazette* will ask "So what?", but, in the fifties, when the Macaulay (Rhodesia) Trust was established, comparatively few Lewis students could even think of higher degrees. They had to get to work as soon as possible. When the Bank told us we could go to something like £400 or £500 a year in suitable cases — a princely sum at 1950 prices — I said to John Smith, "What would you have said, John, if you had been offered £500 a year when you were a student to stay on for a higher degree?" "I wouldn't have said anything," said John. "I would still be at the university!"

Macaulay had indicated in his will a desire to help the fishermen. Here again we came up against a difficulty. We suggested to the Bank that they might give fishermen the down payment for boats which they had to make to qualify for Herring Industry Board or White Fish Authority grants and loans. The Bank demurred at first but we argued, "If we can give a student a grant so that he can get a better degree and earn his living helping people hundreds of miles from Lewis, why should we not help a fisherman to get training and acquire a boat so that he can earn his living at home?" The grant for the down payment, we suggested could be conditional on the fisherman training on an East Coast boat for a specified period. That, we thought, made the scheme directly comparable with a student's bursary. At that point the Bank agreed. But that was only the first hurdle.

"We can't accept a down payment from the Macaulay Trust for a new fishing boat," the authorities told us. "The down payment must be the applicant's own money."

"Why?" we asked.

"A man will look after his own," we were told. "He won't be so careful with a boat, if he hasn't got his own money in it."

"If a man has a win on the football pools and applies for a boat with the money, will you take that?" we asked.

"Yes!" was the reply.

"Right!" we said. "We'll ask Barclay's Bank to agree to a scheme under which the money we are putting up will become the personal property of the applicant five minutes before you grant his application."

At that point the DAFS — God bless them! — changed course. Their problem stemmed from the Treasury, but they were under pressure from the Highlands and Islands Advisory Panel, as well as the Macaulay Fund, to do something for the fishermen. They came up with the first Fishery Training Scheme for the Outer Isles, and persuaded the Highland Fund to put up some money to help fishermen from the islands which could not benefit under Macaulay's will. As long as the Macaulay money lasted — and it wasn't very long, unfortunately — Lewis fishermen had the great advantage that they could get grants of their down payment while those from other islands had to make do with loans.

The Fishery Training Scheme was later greatly extended by the Highlands and Islands Development Board, which added an entirely new dimension, but, rather ironically, when the Board came to publish a report on the scheme, the contribution of the Highland Fund was acknowledged but the remarkable man from Ness, with whom, in a very real sense, it all began, didn't even get a mention in a footnote.

One of the last ploys the Macaulay Fund got involved in was an A1 scheme for Lewis. Archie Gillespie, who was then the College of Agriculture Adviser in the Island, was very keen on the idea and persuaded the Trustees to back him for something like £4,000 or £5,000 — provided the crofters really wanted it!

That was the rub. Could he get the support of the mass of the crofters at that early stage? Archie worked hard on it, holding meetings all over the island in preparation for a great rally in the Town Hall in Stornoway at which the matter would be put to the test. He was not helped by the fact that one of the principal spokesmen at the meeting was decidedly cool. One wondered why he had accepted the invitation to the platform in the first place, unless he was planning to sabotage the scheme. But Archie, and his College boss, John Grant, carried the meeting with them. It was one of the most remarkable gatherings I ever chaired. There must have been more than three hundred crofters in the hall. The idea was novel to many of them. Perhaps repugnant to some. But, by the end of the meeting, the crofters had agreed to the College proposal and had set up a committee to carry it forward, representative of every district in the island.

At that point Robert Macleod, Garenin, who had been a member of the Taylor Committee on Crofting, rose to give some sage advice to the Committee. "Before you do anything, consult DAFS. You will get nowhere without their help."

The Committee took his advice. The Dept agreed to co-operate. Indeed they went very much further. They took the scheme over and ran it as their own. The Macaulay money, which had made the idea possible, was not needed at the end of the day. Fortunately! It was no longer there!

Rhodesia was preparing for its unilateral declaration of independence.

Relations with Britain were deteriorating. Suddenly, while the campaign for the A1 scheme was still in progress, the Macaulay Funds were frozen. The dream was at an end.

It was then I learned how much can be achieved by money you haven't got, so long as people think you have it!

It would be difficult to quantify what Murdo Macaulay did for Lewis. He certainly cared for a great many old folk in Ness at a time when pensions were even less adequate than they are today. And when I visited Washington and called on one of my old class-mates, Roddie Murray from Shawbost, he put me through on the phone to a fellow Lewisman from Carloway who won a Macaulay bursary at a critical point in his university career. Donald Macarthur, he told me, now runs one of the most advanced laboratories in the United States.

"You can guess his standing here," said Roddie, "If I tell you that his next door neighbour in the suburb where he lives is General Haig, the Secretary of State."

Shortly after he went to USA, Donald married a niece of President Johnson, she visited Lewis with him to see his folk in Carloway, and I met them by chance on the Glasgow plane. He was very appreciative of the help the Macaulay Fund had given him.

Not long before my visit to Washington I had a long talk in Inverness with another Macaulay bursar on a visit back to Scotland. Kathleen Nicolson (Mrs Jamieson) was studying the History of Art when she won the Macaulay award. It was rather an exotic subject for a Lewis girl at that time but it was only the beginning of a career that led her into even more unusual paths.

When her husband's work took her to Latin America she became interested in the problems of the under-privileged, and, when his next move took her to Canada, she took up the study of law, and became an authority on the rights of Red Indian women who were heavily discriminated against under the current Canadian legal code.

In the course of our conversation she spoke of the position of the women of her mother's generation in the Lewis of their day. The fight they had to raise their families, and what they achieved with scant resources.

In effect she was talking about the generation represented by the group on Charlie Alexander's lorry at the carnival, cheerfully raising funds for the Hospital between two spells of dirty, disagreeable and ill-paid work, in a brief respite between the war and emigration which left many of them with a bleak future as young widows or ageing spinsters, and the war to come which widowed many more.

Their story was known to me well, but only as social facts which I had observed, and, when they were newsworthy, reported. Often I was moved by a borrowed sense of pride, sometimes I was moved almost to despair, but I did not feel their history in my bones with passion as Kathleen Jamieson clearly did. It was peripheral to my personal experience.

Lewis is a different island to everyone who has ever lived there, although it is essentially the same. None of us sees it comprehensively, or completely. All of us see it from an eclectic, exclusive, idiosyncratic point of view.

But, wherever we stand, and however we look at Lewis, none of us has ever found it dull.

And we are always learning something new about it.